Sustainable Business

Theory and Practice of Business under
Sustainability Principles

Edited by

Geoffrey Wells

University of South Australia

Edward Elgar
Cheltenham, UK • Northampton, MA, USA

Published by
Edward Elgar Publishing Limited
The Lypiatts
15 Lansdown Road
Cheltenham
Glos GL50 2JA
UK

Edward Elgar Publishing, Inc.
William Pratt House
9 Dewey Court
Northampton
Massachusetts 01060
USA

A catalogue record for this book
is available from the British Library

Library of Congress Control Number: 2012946681

ISBN 978 1 78100 185 1

Typeset by Servis Filmsetting Ltd, Stockport, Cheshire
Printed and bound by MPG Books Group, UK

\. S
9/21

Contents

Contributors

John Benson is a Professor and Head of the School of Management, University of South Australia. His research specialities are human resource management and industrial relations, Japanese management and trade unions, Chinese labour and management, outsourcing and firm performance, employee voice, knowledge work, employee commitment, and generations.

Joy Chia is Associate Professor, and Head of School of Applied Media and Social Science, Monash University (formerly School of Management, University of South Australia). Her research specialities are social capital development in regional communities and the communication context of this capital.

Nicholas Chileshe is a Senior Lecturer in Construction and Project Management, and Research Education Portfolio Leader, in the School of Natural and Built Environments, University of South Australia. His research specialities are risk management in construction operational environments, sustainability, project performance, quality and change management, and structural equation modelling for total quality management in small and medium sized construction related organizations.

Nina Evans is the Associate Head of the School of Computer and Information Sciences (CIS), University of South Australia. Her research specialities are knowledge management, information asset management, IT leadership, business-IT fusion, and scholarship of teaching.

Erich C. Fein is a Lecturer and Program Director at the Centre for Human Resource Management in the School of Management, University of South Australia. His research focuses on performance management, personnel selection, leadership development, and managerial ethics.

Sumit K. Lodhia is a Senior Lecturer in Accounting at the Centre for Accounting, Governance and Sustainability, University of South Australia. His research specialities include sustainability accounting, management and reporting in corporations and the public sector, climate change/carbon accounting, integrated reporting, sustainability education and corporate social responsibility.

Stephen Pullen is a Senior Lecturer in the School of Natural and Built Environments. He is a building scientist with over fifteen years experience in the study of sustainability of construction materials, buildings and the urban environment, supported by a number of Federal research grants.

Janek Ratnatunga is a Professor of Accounting in the School of Commerce, University of South Australia. His research specialities include carbon accounting, carbon auditing and carbon finance. He is a consultant on carbon related issues to the United Nations Framework Convention on Climate Change (UNFCCC), to the World Bank and to a number of Asian governments and corporations.

Sukhbir Sandhu is a Lecturer in the School of Management, University of South Australia. Her research and teaching focus on business sustainability. Her research specialities include examining drivers of social and environmental sustainability in businesses, exploring the role of sustainability champions, and examining social and environmental implications of the bottom of the pyramid business approach.

Shruti R. Sardeshmukh is a Lecturer at the School of Management, University of South Australia. Influenced by her work experience, her research investigates the effect of overlap of business and family spheres on the attitudes, behaviours and activities of entrepreneurs and family co-workers.

Janet Sawyer is Head, Business and Regional Enterprise Unit, Centre for Regional Engagement, University of South Australia. Her research interests include accounting education and regional issues.

Christina M. Scott-Young is a Lecturer and Undergraduate Program Director in the School of Management, University of South Australia. She conducts research on family business, group behaviour, ethics and organizational performance.

Martin P. Shanahan is Dean of Research in the Division of Business, and Deputy Director of the Centre for Regulation and Market Analysis, University of South Australia. While he specializes in economic and business history, he has a keen interest in environmental history and has recently written on water markets in Australia.

Anne Sharp is a Senior Research Fellow at the Ehrenberg-Bass Institute for Marketing Science, University of South Australia. Her research specialization is in sustainable marketing. She has a focus on government interventions encouraging behaviour change for improved environmental outcomes, as well as the development of marketing metrics for sustainability activities of consumer goods marketers.

Jie Shen is a Senior Research Fellow in the International Graduate School of Business and the Centre for Human Resource Management, University of South Australia. His research interests are in the effects of human resource management practices, such as socially responsible HRM, on employees and organizations.

Aharon Tziner is Professor of Management, former Dean of the School of Business Administration, present Dean of the School of Behavioral Sciences, and Vice-Rector for Research at Netanya Academic College, Israel. He is widely published in the research areas of staffing organizations, performance appraisal, work adjustment, structure and performance of groups in organizations, and the financial value of human resource management programs and organizational behaviour.

Vicki Waye is a Professor of Law and Dean of Teaching and Learning for the Division of Business, University of South Australia. Her research incorporates international and comparative elements, and spans subject matter such as multilateral and bilateral treaties, international trade, comparative civil procedure, and matters affecting access to justice (including inter-generational justice).

Geoffrey Wells is a Senior Research Fellow in the Centre for Regional Engagement, and former founding director of the sustainable business programs in the International Graduate School of Business, University of South Australia. His research specialities are the theoretical foundations of sustainable business, valuation methods in environmental and natural resource economics, and financial modelling for climate change management.

Lou Wilson is a Senior Lecturer in the School of Natural and Built Environments, University of South Australia. His research focuses on social inclusion, social cohesion, social capital and social, economic and environmental sustainability.

George Zillante is Associate Professor and Head of Building, School of Natural and Built Environments, University of South Australia. He has qualifications in architecture, urban and regional planning, building surveying, business administration and construction, and works at the professional level in those fields, with many Government committees. He represents the Australian Construction Industry on the International Association for the Professional Management of Construction.

Jian Zuo is a Senior Lecturer in the School of Natural and Built Environments, University of South Australia. His research interests include low carbon built environment through stakeholder engagement and competitiveness studies in the construction context.

Acknowledgements

I am grateful to the University of South Australia, and particularly to the Division of Business and to the Centre for Regional Engagement, for making it possible for me to work on this book. The International Graduate School of Business supported me in developing ideas about sustainable business in the context of new graduate programs. Professor Gerry Griffin, Pro Vice Chancellor, Division of Business, provided valuable advice and support to the project. Many colleagues contributed through a range of discussions to the ideas developed here. Michele Cranage was a tireless copy-editor. To all, my grateful thanks.

Introduction: historical and emerging themes in sustainable business

Geoffrey Wells

PRECURSORS

It is usual to trace the historical antecedents of the idea of sustainable business to at least the 1950s. In the course of sixty years the emerging conceptual landscape of that idea has been wide-ranging. Included in it are: corporate philanthropy; corporate social responsibility (CSR); corporate social responsiveness; corporate social performance (CSP); public responsibility; business ethics; stakeholder theory; corporate citizenship; corporate social marketing and so on. These are not paradigms, in the strict sense (Kuhn 1996). Rather they are conceptual frameworks – some more formalized, some better documented than others – through which the wider responsibilities of the firm have been analyzed (Carroll 2008; Lee 2008). This historical trajectory is now briefly described, through some central contributions.

Carroll (2008) notes that from the late 1800s on, critiques of working conditions in the emerging factory system in Great Britain were successfully mounted. The courts began to wrestle with the legitimate limits of corporate philanthropy (Wren 2005). Initiatives such as the Pullman town, a model industrial community, were attempted (Heald 1970). Management theorists began to explore the relationship between corporate profitability and social responsibility: Berle and Means (1932, p. 312) examined the claims of passive owners and articulated the important principle that 'Neither the claims of ownership nor those of control can stand against the paramount interests of the community'; this was, Stretton (2000, p. 362) remarks, 'a proposal to save capitalism, not to replace it.' Similarly in an early work, Drucker (1946, p. 256) argued that there were limits to the operation of the market: '. . . No society can allow labor, physical resources of land or equipment and money to be treated as "commodities". The market cannot be allowed to destroy them nor to destroy their stability.' In two of these factors, labor and physical resources of land, can be seen conceptual roots of the internal and external dimensions of the sustainable firm.

However it is widely agreed that the first codified account of the social dimensions of business was Howard R. Bowen's *Social Responsibilities of the Businessman* (Bowen 1953). Many of the central concepts of CSR and sustainable business theory over the succeeding six decades are prefigured here. Bowen bases his argument on a broadly conceived account of the goals of the economic system: these include not only economic progress and stability, but the wider goals of justice, freedom, the development of the individual person, community improvement and personal integrity. Such goals then become criteria according to which the social performance of business is judged. Moreover they are delivered by ethical conduct: 'Businessmen have always been expected to act according to sanctioned rules of conduct . . . morality is one of the foundations of economic life' (p. 13). Principled action is required; a notion expanded upon by a later generation of economists (Lutz 1999).

Bowen's position challenged a century of unfettered American business. Included in it are many concepts that have now become central to the discourse of CSR and sustainable business. Stewardship is associated with the idea that business leaders are servants of society, for whom 'management merely in the interests (narrowly defined) of stockholders is not the sole end of their duties' (Bowen 1953, p. 44), a central theme of socially responsible business (ICAEW 1975). It is taken for granted that free enterprise is the most productive economic system, and profitability (or at least 'satisfactory' profits) is the first requirement for a firm; but once secured other responsibilities to society must be considered. The directors of a firm are 'trustees, not alone for stockholders or owners, but also for workers, suppliers, consumers, the immediate community, and the general public', amongst whose interests they are required to mediate (Bowen 1953, p. 48). In that task, recourse will be taken to 'ethical connotations which extend far beyond the narrow principle of profit maximization' (p. 50). This model of the firm has its foundation in community values: 'The changing values and attitudes of the public have persuaded businessmen, in a decisive way, to reconsider their social role and the aims of their activity' (p. 53). It is not difficult to see in this analysis the foundations of stakeholder theory (Dunfee 2008), of business ethics (Brenkert 2010), and of the social license to operate (Kurucz et al. 2008).

Among these responsibilities of the firm, those which pertain to employees are among the most unambiguous. Bowen observes that 'the wants and needs of workers extend far beyond wages' and that management must act proactively 'in giving workers the things essential to make of work a satisfying and rewarding human experience'. Bowen's extended list of those things deemed essential present a formidable summary of what have become organizational dimensions of the firm in CSR and sustainable business theory (Bowie 2010).

Bowen faces the challenge this model of the firm poses to competitive business: that since some competitors will not 'accept their social responsibilities' and the costs that come with them the socially responsible firm will be uncompetitive. Bowen counters with the observation that better employment practices historically have resulted in greater productivity; an early approach to the business case for CSR (Carroll and Shabana 2010). Furthermore from an economic point of view, aggregate welfare is increased: 'The welfare of society is related not only to the quantity of final goods and services but also to the conditions under which these goods and services are produced' (p. 113); a principle upon which the modern disciplines of environmental and natural resource economics (Perman et al. 2003) and ecological economics (Common and Stagl 2005) have systematically expanded. There are in any case unavoidable moral obligations, and these extend widely: to immediate moral obligations are added 'obligations that are distant and less clearly seen' (p. 123); a statement which aligns with the later sustainability principles of social justice and intergenerational equity (Rawls 1972; WCED 1987).

Davis (1960, p. 76) adopted a position not far from Bowen's: 'Clearly, economic functions of business are primary, but this does not negate the existence of non-economic functions and responsibilities. The price of social freedom is its responsible exercise.' The considerable power of business is to be balanced in a 'co-equal responsibility': the continuing vitality of business depends upon it; refusal to accept it threatens the foundations of a stable society. In practice, Davis proposes, it is a matter of determining which economic decisions also have social dimensions, and including the latter in business decision making. Those dimensions are recognized as being both internal and external to the firm, as in the conditions of work and in the implications for wider employment. Importantly Davis argues that an ethical imperative may be embedded in the firm's collective beliefs and actions, but that does not relieve the individual of the obligation to act ethically: '. . . in the last analysis it is always the businessman who makes the decision' (p. 71).

Frederick (1960) began a long engagement with CSR theory by accepting the requirement for business to deliver 'broad social ends' and to attend properly to the welfare of its employees. However he counsels an acceptance of the profit motive, on historical and cultural grounds, and from a recognition of limits in actions open to business managers (1960). He looks rather to the public institutional context to attach appropriate social dimensions to business actions.

These themes were treated with increasing rigour in the following decades. Friedman's famous magazine article has been endlessly cited as presenting a fundamentalist neoclassical view of the firm entirely opposed to the idea of a sustainable enterprise (Friedman 1970). A closer reading presents a more nuanced view.

Friedman's thesis is that the sole responsibility of the corporate executive is to his employers, the owners. (This view was later challenged under ethical theory – for example, by Solomon (2004) – but let us see where Friedman takes it.) Owners will normally want 'to make as much money as possible while confirming to the basic rules of the society, both those embodied in law and those embodied in ethical custom'; an interesting constraint, often overlooked in commentary.

In the standard corporate model, then, to incur costs to the company for social purposes, such as improving the environment, is therefore not acting in the interests of the owner: it is 'spending someone else's money for a general social interest', in a different way than the owners would have spent it (unless, of course, the owners were predisposed to act in this way). This is, Friedman argues, in effect a corporate tax, and it represents a breach not of ethical but of political principle. Furthermore it is unreasonable to expect the businessman to be 'simultaneously legislator, executive and jurist' and expert in social matters such as macroeconomic policy or environmental policy.

By contrast, he argues, in standard libertarian mode, under a free market system '. . . no individual can coerce any other, all cooperation is voluntary, all parties to such cooperation benefit or they need not participate. There are no values, no "social" responsibilities in any sense other than the shared values and responsibilities of the individuals'.

Importantly it is accepted that the market mechanism is not always feasible: '. . . I do not see how one can avoid the use of the political mechanism altogether.'

It should be noted that Friedman is not arguing against social goals *per se*: he is arguing that firms should not and cannot (by reasons of both governance and expertise) develop or implement them. Social goals, in his view, belong to social governance: they are political and should be set by the political mechanism in legislation and regulation. The ethical elements of such goals are socially embedded; a view, ironically, that modern critical theorists such as Habermas (1990) have elaborated.

Baumol (1970) examined the long established practice of corporate philanthropy. He cites court opinions that 'corporate giving has been found appropriate so long as it serves the interests of the firm, broadly defined.' A broad business case for corporate giving is proposed: 'The company pays a high price for operating in a region where education is poor, where living conditions are deplorable, where health is poorly protected, where property is unsafe, and where cultural activity is all but dead.' Where that price is greater than the price of corporate giving, corporate philanthropy makes business sense. Particularly if government action is absent, such giving is seen as best handled collectively, by voluntary groupings of firms.

A similar more formal argument was mounted by Wallich and McGowan (1970). The key question, it is proposed, is the appropriability by the firm of returns on social investment. Social arenas include the quality of the environment (air, water) and social stability (equality of opportunity). The analysis points to the rationality of a corporate strategy which pursues all such returns appropriable through the market system but avoids actions which generate non-market returns. Again it is concluded that voluntary cooperation by firms (short of antitrust actions) will yield best financial results.

The plethora of positions unleashed by Friedman's article leads to a demand for greater formalization of the CSR domain. Sethi (1975) proposed a tripartite framework for corporate behaviour: social obligation, based on economic criteria; social responsibility, based on social norms, values and expectations; and social responsiveness, which demands a long term view that is both anticipatory and preventative.

Carroll's (1979) analysis of CSR has been influential over three decades. He offered a four part definition of CSR: 'The social responsibility of business encompasses the economic, legal, ethical, and discretionary expectations that society has of organizations at a given point in time' (p. 500). The first two elements of this definition comprise the basic requirements the society has of business: to make a profit, and to abide by the law (the Friedmanite limit of firms' purposes). In addition, however, Carroll proposes ethical and discretionary elements which go beyond obedience to the law and are answerable to social norms. He later emphasized that, although it is attractive to categorize the first two elements as what the firm does for itself and the second two as what the firm does for others, in reality 'economic viability is something business does for society as well' (Carroll 1999, p. 284). Subsequent versions of the schema were presented as a pyramid, with economic responsibility forming its base.

Carroll (2008, p. 36) notes the extension of the concept during the 1980s to 'environmental pollution, employment discrimination, consumer abuses, employee health and safety, quality of work life, deterioration of urban life, and questionable/abusive practices of multinational corporations', a considerable expansion of scope, both internal and external to the firm. Wartick and Cochran (1985) elaborated Carroll's schema in an integrating framework of corporate social responsibilities, corporate social responsiveness and social issues under dimensions of principles, processes, and policies.

However the dominant contribution to the field during this period came from Freeman's development of stakeholder theory (Freeman 1984; Freeman et al. 2010). Although presented in the context of strategic management, stakeholder theory had a substantial impact on the development of all fields dealing with business and society, and was developed by Freeman himself over more than two decades. Freeman observes that the legal question of corporate responsibility had moved 'to give de facto standing to the claims of groups other than stockholders. It has, in effect, required that the claims of customers, suppliers, local communities, and employees be taken into consideration' (Freeman 2009, p. 58).

He argues against the attempt to separate business decisions from ethical decisions and in favor of an integrated view, which recognizes the inherently ethical nature of business decisions and the obligation of businesses to accept responsibility for it. Stakeholders in the firm are 'groups and individuals who can affect or are affected by, the achievement of an organization's mission' (Freeman 1984, p. 52). They include secondary entities, such as consumer groups, special interest groups, media, government, and even competitors. Freeman cites principles from various traditional and modern ethical theories in support of his position.

At this point the conceptual building blocks of theory relating to the social responsibilities of business were mostly identified, although the form of that theory was not agreed upon. The subsequent two decades saw a further expansion of scope: for example, in management, to strategic giving and social marketing; and in business practice, to community investment and governance. An emphasis on performance, particularly financial performance, drove new research programs. However it is the emergence of sustainability as a framing concept that is the most significant of these more recent developments.

Even with the expansion of scope of CSR and related fields in the 1980s, the application of sustainability principles to business has strongly challenged the adequacy of the conceptual frameworks that CSR theory had developed. The roots of sustainability thinking extend over many decades (Meadows et al. 1972, 1992, 2005). However its modern formulation is identified with the United Nations report, *Our Common Future* (WCED 1987). This report ranged widely over global challenges, predominantly economic and environmental, but including also poverty, inequality and militarization; population growth and food security; biodiversity and ecosystem integrity; energy, industry and urbanization; and the institutional changes needed for sustainable development. It firmly endorsed the concept of global environmental limits. As is well known, it proposed a view of sustainability which has been definitive: 'Sustainable development seeks to meet the needs and aspirations of the present without compromising the ability to meet those of the future' (p. 40). Intra-generational equity is equally emphasized: 'A world in which poverty and inequity are endemic will always be prone to ecological and other crises' (p. 43).

Our Common Future framed the development of sustainability principles and practice for two decades. The *Rio Declaration on Environment and Development* (UNDESA 1999) articulated 27 principles, which are essentially a formalization of the Brundtland report. One is the precautionary principle (Principle 15). Another is the internalizing of external costs (Principle 16): 'National authorities should endeavour to promote the internalization of environmental costs and the use of economic instruments, taking into account the approach that the polluter should, in principle, bear the cost of pollution, with due regard to the public interest and without distorting international trade and investment.' The recent Rio + 20 deliberations have essentially confirmed these principles.

On these readings it is evident that when applied to business, sustainability principles represent a dramatic expansion of the earlier scope of CSR and its affiliates. The responses of the academic and professional communities have varied widely. An early contribution which directly reflected the WCED analysis was Hart (1997), who proposed a context for sustainable business which required developed, emerging, and survival economies to be evaluated against the major sustainability challenges of pollution, depletion (of renewable resources), and poverty.

Montiel (2008) investigated the relationship between CSR and CS (corporate sustainability) in a quantified review of articles in selected leading journals over the period 1970–2005. The study demonstrated some expected trends: a longer history of CSR research; an increase in CS and EM (environmental management) articles since 1990; and a shift of interest from CSR to corporate social performance (CSP) after 1990. Definitions of CSR reflected the wide range of perspectives outlined above. On the other hand, CS definitions were more focused: on ecological sustainability, identifying CS primarily with the environmental dimension of business; and on the tripartite construct – environmental, economic, and social – associated with the WCED approach and its successors (Elkington 1997).

Montiel identified several points of difference emerging from the research between CSR and CS. CS treats economic, social and environmental dimensions as integrated; CSR deals only with the social and economic, and maintains their separation. CS tends to be eco-centric; CSR anthropocentric. CSR, as we have seen, has come to centre on stakeholder theory; CS has moved to resource based views, motivation theory and institutional theory. At the same time CSR has begun to incorporate environmental elements, such as pollution abatement and conservation of natural resources; and CS is placing increasing importance on the social dimension, in areas such as government relationships, stakeholder interests, health and safety, and community development. Montiel concluded that the two fields are converging: 'Contemporary businesses must address economic prosperity, social equity, and environmental integrity before they can lay claim to social responsible behavior or sustainable practices' (Montiel 2008, p. 260).

This conclusion was supported by Dahlsrud (2008), who conducted a review of CSR definitions in both journal articles and web pages over the period 1980–2003. Utilizing frequency scores, five dimensions of CSR were identified: environmental; social; economic; stakeholder; and voluntariness. Of these the environmental dimension is somewhat lower in frequency. Importantly Dahlsrud notes that most of the definitions are descriptive, rather than normative: rather than arguing for the social responsibility of business, they 'describe CSR as a phenomenon.' He concludes from the data that CSR 'is nothing new at a conceptual level' but is being brought into new operational focus in a globalized economy: 'New stakeholders and different national legislations are putting new expectations on business and altering how the social, environmental and economic impacts should be optimally balanced in decision making' (p. 6).

The general thesis of CSR/CS convergence is developed further by Dyllick and Hockerts (2002). They observe that to the themes of economic growth and social equity has now been added 'concern for the carrying capacity of natural systems.' It is proposed that none of the three can be developed on its own. Sustainability interpreted as eco-efficiency – the entry point for most firms – is judged inadequate, even on sustainability criteria. Stakeholder concepts are used to present an integrated definition: '. . . corporate sustainability can accordingly be defined as meeting the needs of a firm's direct and indirect stakeholders (such as shareholders, employees, clients, pressure groups, communities, etc.), without compromising its ability to meet the needs of future stakeholders as well.'

A triple-bottom line approach is thus proposed, along with a demand to integrate short with long term perspectives and strategies. In practice sustainability is to be implemented by managing three types of capital. Economic capital includes financial, tangible and intangible components (Stewart 1999). Natural capital includes natural resources and ecosystem services (Hawken et al. 2008; Heal 2005). Social capital includes human capital (of employees and business partners) and societal capital (public services) (Putnam 2001). Sustainable enterprise requires all three types of capital to be at least maintained, and ideally increased. It is emphasized that natural capital cannot always be substituted for by economic capital, and is characterized by non-linear processes, thresholds and irreversibility, which support the application of the precautionary principle in practice.

EMERGING THEMES OF SUSTAINABLE BUSINESS IN THIS BOOK

The chapters in this volume come from researchers in sustainable business at one university, the University of South Australia. They reflect the wide range of themes now emerging in the international exploration of sustainability principles in management and business.

The first group of chapters focuses on the foundations of the sustainable firm and sustainable business. Sandhu addresses a principal challenge of sustainability theory, that of complexity. The focus here is the environmental and social responsiveness of firms. Sandhu argues for a more holistic view of the sustainable firm and its activities derived from cross-theoretical analysis. Stakeholder and resource dependence theories offer an account of stakeholder influence on the environmental and social responsiveness of firms. Institutional theory illuminates stakeholder legitimization and approval. The resource based perspective provides a firm-specific view of how firms may break free of institutional influences. Integrating these approaches thus points the way to a more holistic model of the drivers of corporate responsiveness to sustainability at many levels.

In the tripartite model of sustainability, the social dimension has been the least addressed. Chia examines the importance of social capital for organizational outcomes. Drawing on community research in Australia and Canada, the importance of the business organization's networks, connections and relationships with its community base is explored. Among an array of grass roots communication methods the emerging role of social media in providing a focus for connection and inclusion is emphasized. Diverse and meaningful communication establishes trust between the business organization and its community, and lays the ground for business activity that is on the one hand more competitive and on the other more socially responsible.

The ethical theme in the history of socially responsible business models was established at its inception. Wells argues for the fundamentally ethical character of conceptions of the sustainable firm: in particular, that from Kantian ethics and common morality theories can be derived the essential features of the sustainable firm and its activities. Four concepts generally regarded as central to the idea of sustainable business – stakeholders, the extension of the firm's boundaries and responsibilities, sustainable organization, and future generations – are considered as consequences of this ethical theory. In contrast to historical classificatory schemes, it is proposed that the higher-order principle of an ethical foundation offers a coherent basis on which the theory and practice of the sustainable firm can systematically be constructed.

The second group of chapters applies sustainability concepts to core management disciplines. As each discipline has grappled with the implications of sustainability principles the reconfiguration of theory required for a coherent account of sustainable business has been developed.

Lodhia reviews the history of this work in the accounting disciplines, from both internal (sustainability management) and external (sustainability reporting) perspectives. The intellectual tensions that have emerged in the literature – for example, between accounting and sustainability metrics of success – are a particular focus. These differences are critical to the emerging account of the sustainable firm, as in business practice the firm is largely defined by the assumptions which underpin the conceptual framework of accounting. The application of these perspectives to two contemporary developments in accounting theory and practice, carbon accounting and integrated reporting, are examined, and emergent research directions in sustainable accounting are outlined.

As climate change has moved to the forefront of the global sustainability agenda, carbon measurement, accounting and auditing have become critical to the public policy responses, particularly in emissions tax or trading regimes. Ratnatunga provides a detailed review of conceptual and professional progress in this critical arena. He notes that these carbon measurement issues are important to government in the development and implementation of economic instruments; to business entities in trading, investment and cost control; and to consumers, in the provision of information for buying decisions. Current accounting and assurance frameworks are found to be inadequate to these tasks, in part because of the non-monetary character of critical carbon elements. New costing techniques incorporating whole-of-life carbon costs in products and services, and new approaches to the provision of strategic management accounting information for investment and performance evaluation are envisaged.

The role of marketing as the consumer-facing management discipline is central to the shaping and success of sustainable business. Sharp examines the tensions that are emerging for marketers between longer term social and environmental imperatives and the immediate concerns and buying behaviour of consumers. Firms increasingly view sustainability as a competitive imperative and a strategic goal, and the development of green brands as an emerging marketing responsibility and tactic. Central principles of marketing science, such as the routinized behaviour of consumers and their split loyalty across brands, have implications for meeting this responsibility. Well-established principles of marketing, such as under-standing the market, using messages and calls to action, ensuring visibility on the shelf and in the consumer's mind, and growing sustainable brands are all found to have valuable applications to sustainability challenges.

Shen and Benson explore the internal dimensions of sustainable busi-ness through socially responsible human resources management (SR-HRM). Reviewing a large body of theoretical and empirical research, they develop a nuanced conceptual framework of CSR and SR-HRM dimensions. External dimensions of SR-HRM are distinguished from internal. It is argued that it is employee-oriented SR-HRM practice which builds employee support for socially responsible acts of the organization. Addressing the interest and needs of employees is proposed as likely to minimize negative impacts on employees of external CSR initiatives and to build support for them. Enhanced organizational performance and long term sustainability are held to be organizational outcomes of this approach.

A second analysis of internal sustainability is undertaken by Fein and Tziner in a consideration of leadership and organization under sus-tainability principles. Leadership is approached through the relational concept of the Leader-Member Exchange (LMX), which is embedded in an integrated organizational model of individual and organizational per-formance. It is argued that historical core virtues of courage, justice, tem-perance and wisdom directly influence the leader-follower relationship, individual performance and group performance in promoting sustainabil-ity outcomes. A research program is proposed which points to the poten-tial relevance of other core virtues, such as humanity and transcendence, and which, through appropriate operationalization of these concepts, is open to empirical testing.

The evaluation of business risk has assumed new prominence in an era characterized by high volatility, in both the physical and business environ-ment. Chileshe et al. apply sustainability concepts to strategic risk assess-ment, in the context of the construction industry. A diagnostic model, framing internal, external and competitive dimensions, is used to evaluate organizational effectiveness in sustainability initiatives. The countervail-ing concepts of agency (human capacities) and structure (organizational rules) offer a dynamic view of sustainability initiatives in project manage-ment. These concepts are then applied to the management of project risk of two kinds: those that derive from not meeting sustainability demands, and those that accompany action to meet those demands. A sequence of actions designed to identify and respond to these risks is then derived.

The third group of chapters examines the shape sustainability princi-ples give to businesses, particularly small and medium sized enterprises

(SMEs), in practice. The first two of these essays focus on family firms, which, as is well known, can make up the majority of business organizations in developed economies. Most SMEs are family companies (European Commission 2009).

Sardeshmukh proposes that family firms are well suited to sustainable entrepreneurship focused on ecological sustainability. Family firms typically display stewardship, under principles of continuity and long-term preservation. Their behaviours extend beyond financial concerns to the community and the external environment. The opportunity recognition characteristic of entrepreneurial firms is thus, in the family firm, well aligned with the emerging sustainable business sector. Family firms are more likely to reduce unsustainable inefficiencies, mitigate externalities harmful to the community, position products and services with fair pricing, and address information asymmetries on sustainability with consumers. Such strategies will benefit both the firms themselves and the community at large.

Scott-Young reports an illuminating case study of an environmentally innovative medium sized family food manufacturer. The firm is a recognized leader in integrating eco-sustainability with profitability and business growth. The case study draws on theories of sustainable business practice which identify as drivers factors of economic opportunity recognition, owner-CEO environmental values, and the presence of an innovation culture. It further examines the family business concept of socioemotional capital. The value of these factors in practice is confirmed by the study. Further the importance of the external dissemination of sustainability knowledge is recognized, a finding which extends the eco-sustainability literature. Links to family values and innovation emerge as future research directions.

Further insight into real world approaches taken by SMEs in implementing sustainable business practices emerges from a study of rural firms undertaken by Sawyer and Evans. Their study of 18 firms in the retail and services sector explored attitudes, values, opportunities and barriers with respect to social and environmental initiatives. In handling a range of business challenges, including employee attraction and retention, competitiveness, customer values, financial viability and so on, sustainable practice was found to have real value. Factors such as honesty and trust, responsibility to community, workplace culture, ethical approaches to the supply chain, environmental responsibility and reputation were all found to support the development of business value.

Zuo et al. focus attention on the appraisal of corporate sustainability in the construction industry. A critique of existing measurement frameworks is undertaken, and an alternative conceptual framework proposed.

Company and project stakeholder analysis is coupled with a longer term time horizon, and applied to both products and processes. Given the dominance of SMEs in the construction industry, the scale of firms is also taken into consideration. Project culture and knowledge, with reference to sustainability principles, products and processes, is central, as is the early and ongoing participation of stakeholders. Such a framework, it is argued, can be operationalized both to generate and to measure sustainability outcomes.

The international dimension of environmental sustainability is one of its characteristic features, a physical analogue to the global economy. The final two chapters focus on international dimensions of sustainability relevant to sustainable business.

Waye addresses international legal aspects of climate change, perhaps the preeminent global issue of our time, and one which presents formidable challenges to the global business environment. The chapter outlines features of the international legal system as it has attempted, often slowly, to respond to these challenges in the arena of international trade. An account of the relevant instruments, including the Kyoto Protocol and recent international conventions and agreements, is supported by two case studies of WTO disputes. Implications for business are explored. The specific difficulties for international legal frameworks of different methods and standards for measuring carbon footprint are then examined. Harmonization of these approaches is argued to be essential.

One of the hallmarks of sustainability thinking is its attempt to coordinate physical and social factors of human well-being. Climate change presents this challenge of coordination at the highest level. A key framework for analyzing it has been provided by economics. Shanahan examines two central economic analyses of climate change, the UK Stern Report and the Australian Garnaut Reports. It is observed that conditions differ in national economies, making generalized analysis difficult. However both reports have been instrumental in deriving from the science of climate change the physical impacts on human well-being, strategies for mitigating and adapting to it, and benefit-cost analyses of different response strategies. The chapter addresses technical criticisms of the reports and explores their business implications for firms. Both reports are seen as optimistic, grounded in the demonstrated abilities of societies to make changes, both technological and institutional, when the need for change is clearly demonstrated.

The exploration of ways in which sustainability principles apply to the theory and practice of business is no small undertaking. As the chapters in this book demonstrate, its implications run wide and deep. No discipline of management stands outside it and no business practice can ignore it.

It requires systematic work in the development of business theory, and adaptive, emergent management in the development of business practice. Ultimately, like any new paradigm, its elaboration must be a collaborative enterprise among its intellectual leaders and its practitioners, and between them. It is, we believe, an enterprise worth entering upon, in its potential to make crucial contributions to the greater well-being of people at all levels of society across the world.

REFERENCES

Baumol, W. (1970), 'Enlightened self-interest and corporate philanthropy', in W. Baumol, R. Likert, H. Wallich and J. McGowan (eds), *A New Rationale for Corporate Social Policy*, New York: Committee for Economic Development.

Berle, A. and G. Means (1932), *The Modern Corporation And Private Property*, New York: Harcourt Brace and World Inc.

Bowen, H. (1953), *Social Responsibilities of the Businessman*, New York: Harper & Brothers.

Bowie, N. (2010), 'Organizational integrity and moral climates', in G. Brenkert and T. Beauchamp (eds), *The Oxford Handbook of Business Ethics*, Oxford, UK: Oxford University Press.

Brenkert, G. and Beauchamp, T. (eds) (2010), *The Oxford Handbook of Business Ethics*, Oxford, UK: Oxford University Press.

Carroll, A. (1979), 'A three-dimensional conceptual model of corporate social performance', *Academy of Management Review*, **4**, 497–505.

Carroll, A. (1999), 'Corporate social responsibility: evolution of a definitional construct', *Business & Society*, **38** (3), 268–95.

Carroll, A. (2008), 'A history of corporate social responsibility', in A. Crane, A. McWilliams, D. Matten, J. Moon and D. Siegel (eds), *The Oxford Handbook of Corporate Social Responsibility*, Oxford, UK: Oxford University Press.

Carroll, A. and Shabana, K. (2010), 'The business case for corporate social responsibility: a review of concepts, research, and practice', *International Journal of Management Reviews*, 85–105. DOI: 10.1111/j.1468-2370.2009.00275.x

Common, M. and S. Stagl (2005), *Ecological Economics: An Introduction*, Cambridge, UK: Cambridge University Press.

Dahlsrud, A. (2008), 'How corporate social responsibility is defined: an analysis of 37 definitions', *Corporate Social Responsibility and Environmental Management*, **15**, 1–13.

Davis, K. (1960), 'Can business afford to ignore social responsibilities?', *California Management Review*, **2** (Spring), 70–76.

Drucker, P. (1946), *The Concept of the Corporation*, New Jersey: Transaction Publishers Rutgers University.

Dunfee, T. (2008), 'Stakeholder theory: managing corporate social responsibility in a multiple actor context', in A. Crane, A. McWilliams, D. Matten, J. Moon and D. Siegel (eds), *The Oxford Handbook of Corporate Social Responsibility*, Oxford, UK: Oxford University Press.

Dyllick, T. and K. Hockerts (2002), 'Beyond the business case for corporate sustainability', *Business Strategy and the Environment*, **11**, 130–41.

Elkington, J. (1997), *Cannibals With Forks: The Triple Bottom Line of 21st Century Business*, Oxford: Capstone.

European Commission (2009), *Final Report of the Expert Group: Overview of Family Business Relevant Issues: Research, Networks, Policy Measures and Existing Studies*, Brussels, Belgium: European Commission Enterprise and Industry Directorate-General.

Frederick, W. (1960), 'The growing concern over business responsibility', *California Managment Review*, **2** (Summer), 54–61.

Freeman, R. (1984), *Strategic Management: A Stakeholder Approach*, Boston: Pitman.

Freeman, R. (2009), 'Managing for stakeholders', in T. Beauchamp, N. Bowie and D. Arnold (eds), *Ethical Theory and Business*, London: Pearson Education, pp. 56–68.

Freeman, R., J. Harrison, A. Wicks, B. Parmar and S. de Colle (2010), *Stakeholder Theory: The State of the Art*, Cambridge, UK: Cambridge University Press.

Friedman, M. (1970), 'The social responsibility of business is to increase its profits', *The New York Times Magazine*, 13 September, available at http://graphics8. nytimes.com/packages/pdf/business/miltonfriedman1970.pdf (accessed 22 June 2012).

Habermas, J. (1990), *Moral Consciousness and Communicative Action*, Cambridge, MA: The MIT Press.

Hart, S. (1997), 'Beyond greening: strategies for a sustainable world', *Harvard Business Review*, January–February, 68–76.

Hawken, P., A. Lovins and L. Lovins (2008), *Natural Capital: Creating the Next Industrial Revolution*, New York: Back Bay Books.

Heal, G. (2005), *Valuing Ecosystem Services*, Washington, DC: The National Academies Press.

Heald, M. (1970), *The Social Responsibilities of Business: Company and Community, 1900–1960*, Cleveland OH: The Press of Case Western University.

ICAEW (1975), *The Corporate Report*, London: Institute of Chartered Accountants of England and Wales.

Kuhn, T. (1996), *The Structure of Scientific Revolutions*, Chicago IL: University of Chicago Press.

Kurucz, E., B. Colbert and D. Wheeler (2008), 'The business case for corporate social responsibility', in A. Crane, A. McWilliams, D. Matten, J. Moon and D. Siegel (eds), *The Oxford Handbook of Corporate Social Responsibility*, Oxford, UK: Oxford University Press.

Lee, M. (2008), 'A review of the theories of corporate social responsibility: its evolutionary path and the road ahead', *International Journal of Management Reviews*, **10** (1), 53–73.

Lutz, M. (1999), *Economics for the Common Good*, Abingdon, UK: Routledge.

Meadows, D.H., D.L. Meadows and J. Randers (1992), *Beyond the Limits to Growth: Global Collapse or Sustainable Future*, London: Earthscan.

Meadows, D.H., D.L. Meadows and J. Randers (2005), *Limits to Growth: The 30-Year Update*, London: Earthscan.

Meadows, D.H., D.L. Meadows, J. Randers and W. Behrens (1972), *The Limits to Growth: A Report for the Club Of Rome's Project on the Predicament of Mankind*, New York: Earth Island, Universe Books.

Montiel, I. (2008), 'Corporate social responsibility and corporate sustainability: separate pasts, common futures', *Organization & Environment*, **21** (3), 245–69.

Perman, R., Y. Ma, J. McGilvray and M. Common (2003), *Natural Resource and Environmental Economics*, Harlow, Essex, UK: Pearson Education.

Putnam, R. (2001), *Bowling Alone: The Collapse and Revival of American Community*, Clearwater, FL: Touchstone Books, Simon and Schuster.

Rawls, J. (1972), *A Theory of Justice*, Oxford, UK: Oxford University Press.

Sethi, P. (1975), 'Dimensions of corporate social performance: an analytic framework', *California Management Review*, **17** (Spring), 58–64.

Solomon, R. (2004), 'Aristotle, ethics and business organizations', *Organization Studies*, **25** (6), 1021–43.

Stewart, T. (1999), *Intellectual Capital: The New Wealth of Organizations*, New York: Doubleday.

Stretton, H. (2000), *Economics: A New Introduction*, London: Pluto Press.

UNDESA (1999), *Rio Declaration on Environment and Development*, New York: United Nations Department of Economic and Social Affairs.

Wallich, H. and J. McGowan (1970), 'Stockholder interest and the corporation's role in social policy', in W. Baumol, R. Likert, H. Wallich and J. McGowan (eds), *A New Rationale for Corporate Social Policy*, New York: Committee for Economic Development.

Wartick, S. and P. Cochran (1985), 'The evolution of the corporate social performance model', *Academy of Management Review*, **10**, 758–69.

WCED (1987), *Our Common Future*, Oxford: The World Commission on Environment and Development/ Oxford University Press.

Wren, D. (2005), *The History of Management Thought*, Hoboken NJ: John Wiley & Sons Inc.

PART I

The Sustainable Firm

1. Towards an integrated conceptual framework for corporate social and environmental sustainability

Sukhbir Sandhu

INTRODUCTION

Governments and societies throughout the world are increasingly calling on businesses to be environmentally and socially responsible, and many businesses appear to be responding to this call (Hart, 2007; Lubin and Esty, 2010). This inclusion of social and environmental sustainability in the business agenda has also resulted in enhanced academic attention. Thus in the last two decades, a growing number of academic studies have focussed on examining various aspects of corporate sustainability (for example, Bansal, 2005; Hart, 2007; Madsen, 2009; Wells, 2011). While these studies have considerably extended the understanding about corporate sustainability, researchers have yet to reach a definitive conclusion regarding the relative importance of the various factors that can drive organizations towards sustainability (Delmas and Montes-Sancho, 2010; Kassinis and Vafeas, 2006; Russo and Harrison, 2005).

One explanation for this ambivalence is that researchers have used an either/or approach to theoretical frameworks while examining drivers of corporate social and environmental responsiveness. Researchers have thus been guided by either stakeholder theory (Eesley and Lenox, 2006; Henriques and Sadorsky, 1996), or institutional theory (Bansal and Clelland, 2004; Hoffman, 1999; King et al., 2005), or by the perspectives from the resource based view (RBV) (Aragon-Correa and Sharma, 2000; Christmann, 2000; Hart and Ahuja, 1996), or the resource dependence perspectives (Kassinis and Vafeas, 2006; Rowley and Moldoveanu, 2003; Sharma and Henriques, 2005).

One limitation of being guided by a singular theoretical perspective is that the enquiry will, of necessity, be constrained and scoped in accordance with the prescriptions of the given framework (Oliver, 1991, 1997). While a singular framework might be suitable for examining linear relationships, for complex phenomena such as corporate sustainability (which are characterized by radical uncertainty – Perman et al., 2003), decision making involves an interplay between multiple determinants at multiple levels, which may not necessarily be captured and explained by a singular theoretical framework (Delmas and Montes-Sancho, 2010). Additionally social and environmental sustainability issues in business are often viewed as being relatively nascent. While one-dimensional frameworks may appear to provide a useful starting point as sustainability issues mature in their socio-political dimensions, and as organizational, institutional and stakeholder environments evolve, there will be a need to understand the complexities surrounding sustainability issues through combining perspectives from multiple theoretical insights.

Researchers are therefore increasingly stressing the need to combine perspectives from multiple theoretical viewpoints for obtaining a more complete account of the phenomenon being investigated (Sparrowe and Mayer, 2011). Thus Okhuysen and Bonardi (2011, p. 6) suggest that in order to move research into complex phenomena forward, especially at multiple levels of analysis (for example, organizational, national, and international levels), there is an urgent need for 'developing explanations that are matched in complexity . . . (and) explanations that can be built from combination of perspectives' (Okhuysen and Bonardi, 2011, p. 6).

This chapter responds to this call and integrates perspectives from four distinct theoretical perspectives (stakeholder, resource dependence, institutional, and resource based theories) to provide an integrated framework for research into drivers of corporate social and environmental sustainability. Each of these theoretical perspectives when considered in isolation is unable to comprehensively untangle the drivers of corporate sustainability (Table 1.1). In an attempt to remedy this some scholars have attempted partial combinations of theoretical frameworks. Thus Bansal's (2005) exploration of sustainable practices in businesses relies on a combination of resource based and institutional explanations. While this is a valuable development it still leaves unaddressed the importance of stakeholder pressure. The contribution of the current chapter is in systematic integration of the main theoretical frameworks that have been previously used in sustainability literature. The proposed integrated framework can anchor a comprehensive enquiry into drivers of corporate social and environmental sustainability.

Combining insights from these multiple theoretical perspectives promises better explanatory capabilities at an organizational, national and international level of analysis. Corporate sustainability in any given organization is often not a one-dimensional construct. Thus at an organizational

Table 1.1   Limitations of singular theoretical frameworks in guiding research in corporate sustainability

Theoretical perspective	Contribution to framework	Issues the theory is ambivalent about
Stakeholder theory	Pressure from stakeholders can contribute towards corporate sustainability.	What are the mechanisms that govern stakeholder salience? This is where resource dependence theory informs stakeholder theory.
Resource dependence theory	Stakeholder salience can in part be explained on the basis of a firm's dependence on stakeholders for critical external resources.	Firms however compete not only for resources but also for legitimacy. Inputs from institutional theory provide a framework for understanding legitimacy drivers.
Institutional theory	Explains how desire for social legitimacy leads firms to conform to institutionalized sustainability norms.	Does not explain why firms facing similar institutional pressures differ in their sustainability strategies. Resource based view addresses this issue.
Resource based theory	Focuses on the role of internal resources of a firm as a source for differentiating social and environmental strategies.	Resource based view does not explicitly focus on the 'outside in' determinants

Synthesis of perspectives from the above four theoretical viewpoints can provide a holistic explanation of the *external* (institutional and resource dependence factors) and the *internal* (resource based) dynamics.

level different sustainability initiatives are best understood through combining perspectives from different theoretical frameworks (Sandhu et al., 2010). As an example, effluent treatment in any given organization might be dictated by regulatory pressures. However in the same organization, new green product development might be driven by resource based competencies. Therefore relying only on stakeholder analysis might result in an incomplete or partial understanding. This argument can be extended to the national level of analysis: when researchers explore the drivers of corporate sustainability across different countries (for example across developing and developed countries), multiple theoretical lenses can provide more useful explanatory capabilities than relying on singular or a partial combination of these theoretical viewpoints. As an example, similar sustainability initiatives (such as investing in waste management systems) may have institutional explanations (coercive isomorphism due to regulatory pressures) in developed countries but resource dependence and resource based explanations (supply chain pressures from powerful MNC buyers and internal organizational capabilities in investing these initiatives) in developing countries (Sandhu et al., 2010).

Combining perspectives across theoretical viewpoints can therefore provide a comprehensive conceptualization for understanding the drivers of corporate sustainability at different levels of analysis. This will benefit managers of MNCs and also researchers and policy makers who are engaged in exploring the drivers of corporate sustainability across organizational, national and international levels.

The chapter is structured as follows. It commences with a discussion of how stakeholder and resource dependence theories together can provide a starting point for identifying stakeholders that can potentially leverage business organizations into being environmentally and socially responsive. However organizations are not just beholden to stakeholders who control resources; their policies also result from a desire to confirm and to seek social approval and legitimacy. This desire for legitimacy has its roots in institutional theory and this leads to perspectives from institutional theory being incorporated into the framework. However while institutional theory explains legitimacy driven acceptance of socially sanctioned sustainability norms, it does not explain why firms in a given industry facing similar institutional pressures, might choose to react differently to social and environmental issues (for example in the sustainability realm, when do firms break free of the isomorphic institutional cage?) This is where the Resource Based View (RBV) – with its focus on costly-to-copy, firm specific, internal resource (as factors that differentiate the strategic choices of a firm) – enters the framework and helps explain how firms break free of institutional influences.

The major contribution of this chapter thus lies in combining the insights from the RBV (regarding the significance of internal resources) with the importance of the role of external stakeholder (from resource dependence and institutional theories). The chapter integrates these insights to develop a holistic framework for anchoring an enquiry into the drivers of corporate social and environmental responsiveness at multiple levels of analysis.

TOWARDS AN INTEGRATED CONCEPTUAL FRAMEWORK

Stakeholder Theory and Corporate Social and Environmental Sustainability

Freeman (1984, p. 46) defines stakeholders as 'any group or individual who can affect or is affected by the achievement of the organization's objectives'. Stakeholder theory (Berman et al., 1999; Freeman, 1999; Jones, 1995; Jones and Wicks, 1999) suggests that organizations are driven to be environmentally and socially sustainable due to pressures from stakeholders. Stakeholder theory can thus provide a useful starting point for anchoring an enquiry into corporate sustainability practices. However the broad inclusiveness of stakeholder theory makes it difficult to determine which stakeholders (amongst the many possible –'can affect or be affected by') are genuinely important in influencing an organization's social and environmental sustainability practices (Mitchell et al., 1997). In an attempt to resolve the issue of 'who or what really counts' (Freeman, 1994, p. 411) stakeholders have been classified as primary or secondary, based upon their importance to an organization (Clarkson, 1995). However the value of this to both research and practice is limited. This is because stakeholder attributes are neither in a steady state nor an objective reality; instead they are socially constructed and variable (Mitchell et al., 1997). Stakeholder importance is thus transitory and subject to change. Pressures from stakeholders who were considered secondary in the past (such as environmental groups, scientific agencies like the Intergovernmental Panel on Climate Change (IPCC)) have now become significant catalysts for social and environmental changes in many organizations (Anderson, 2005; Hart and Sharma, 2004). Thus classifying stakeholders as primary and secondary is tenuous; the status can be attained or lost.

In attempting to apply a sorting logic to this transitory nature of stakeholder importance, Mitchell et al. (1997) proposed that stakeholders with power, legitimacy and urgency will be regarded as important by managers of a firm. This seminal work helps unpack stakeholder saliency and allows stakeholders to be grouped according to the attributes that they possess (in terms of power, urgency and legitimacy). Thus, at one end there are *definitive* stakeholders (who have all three attributes) and at the other extreme are *non stakeholders* (who lack all three attributes). A range of stakeholder saliency can be observed in between these extremes – depending on the type and number of attributes possessed by any given stakeholder. Thus for example, *dormant* stakeholders (such as retrenched employees) may have power (as they can engage in potential lawsuits), but currently may have neither legitimacy nor urgency; *dangerous* stakeholders, such as terrorist groups, may have power and urgency but no legitimacy.

In proposing this saliency typology Mitchell et al's. (1997) seminal work starts to integrate perspectives from resource dependence theory into stakeholder theory. However while Mitchell et al.'s work is a useful starting point towards integrating perspectives from these two theoretical viewpoints, it leaves unaddressed the dynamics by which stakeholders gain (or lose) these attributes of power, urgency and legitimacy (for example when and how can a dormant stakeholder become a dangerous or definitive stakeholder).

What further complicates the issue of stakeholder saliency is Rowley's (1997) research which suggests that stakeholder concerns do not present themselves in an ordered dyadic relationship between individual stakeholders and a focal organization; instead managers are confronted with simultaneous influences of multiple stakeholders many of whom are interdependent and acting in collusion with each other to achieve their own ends (Rowley, 1997). Recent work by Neville et al. (2011) on stakeholder salience suggests that there is an urgent need to bring in other theoretical frameworks to better understand and explore the basis of stakeholder saliency.

Thus, there are two issues here. (1) Despite the fact that Mitchell et al. (1997) integrate aspects of resource dependence theory into stakeholder theory, there is potential for resource dependence theory to further inform stakeholder salience especially with regards to the dynamics of stakeholder salience. (2) Recent research (Neville et al., 2011) suggests that there is a need to further explore stakeholder salience through integrating insights from theoretical perspectives such as institutional theory. This chapter addresses both these issues.

The following section will provide a brief explanation of resource dependence theory and discuss the potential for its further integration with stakeholder theory in exploring the drivers of corporate social and environmental sustainability. The subsequent section will discuss how institutional and resource based perspectives inform the framework being developed.

Resource Dependence Theory and Corporate Social and Environmental Sustainability

Drawing from resource dependence theory (Pfeffer and Salancik, 1978), Frooman (1999) argues that the more dependent an organization is on a stakeholder for critical resources, the greater the extent to which that stakeholder can influence the firm's response. It is this dependence of organizations on stakeholders for critical resources that gives stakeholders leverage over organizations and creates differentials among stakeholders. To assist managers with the process of identifying stakeholder salience, Frooman (1999) has organized stakeholder influences into four strategies (withholding, usage, direct and indirect).

The first two strategies (withholding and usage) involve the extent of firm-stakeholder interdependence. A withholding strategy will be used when stakeholders have absolute discretion over allocation of resources. The stakeholder can walk out of the relationship with no harm to itself. Stakeholders can thus withhold critical resources needed by a firm with the intention of making the firm change its behaviour. Frooman's (1999) insights are particularly useful in exploring sustainability drivers. Thus the use of withholding strategy by consumers through boycotting Shell's products in the 1990s (involving the Brent Spar and the Ogoni controversies) led Shell to redefine its mission worldwide to include environmental and human rights concerns (Shell, 2007; Shell (Nigeria), 2007a, 2007b). Withholding strategies can thus be used when the balance of resource dependence favours the stakeholder.

A usage strategy on the other hand is used when there is a mutual dependence between the firm and the stakeholder (the welfare of each is linked to the other). In a usage strategy, stakeholders therefore do not withhold outright but attach conditions for the continued use of a resource (for example Mattel toys had to attach more stringent requirements for quality control on their suppliers in China, after lead was detected in paint used for children's toys (Mattel Toys, 2007).

The next set of strategies involves pathways (direct and indirect) used for influencing a firm. Direct strategies are used when the stakeholder has enough influence over the firm to manipulate the flow of resources by itself (through withholding or by usage) without assistance from other stakeholders. For example governments can cancel the '*license to operate*' (Elkington, 1997) or attach stringent conditions if firms violate the conditions of their license. Indirect influence pathways are employed when a stakeholder has little or no control over firm resources and thus has limited influence over a firm. The stakeholder can then choose to act through other influential stakeholders who act as allies by manipulating the flow of resources (again through withholding or usage). The purpose of adding the ally is to shift the balance of the power towards the weaker stakeholder. An example of this is social activist groups acting through mobilizing consumers to boycott Nike sweat shop products. These four strategies result in the matrix shown in Table 1.2 (Frooman, 1999).

Applying the resource based logic to corporate social and environmental practices provides a theoretical rationale for understanding stakeholder

Table 1.2   Resource dependence dynamics (based on Frooman, 1999)

Is the firm dependent on the social stakeholder?	Is the social stakeholder dependent on the firm?	
	No	Yes
Yes	Stakeholder power (direct-withholding strategy) 1 (For example, consumers of multinational products who can easily switch brands without any real loss to themselves; for example between Nike shoes and Adidas shoes)	High interdependence (direct-usage strategy) 3 (Local communities, where the organization is also a major employer. The community members may be concerned about the ill effects of the operations of the organization but may attach conditions to continued operations rather than direct action campaigns.)
No	Low interdependence (indirect-withholding strategy 2 (For example, environmental NGOs acting through alliances with consumers. Thus the NGOs themselves may not have the requisite power, but can incite consumers against the 'guilty' organization)	Firm power (indirect-usage strategy) 4 (Civil society protests are not very effective in this scenario, unless they can find powerful allies such as government)

saliency and provides a basis for understanding how secondary stakeholders can become important catalysts for driving corporate social and environmental sustainability. Monsanto's withdrawal from genetically modified (GM) foods presents an interesting example of resource dependence dynamics at work. Protests by millions of small farmers in India (traditionally considered fringe or dormant secondary stakeholders) in combination with NGOs who leveraged the consumer fear for GM foods are reported to be instrumental in forcing Monsanto to re-evaluate its multibillion genetically modified seed business (Hart and Sharma, 2004).

It is thus not sufficient to view stakeholder salience in terms of absence or presence of power, urgency and legitimacy; instead it is important to understand the processes by which stakeholders can gain the resources

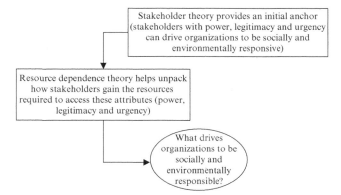

Figure 1.1   Role of stakeholder and resource dependence theories in informing the drivers of corporate social and environmental responsiveness

required to become catalysts of change (Figure 1.1). Integrating perspectives from resource dependence theory (using Frooman's strategies) into stakeholder theory suggests that stakeholders who can marshal the requisite resources will be successful in driving organizations towards social and environmental sustainability.

Organizations however are not just beholden to stakeholders who control resources. As DiMaggio and Powell (1983, p.150) point out 'organizations compete not just for resources and customers but also for institutional legitimacy'. Organizations as social actors thus do not always act as rational profit maximizers; their policies also result from a desire to confirm and to seek social approval and legitimacy (Myers and Rowan, 1977; Scott, 1987; Oliver, 1991). This desire for legitimacy has its roots in institutional theory. The following section will discuss how inputs from institutional theory can further enrich the capabilities of stakeholder and resource dependence theory in providing a framework for understanding the drivers of social and environmental sustainability.

Institutional Theory and Corporate Social and Environmental Sustainability

Institutional theory emphasizes the social context in which firms operate and explains the role of institutions (for example governments, professional associations, media and public opinion) in shaping organizational responses (DiMaggio and Powell, 1983). Institutional theory explains how pressures from these social institutions become 'institutionalized' and accepted as given over a period of time (Myers and Rowan, 1977; Oliver, 1991; Scott, 1987). Through adhering to commonly accepted and institutionalized norms, organizations seek to obtain social approval and legitimacy and failure to conform to critical institutional norms can threaten an organization's legitimacy and survival (DiMaggio and Powell, 1983; Myers and Rowan, 1977; Oliver, 1991).

DiMaggio and Powell (1983) attribute the reason for certain norms gaining institutional acceptance to the tendency of organizations (in a given organizational field) to move towards isomorphism. Isomorphism results in an 'inexorable push towards homogenization' (DiMaggio and Powell, 1983, p. 148). Institutional theory thus suggests that through adopting institutionalized social and environmental norms (which have penetrated the social contexts and are seen as intractable) organizations seek social approval and legitimacy. According to DiMaggio and Powell (1983) coercive, mimetic and normative pressures push organizations towards homogenous responses. These three pressures provide a theoretical grounding for understanding legitimacy inspired drivers of organizational environmental and social practices.

Coercive pressures stem from political influence. Thus the existence of a common legal environmental framework affects all organizations in a given field similarly and leads to homogeneity in organizational responses. For example most countries have regulations regarding the specific types and quantities of contaminants that businesses can discharge. Failure to conform attracts fines and penalties and threatens the firm's legitimacy. Thus coercive regulatory pressures, over a period of time lead to isomorphic and institutionalized responses, wherein all firms will tend to comply with the regulatory discharge requirements.

Another source of isomorphism is mimetic pressure. Mimicry results when organizations operate under conditions of uncertainty. Organizations tend to mimic other more successful and legitimate organizations when there is uncertainty in the business environment. Thus uncertainty resulting from poorly understood environmental challenges is a powerful institutional driver for isomorphism (DiMaggio and Powell, 1983). Environmental and social risks are not yet fully understood by the entire spectrum of organizations (Porter and Reinhardt, 2007). Under such conditions of uncertainty (what policies and technologies should be employed, should an organization aim for leadership position on climate change or wait and watch) organizations tend to model their sustainability practices after other organizations who are perceived to be more legitimate or successful (DiMaggio and Powell, 1983). An increasing number of multinationals thus now have sustainability reports, whereas only a handful of them reported on their sustainability practices just a decade earlier

(Rondinelli and Berry, 2000). In doing so organizations are attempting to gain legitimacy through mimicking the organizations deemed to be social and environmental leaders (Lubin and Esty, 2010).

The third basis for isomorphism is normative pressures. The normative basis is associated with professionalization. Professionalization stems from the fact that most managers at a given level have commonalties based on similar educational qualifications and through socialization in common professional associations. Moreover the mobility of managers through turnover and head hunting further ensures that these managers 'drawn from the common pool of universities and filtered on a common set of attributes' (DiMaggio and Powell, 1983, p.153) will arguably respond to problems and policies within the constraints of normatively sanctioned isomorphism. In the context of social and environmental management this points to the fact that in a given organizational field since most of the senior managers dealing with social and environmental issues might have similar educational qualifications, attend same or similar professional workshops, and will be members of similar professional bodies and industry associations, their responses to sustainability problems will, to the extent of sharing common frames, be bound by collective normative and ethical guides. Thus to a certain extent professionalization leads managers to have a shared world view of socially sanctioned legitimacy, and to that extent, results in isomorphic responses to social and environmental challenges (Jennings and Zandbergen, 1995; Cramer, 2005). These normative isomorphic influences are being currently evidenced in the collective opposition of the business leaders to the carbon tax in Australia.

Based on the above discussion research into drivers of corporate sustainability can thus be further informed by the perspectives gained from the institutional lens. Incorporating the institutional perspectives allows researchers to account for the role of institutions in driving corporate environmental and social responsiveness (Figure 1.2). Thus apart from stakeholders who control resources, sustainability initiatives are also explained by institutional insights into coercive, mimetic and normative bases of legitimacy.

However within an institutional framework firms aim to 'meet not exceed' (Bansal and Clelland, 2004, p.94) established norms. Hence institutional theory cannot explain why organizational responses to sustainability challenges are not always constrained by the 'iron cage' (DiMaggio and Powell, 1983, p.147) of institutionalized norms. Research suggests that firms operating in similar social, regulatory and public policy environments can vary in their social and environmental strategies (Aragon-Correa, 1998; Hart and Ahuja, 1996). Even in a single industrial context where organizations face very strong and similar institutional pressures,

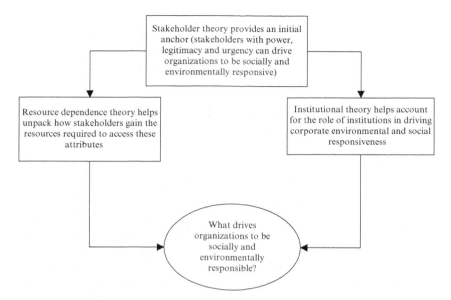

*Figure 1.2   Incorporating institutional explanations of corporate social
and environmental responsiveness*

organizational responses to social and environmental challenges may
vary from substantive to symbolic practices (Delmas and Montes-Sancho,
2010). Thus while institutional theory explains legitimacy driven acceptance of socially sanctioned sustainability norms, it does not explain why
firms in a given industry facing similar institutional pressures might
choose to react differently to social and environmental issues (Sharma and
Vredenburg, 1998).

WHAT ABOUT THE ROLE OF FIRM-SPECIFIC FACTORS?

Summarizing the above discussion, combining perspectives from stakeholder, resource dependence and institutional lenses provides a theoretical basis for understanding drivers of corporate sustainability, but only
insofar as the drivers are explained by a firm's resource dependence or its
search for legitimacy. These three theories however, essentially focus on
forces that lie beyond the organizational boundaries (Hoffman, 1999).
They ignore the dynamics happening inside the black-box: the firm. It
must be pointed out that these theories do not completely rule out internal

pressures (for example stakeholder theory recognizes employees as having a stake) but as discussed above, their theoretical capabilities fall short of explaining why firms with similar kinds of employees (institutional), and with similar level of dependence on employees (resource dependence), might choose different social and environmental strategies. The resource based theory with its focus on costly-to-copy, firm specific, internal resources as factors that differentiate the strategic choices of a firm, helps explain the above dilemma.

RESOURCE BASED THEORY AND CORPORATE SOCIAL AND ENVIRONMENTAL SUSTAINABILITY

Penrose's seminal work (1959) guided early resource based researchers who focused on the valuable and inimitable internal resources of a firm as a source of securing competitive advantage (Grant, 1991; Hamel and Prahalad, 1994; Wernerfelt, 1984). The RBV combines the analysis of resource based competencies rooted inside a firm with the external analysis of the business environment. According to Collis and Montgomery, (1995, p. 120) 'the RBV inextricably links a company's internal capabilities (what it does well) and its external environment; what the market demands and what competitors offer'. Thus through combining the internal and the external analysis, the RBV offers a very useful perspective for strategic management research (Barney, 1991; Hart, 1995; Oliver, 1997; Bansal, 2005).

It may help to point out that despite what may perhaps be perceived as nomenclature similarities, the resource *based* theory is distinct from the previously discussed resource *dependence* perspective. The previously explained resource *dependence* perspective helps explain the processes through which stakeholders can leverage organizations into meeting their demands. The resource *based* theory in contrast helps unpack how internal competencies of the firm can influence its strategy.

According to RBV (Barney, 1991, 2001; Conner, 1991; Grant, 1991; Oliver, 1997; Wernerfelt, 1984), resources which are valuable, rare, imperfectly imitable and non-substitutable can lead to the development of internal competencies which when applied to the appropriate external environment, can secure competitive advantage. According to Barney (1991) these resources can be physical resources, human capital resources and organizational resources. Having valuable resources is however a necessary but not a sufficient condition for securing a competitive edge. Firms have to continuously evaluate choices regarding resource employment with respect to the external environment (Collis and Montgomery, 1995).

Major transformations are now occurring in the business environment due to the constraints imposed and opportunities offered by the changes in the natural and social environment (Hoffman, 2007; Porter and Reinhardt, 2007; Schwartz, 2007). Under these conditions of flux, resource and capability development in organizations is also being driven by the need to adapt to these changes in the natural environment (Nidumolu et al., 2009). Hart's (1995) expansion of the resource based theory to include the challenges posed by sustainability (in the form of the natural resource based view (NRBV) allows an examination of the role of firm specific factors in driving corporate social and environmental responsiveness.

The natural resource based view has thus been developed on the premise that businesses will be now increasingly constrained by sustainability risks and opportunities (Hart, 1995). According to Hart (1995, p. 991) 'competitive advantage in the coming years will be rooted in capabilities that facilitate environmentally and socially sustainable economic activity'. Drawing from the resource based view, Hart (1995) contends that to be able to develop a successful sustainability strategy, firms need resources that are valuable, non substitutable and difficult to replicate.

The NRBV states that firms possessing valuable, rare, non substitutable, tacit and socially complex resources can develop strategic capabilities in strategies such as pollution prevention, product stewardship and sustainable development. These strategies can lead to competitive advantage (lower costs, pre-empt competition and secure future position). The choice of the strategy that the firm can or will actually adopt will in turn be dependent on the resource endowments of that firm (Nidumolu et al., 2009). The stress in NRBV is on the significance of the internal organizational resources and characteristics in influencing corporate sustainability. According to NRBV firms will differ in their environmental and social initiatives depending on the disparity in the organizational resources that they can marshal. Social and environmental capabilities resulting from these resources can be difficult to replicate either because they are tacit (skill based and people intensive or accumulated through experience) or socially complex (such resources depend on a large number of people or teams engaged in coordinated activity). This view is empirically supported by a number of studies which have found a positive relationship between development of resource based environmental capabilities and improved competitive advantage (Hart and Ahuja, 1996; Menguc and Ozanne, 2005). NRBV thus allows researchers to extend the investigation into the drivers of social and environmental sustainability from stakeholder and legitimacy based drivers to include the role of internal organizational resources and characteristics in influencing corporate social and environmental responsiveness (Figure 1.3).

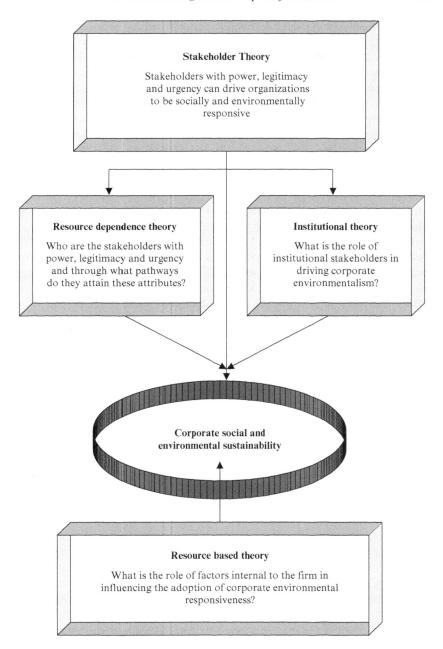

Figure 1.3   Holistic conceptual framework using multiple theoretical lenses

DISCUSSION AND CONCLUSION

The central argument of this chapter is that to enable a more complete understanding of the complex motivations that drive organizations to be socially and environmentally sustainable, we need a theoretical framework that matches the complexity of the phenomenon being investigated. Combining insights from the NRBV (regarding the significance of internal resources) with the importance of the role of external stakeholders (from resource dependence and institutional theories) allows the development of such a holistic framework.

The benefits of such a framework extend to organizational, national, and international levels of analysis. At an organizational level an integrated framework will help managers and researchers have a more nuanced understanding of the drivers for different sustainability initiatives. Thus at an organizational level pollution control initiatives might be best explained by resource dependence explanations (community groups collaborating with NGOs and media, in protesting against the toxic emissions of the organizations). However the same organization might be currently unwilling to respond to potential climate change challenges. This lack of action may be explained by its unwillingness to depart from current institutional norms in its industry. Therefore a straitjacket approach that tries to explain different levels of responsiveness by relying on a singular theoretical framework can yield incomplete and misleading findings.

An integrated conceptual framework is also useful when exploring drivers of corporate social and environmental sustainability from a national and international perspective. Thus within a given national socio-political context, organizations will differ in both the sustainability initiatives that they adopt, and also in their motivations for these. A cohesive and holistic framework allows researchers and policy makers to make sense of complex motivations that trigger the wide range of social and environmental responses. For example within a given national context, organizations might respond to a combination of institutional (mimicking industry response), resource dependence (pressure from communities and NGOs) and resource based motivations (internal organizational competencies). Similarly in an international context, an integrated framework will help managers in MNCs distinguish between different drivers for very similar initiatives in their businesses across nations. As discussed in the introductory section similar sustainability initiatives (for example investing in waste management systems), may have institutional explanations (coercive isomorphism due to regulatory pressures) in developed countries but resource dependence explanations (supply chain pressures from powerful MNC buyers) in developing countries (Sandhu et al., 2010).

An integrated framework thus allows researchers to conduct an in-depth enquiry into the factors that can propel business organizations to be environmentally and socially sustainable. To borrow Porter and Reinhardt's (2007) terminology such a framework permits an exploration with both 'inside out' (understanding the impact of a firm's resources on corporate environmentalism) and 'outside in' focus (how external factors impact a firm's corporate environmentalism).

Uncovering and testing these relationships using such a comprehensive framework will have clear benefits for furthering research knowledge and also for policy makers and managers. Thus research based on this framework can help policy makers in gaining a better understanding of the institutional areas that need to be strengthened to assist further adoption of social and environmental sustainability. Similarly managers can gain a better and more comprehensive understanding of how stakeholders liaise with each to pressurize organizations into being more sustainable. It will also allow managers to reflect on how they can leverage their internal competencies, to achieve greater sustainability. Overall this framework, with its focus on synthesis across multiple theoretical frameworks, will allow researchers, organizations and policy makers to better understand the risks posed and opportunities offered by social and environmental sustainability challenges at organizational, national and international levels.

REFERENCES

Anderson, D.R. (2005), *Corporate Survival: The Critical Importance of Sustainability Risk Management*, New York: iUniverse Inc.

Aragon-Correa, J.A. (1998), 'Strategic proactivity and firm approach to the natural environment', *Academy of Management Journal*, **41** (5), 556–67.

Aragon-Correa, J.A. and Sharma, S. (2000), 'A contingent resource based view on proactive corporate environmental strategy', *Academy of Management Review*, **28** (1), 71–88.

Bansal, P. (2005), 'Evolving sustainably: a longitudinal study of corporate sustainable development', *Strategic Management Journal*, **26** (3), 197–218.

Bansal, P. and Clelland, I. (2004), 'Talking trash: legitimacy, impression management, and unsystematic risk in the context of the natural environment', *Academy of Management Journal*, **47** (1), 93–103.

Barney, J. (1991), 'Firm resources and sustained competitive advantage', *Journal of Management*, **17** (1), 99–120.

Barney, J. (2001), 'Is the resource based "view" a useful perspective for strategic management research? Yes', *Academy of Management Review*, **26** (1), 41–56.

Berman, S.L., Wicks, A.C., Kotha, S. and Jones, T.M. (1999), 'Does stakeholder orientation matter? The relationship between stakeholder management models and firm financial performance', *Academy of Management Journal*, **42** (5), 488–506.

Christmann, P. (2000), 'Effects of "best practices" of environmental management on cost advantage: the role of complementary assets', *Academy of Management Journal*, **43** (4), 663–80.

Clarkson, M.B.E. (1995), 'A stakeholder framework for analyzing and evaluating corporate social performance', *Academy of Management Review*, **20** (1), 92–117.

Collis, D.J. and Montgomery, C.A. (1995), 'Competing on resources: strategy in the 1990s', *Harvard Business Review*, **73** (4), 118–28.

Conner, K.R. (1991), 'A historical comparison of resource based theory and five schools of thought within industrial organization economics: do we have a new theory of the firm', *Journal of Management*, **17** (1), 121–54.

Cramer, J. (2005), 'Company learning about corporate social responsibility', *Business Strategy and the Environment*, **14** (4), 255–66.

Delmas, M.A. and Montes-Sancho, M.J. (2010), 'Voluntary agreements to improve environmental quality: symbolic and substantive cooperation', *Strategic Management Journal*, **31** (6), 575–601.

DiMaggio, P.J. and Powell, W.W. (1983), 'The iron cage revisited: institutional isomorphism and collective rationality in organizational fields', *American Sociological Review*, **48** (2), 147–60.

Eesley, C. and Lenox, M.J. (2006), 'Firm response to secondary stakeholder action', *Strategic Management Journal*, **27** (8), 765–81.

Elkington, J. (1997), *Cannibals with Forks: The Triple Bottom Line of 21st Century Business*, Oxford, England: Capstone.

Freeman, R.E. (1984), *Strategic Management: A Stakeholder Approach*, London: Pitman Books.

Freeman, R.E. (1994), 'The politics of stakeholder theory: some future directions', *Business Ethics Quarterly*, **4** (4), 409–421.

Freeman, R.E. (1999), 'Divergent stakeholder theory', *Academy of Management Review*, **24** (2), 233–6.

Frooman, J. (1999), 'Stakeholder influence strategies', *Academy of Management Review*, **24** (2), 191–205.

Grant, R.M. (1991), 'The resource based theory of competitive advantage: implications for strategy formulation', *California Management Review*, **33** (3), 114–35.

Hamel, G. and Prahalad, C.K. (1994), *Competing for the Future* (1st edn). Boston: Harvard Business School Press.

Hart, S.L. (1995), 'A natural resource based view of the firm', *Academy of Management Review*, **20** (4), 986–1014.

Hart, S.L. (2007), *Capitalism at the Crossroads: Aligning Business, Earth and Humanity*, New Jersey: Wharton School Publishing.

Hart, S.L. and Ahuja, G. (1996), 'Does it pay to be green? An empirical examination of the relationship between emission reduction and firm performance', *Business Strategy and the Environment*, **5** (1), 30–37.

Hart, S.L. and Sharma, S. (2004), 'Engaging fringe stakeholders for competitive imagination', *Academy of Management Executive*, **18** (1), 7–18.

Henriques, I. and Sadorsky, P. (1996), 'The determinants of an environmentally responsive firm: an empirical approach', *Journal of Environmental Economics and Management*, **30** (3), 381–395.

Hoffman, A.J. (1999), 'Institutional evolution and change: environmentalism and the U.S. chemical industry', *Academy of Management Journal*, **42** (4), 351–71.

Hoffman, A.J. (2007), 'If you're not at the table you're on the menu', *Harvard Business Review*, **85** (10), 34–8.

Jennings, P.D. and Zandbergen, P.A. (1995), 'Ecologically sustainable organizations: an institutional approach', *Academy of Management Review*, **20** (4), 1015–52.
Jones, T.M. (1995), 'Instrumental stakeholder theory: a synthesis of ethics and economics', *Academy of Management Review*, **20** (2), 404–37.
Jones, T.M. and Wicks, A.C. (1999), 'Convergent stakeholder theory', *Academy of Management Review*, **24** (2), 206–21.
Kassinis, G. and Vafeas, N. (2006), 'Stakeholder pressure and environmental performance', *Academy of Management Journal*, **49** (1), 145–59.
King, A., Lenox, M.J. and Teralaak, A. (2005), 'The strategic use of decentralized institutions: exploring certification with the ISO14001 management standard', *Academy of Management Journal*, **48** (6), 1091–1106.
Lubin, D.A. and Esty, D.C. (2010), 'The sustainability imperative', *Harvard Business Review*, **88** (5), 42–50.
Madsen, P.M. (2009), 'Does corporate investement drive a "race to the bottom" in environment protection? A reexamination of the effect of environmental regulation on investment', *Academy of Management Journal*, **52** (6), 1297–1318.
Mattel Toys (2007), 'Voluntary recall', available at http://corporate.mattel.com/safety/, (accessed 12 April 2012).
Menguc, B. and Ozanne, L.K. (2005), 'Challenges of the "green imperative": a natural resource based approach to the environmental orientation-business performance relationship', *Journal of Business Research*, **58** (4), 430–439.
Mitchell, R.K., Agle, B.R. and Wood, D.J. (1997), 'Towards a theory of stakeholder identification and salience: defining the principle of who and what really counts', *Academy of Management Review*, **22** (4), 853–86.
Myers, J.W. and Rowan, B. (1977), 'Institutional organizations: formal structure as myth and ceremony', *American Journal of Sociology*, **83**, 340–63.
Neville, B.A., Bell, S.J. and Whitwell, G.J. (2011), 'Stakeholder salience revisited: refining, redefining, and refueling an underdeveloped conceptual tool', *Journal of Business Ethics*, **102** (3), 357–78.
Nidumolu, R., Prahalad, C.K. and Rangaswami, M.R. (2009), 'Why sustainability is now the key driver to innovation', *Harvard Business Review*, **87** (9), 57–64.
Okhuysen, G. and Bonardi, J.P. (2011), 'The challenge of building theory by combining lenses', *Academy of Management Review*, **36** (1), 6–11.
Oliver, C. (1991), 'Strategic response to institutional processes', *Academy of Management Review*, **16** (1), 145–79.
Oliver, C. (1997), 'Sustainable competitive advantage: combining institutional and resource based views', *Strategic Management Journal*, **18** (9), 697–713.
Penrose, E. (1959), *The Theory of the Growth of the Firm*, New York: Wiley.
Perman, R., Ma, Y., McGilvray, J. and Common, M. (2003), *Natural Resource and Environmental Economics* (3rd edn), London: Pearson.
Pfeffer, J. and Salancik, G.R. (1978), *The External Control of Organizations*, New York: Harper and Row.
Porter, M.E. and Reinhardt, F.L. (2007), 'A strategic approach to climate', *Harvard Business Review*, **85** (10), 22–6.
Rondinelli, D.A. and Berry, M.A. (2000), 'Environmental citizenship in multinational corporations: social responsibility and sustainable development', *European Management Journal*, **18** (1), 70–84.
Rowley, T.J. (1997), 'Moving beyond dyadic ties: a network theory of stakeholder influences', *Academy of Management Review*, **22** (4), 887–910.

Rowley, T.J. and Moldoveanu, M. (2003), 'When will stakeholder groups act? An interest- and identity-based model of stakeholder group mobilization', *Academy of Management Review*, **28** (2), 204–19.

Russo, M.V. and Harrison, N.S. (2005), 'Organizational design and environmental performance: clues from the electronic industry', *Academy of Management Journal*, **48** (4), 582–93.

Sandhu, S., Ozanne, L., Smallman, C. and Cullen, R. (2010), 'Consumer driven corporate environmentalism: fact or fiction?', *Business Strategy and Environment*, **19** (6), 356–66.

Schwartz, P. (2007), 'Investing in global security', *Harvard Business Review*, **85** (10), 26–8.

Scott, W.R. (1987), 'The adolescence of institutional theory', *Administrative Science Quarterly*, **32** (4), 493–511.

Sharma, S. and Henriques, I. (2005), 'Stakeholder influence on sustainability practices in the Canadian forest products industry', *Strategic Management Journal*, **26** (2), 159–80.

Sharma, S. and Vredenburg, H. (1998), 'Proactive corporate environmental strategy and the development of competitively valuable organizational capabilities', *Strategic Management Journal*, **19** (8), 729–53.

Shell (2007), 'Brent Spar', http://www.shell.co.uk/, accessed 7 June 2007.

Shell (Nigeria) (2007a), 'Human Rights', http://www.shell.com/home/content/nigeria/about_shell/issues/human_rights/hum_rights.html, accessed 12 April 2012.

Shell (Nigeria) (2007b), 'The Ogoni Issue', http://www.shell.com/home/content/nigeria/about_shell/issues/ogoni/ogoni.html, accessed 7 June 2007.

Sparrowe, R.T. and Mayer, K.J. (2011), 'From the editors, publishing in AMJ – Part 4: Grounding Hypothesis', *Academy of Management Journal*, **54** (6), 1098–1102.

Wells, G. (2011), *Sustainability in Australian Business*, Milton: John Wiley & Sons.

Wernerfelt, B. (1984), 'A resource based view of the firm', *Strategic Management Journal*, **5** (2), 171–80.

2. Developing and communicating social capital for sustainable organizations and their communities

Joy Chia

INTRODUCTION

This chapter focuses on social capital and organizations as active community members and investors in sustainable programs. Social capital development, community engagement and engaging communication that aims to be inclusive are some of the core ingredients which are suggested for the sustainability of organizations. The changing role of social media is also considered as grass roots communication in opening up dialogue between organizations and community members which may affect the reputation of organizations.

If the business of organizations is to be sustainable, developing social capital is critical. Social capital includes the networks, relationships and connections which organizations cultivate and which are important to their internal and external operations. As Putnam (1995a, p.664) puts it: 'by "social capital" I mean features of social life-networks, norms and trust that enable participants to act together more effectively to pursue shared objectives. Whether or not their shared goals are praiseworthy is, of course, entirely another matter.' Putnam identifies the strength of networks and their importance to the business of an organization, but he also alerts us to their limitations. These connections and networks may not be readily identifiable, and they can be fragile, but they underpin the way organizations progress their business, or in their absence, may adversely affect their business.

Realizing social capital potential depends on the 'trustworthiness of the social environment' (Coleman, 1988, p.102). Where relational obligations and reciprocity can develop credit for organizations Putnam (1995a) refers to the social glue that strengthens and sustains organizations' commitment to their communities. It is important that organizations support the networks that open opportunities for community engagement and that they are also aware that there may be a decline in business when connections and relationships become fragmented and weak. The premise of this chapter is that as connections are developed and nurtured, the communication critical to connectivity and to strong organizational community networks and relevant, meaningful relationships, will be effective if it is inclusive and engaging. Open communication through varied media, including social media, engages organizations with their communities so that partnerships develop and grow their business and, simultaneously, businesses take part in community programs that promote community goodwill.

Scholars such as Stuart Hart (2008, p. 321) indicate that 'a vision of sustainability for an industry or a company is like a road map to the future, showing the way products and services evolve and what new competencies will be needed to get there'; that is one aspect of sustainability. In this chapter sustainability is viewed as much more, as even the best products and new competencies cannot replace the need to also develop organizations' social capital to participate, and fully immerse themselves in the 'business of community'. As Burt (1997, p. 339) contends, organizations' 'managers with more social capital get higher returns to their human capital because they are positioned to identify more rewarding opportunities.' In this chapter opportunities for civic or community engagement are considered important to organizations' social capital investment. Community engagement involves 'communication strategies to inform and raise awareness, seek involvement, opinions and provide feedback, and create real partnerships through community problem solving' (Johnston, 2010, p. 218), thereby developing meaningful and productive affiliations. Johnston points to the importance of managing community expectations for programs that will be diverse and complex; I would argue that community engagement is also about developing programs that are in the best interest of communities.

Three components central to sustainability are emphasized in this chapter: social capital, communication, and community engagement. This approach takes particular account of qualitative Australian and Canadian research which indicates that organizations can only be sustainable if they also value the relationships important to their business, both within their organizations and external to them.

UNDERSTANDING SOCIAL CAPITAL AND COMMUNITY ENGAGEMENT

In order to grasp the context of community social capital one of the key theorists that frames this discussion is Robert Putnam (1995a). Putnam's work is important as the bridging and bonding capital that he proposes is part of 'bridging or inclusive, and bonding, or exclusive, social networks' (Luoma-aho, 2009) integral to group cohesiveness, and group members networking and developing bridges or connections, outside of the group. Strong internal networks with employees (bonding capital) are as important as networks and partnerships with other organizations (bridging capital) and community groups; one could say that development of social capital is embedded in their business operations from the inside out and vice versa.

Putnam's theory of social capital involves 'the norms of reciprocity and networks of civic engagement that encourage social trust and cooperation' (Blanchard and Horan, 1998, p. 294). Developing trust progresses as partners spread the word about who can be trusted, a very important consideration for sustainable businesses as they aim to build a reputation of goodwill and trustworthiness in their business and community dealings.

Putnam's reference to civic engagement refers to the connection with community members and with 'the life of the community' (Blanchard and Horan, 1998 p. 294), its vibrancy, energy and livelihood. The 'networks of civic engagement foster sturdy norms of generalized reciprocity and encourage the emergence of social trust' (Putnam, 1995b, p. 66) where shared resources are effectively managed between partners who trust and respect each other's contributions. The premise of Putnam's stance is that through collaboration and established networks a template for future collaboration is created. This tends to present the ideal though, as networks are constantly changing and being challenged, so it is important to consider threats to collaboration and recognize the risks inherent in social capital development. Social capital may not be recognized as important to organizations (Tsai and Ghoshal, 1998). Scholars such as Ihlen (2007; Ihlen et al., 2009) posit that the economic viability of organizations might also be hampered when social capital interests are marginalized. Putnam (1995a) considers that there are societal factors that are contributing to this. He recognizes that a sense of community is under threat and he is despondent about the individualistic nature of our society, and the 'lost sense of a community which makes collaboration and relationships difficult to establish and maintain' (Luoma-aho, 2009, p. 232). Macnamara (2010) argues that even though 'increasing individualism' (p. 147) may be evident in western societies much of the research that supported the notion of individualism predated Web 2 and social media development. As such the place of social media needs to be understood in terms of its role in organizational, social capital development and whether it is adding to a sense of community, fostering connectivity and thereby contributing to sustainable organizations and their communities.

With its focus on relationships and connections social capital might be developed for all the wrong reasons (Svenden, 2006). Svenden asserts that bonding capital (the connections and relationships within groups) might be part of the 'dark side' (Svenden, 2006, p. 57) of social capital. He highlights Putnam's Italian community study, where 'bonding capital is thriving among mafia groups in the South' (p. 56) creating distrust, and a 'lack of cooperation' (p. 65) within the community. Similarly, Svenden's regional Danish study focusing on newcomers to a community, found that 'exclusive social networks' (p. 65) existed that excluded newcomers. When communities exclude those who could, and ought to, contribute to social capital, then the sustainability of these communities, and the businesses important to them, can also be threatened.

The embedded concepts of social capital and community engagement indicate that 'social capital can only be generated collectively thanks to the presence of communities, or particular networks' (Ferragina, 2010, p. 75). Ferragina goes on to say that 'individuals and groups can exploit it at the same time,' and 'organizations sometimes exploit their communities' social capital.'

This was evident in the Chia and Peters (2009) study of Australian and Canadian credit unions: their narrow focus on networking to market their products was unsuccessful because they were conducting their businesses to take advantage of their communities, rather than engaging with them. In 2008 when the global financial crisis took hold, new thinking was required as the existence of credit unions in Australia and Canada was under threat and many branches were closing: in these situations being sustainable meant that they needed to rebuild trust, and simultaneously consider business and social capital initiatives to re-engage with their members. They reported that they were now focusing more on the relationship dimension of their businesses as they supported programs for their members, and for the families of their employees.

Similarly in a follow up study on social capital and community engagement (Chia, 2011b), in Vancouver Island, Canada, the credibility of credit unions was maintained because their bridging capital was established through sound connections important to their project support of small business, which in turn contributed to their business viability and sustainability. There was considerable respect for these credit unions and for other businesses in the community that actively supported community youth programs and housing projects. Their role in giving micro-loans to those who were rejected by banks and other financial institutions was reported in the local and national media, with considerable coverage about small business success. In one instance a mother and daughter who had been refused bank loans but were given a credit union micro loan, established a horse riding school that was so successful that they were able to support other businesses. Their story appeared in local media, they were interviewed on radio and it was also talked about on Facebook and in credit union blogs. This example indicated that the communication about the way they moved from a struggling family to owners of a viable business presented a pathway, and developed knowledge and understanding important to other community members considering similar business ventures. In this example and in others noted in east and west Canadian communities, the sense of community was evident, and the need to communicate what was happening and who was involved continued to build community dialogue and relationships between organizations and between community groups in the private, business, and not-for-profit sectors.

Ferragina (2010) advocates for social capital development that closes the gap between income inequalities; conversely he suggests that declining social capital results in the generation of 'income inequality' (p. 93). Ferragina's perspective is one that aligns with Luoma-aho's (2009) stance that social capital development promotes a sense of inclusiveness where participation in society, and all that it stands for, are possible. The above example highlights this.

The philosophical and ideological arguments that could be discussed here are extensive, but the notion that businesses take into account inclusion of all community members that they support and engage with as part of their business, leverages their prospects to also be sustainable. Conversely when organizations become exclusive and their bonding capital includes only those who participate in elite networks, the outcomes can be catastrophic. Lyon's (2008, p. 385) study of the collapse and demise of the Enron Corporation concluded that internal and external development of social capital was affected by the 'power laden feature of organizational life'. This led to practices where Enron 'executives made many of these changes (concerning their business) through social capital by excluding individuals who disagreed with their approach.' Similar to the exclusivity of social capital highlighted by Svenden, Enron executives did not take into account that selective work practices were unsustainable as they spiralled inwards, into narrow self-serving partnerships. Conversely Cunningham (2002) posits that organizations have an advantage in tough, competitive markets providing that their business is conducted strategically, with an ethical stance as social capital is developed through collaboration and shared learning.

If therefore collaboration, relational growth and connectivity are so important I propose that communication about what this means to the social capital growth of organizations necessitates public relations and communication professionals to make it happen; they are important connectors and social capital investors.

COMMUNICATION IMPORTANT TO SUSTAINABLE BUSINESSES AND THEIR COMMUNITIES: SOCIAL MEDIA LEADING THE WAY

If we communicate we liaise, connect, and inform, and we begin to include others in our conversations, dialogue and plans. This is especially so within the network society that Tampere (2011, p. 60) contends is part of the flexible approach of organizations, where 'interactivity is applied in those organizations whose structure resembles a network and whose nature is flexible and sensitive to the surroundings, to its stakeholders'. Tampere proposes that social media is taking a key role in opening up organizations to their communities. As part of a communication management and public relations role Tampere argues that 'PR needs to take a reflexive role and focus its critical eye on the needs of society and actions of the organization' (p. 50). Australian-Canadian research (Chia, 2011b) points to the increasing role of social media, within a broader media framework, in playing an important part in regional communities, as organizations increasingly seek to communicate with each other, and include many new voices and newcomers in discussion and dialogue. Organizations are seeking to tap into the network society as they develop social capital, but they are still coming to terms with the diversity of social media and online communication exchange and what it means to their businesses. Sander and Putnam (2010) recognize that the internet and social media are playing a role in engagement and dialogue with many groups in the community, but these scholars are sceptical that social media is the answer to social capital development and fully engaged communities. They argue that 'in a world where Facebook "friendship" can encompass people who have never actually met we remain agnostic about whether internet social entrepreneurs have found the right mix of virtual and real strands to replace social ties.' Understanding the role of social media integral to social capital is an emerging area of research and one that was found to be important to the Australian-Canadian study that frames much of this discussion. The study followed earlier research on the response of employees to their organizations' social capital (Chia and Peters, 2008). In that study organizations such as credit unions were active in their communities as they used varied communication to connect with their stakeholders, community leaders and activists.

The Australian-Canadian study is a good one to consider in terms of its focus on social capital and community engagement (Chia, 2011b). Through on-site visits, interviews and focus groups conducted in the remote mining township of Roxby Downs, South Australia, the provincial farming centre of Mount Gambier, South Australia, and Victoria,

Vancouver Island, Canada, a qualitative analysis indicated that communication, especially through social media, was becoming important to community engagement. The study revealed that there were challenges for public relations practitioners and communication professionals as they aimed to include those who had not previously engaged with their communities. Social media acted as a point of connection and inclusivity alongside face-to-face communication, and communication through regional media. It was notable that the initial research focus was not on social media but it became an important component as the research progressed (Chia, 2011a). There were frequent references to the way social media acted as a platform for community members and contributed to their understanding of community goals. Some of the findings of the Australian-Canadian research important to engaged and sustainable communities include:

- Social media is giving more community members the opportunity to engage and it is including those who often do not turn up for meetings, or for face-to-face discussion. This is important as sustainable organizations need to communicate with and reach all possible community members to partner with them, and maybe do business with them, or be part of their business.
- Social media continues to link community members even when they move away from a locality. Businesses and organizations often exist in various localities: they have branches, agencies or outlets. Social media plays a role in ongoing connection, supporting sustainable practice in wider communities.
- Social media opens up media opportunities as community members send in photos on YouTube, participate in blogs and send in local reports. These reports can be negative or positive. Organizations ought to be aware that there are two sides to engagement. The reputation of an organization is open to scrutiny as social media reports what is happening in organizations, and in communities, that may not be part of conventional, traditional media.
- Twitter is often used to communicate short messages, or make announcements and it has an important place in communicating core needs, concerns and ideas between organizations, from organizations to the communtiy, and between community groups.
- Social media encouraged many young people to participate in community discussion as it is their way of communicating. The youth of today are an important demographic and they are important to organizations and their communities' future. They also contribute to innovative and new ideas and planning.

A public relations practitioner in a Canadian credit union emphasized that organizations need to invest in things that matter to neighbourhoods as she discussed youth housing project support and neighbourhood corporations. To be successful grass roots communication is as important as communication through social media. This practitioner found that Twitter was helpful in communicating short but important messages and updates about her work on community projects, but she also valued face-to-face discussion with community leaders and advocates for change. Her focus along with others in the study indicated the need to communicate according to varied community needs and contexts.

In the current environment a paradigm shift in public relations and communication management is taking place as the goal is to is 'to use interaction in a positive way' (Lattimore et al., 2012, p. 15) as the 'social uses of the internet through Facebook, Twitter and blogs have allowed the constituencies to get involved in a two-way communication not only with the organization, but also with each other' (p. 15). These scholars point to the two sides of communication that organizations need to consider. Firstly that they are now more approachable, or as I would put it they are more open to connecting and building social capital, and secondly, they are also open to reputation challenges and scrutiny about their brands and what they stand for.

Social media is connecting different players and different businesses, and alerting the business community to the needs of their communities, but it also needs to be supported through personalized responses that develop trust and understanding between disparate groups, between activists and supporters, and between stakeholders and shareholders.

Hart (2011) found that 'a number of companies are using social media to ask customers and the general public to help them shape the future of the company and its products' (p. 121) as they 'engage with, and build online communities' (p. 120). Hart suggests that social media is growing communities. I would add that it is redefining community engagement and what it means, as so many more participants, compared to the pre-Web 2 business environment, are interacting with organizations. This can be viewed as changing the way organizations manage, sustain and develop their businesses as there are many more players, many more ideas and possibilities for organizations and their communities.

More needs to be understood about social capital development and the role of social media in advancing dialogue and building networks and relationships, but indications are that it will be essential for organizations to actively embrace social media strategically and proactively. Organizations will also find their sustainability threatened when social media exposes practices that are profit driven and where communities have been disadvantaged by this action. As Hart puts it, 'it is important for any organization participating in social media to begin with a focus on their audience, not with a focus on themselves' (p. 131). As such organizations need to look beyond their day-to-day operations taking into account the changing circumstances of their businesses as society becomes more involved in what businesses do, how they carry out their key functions, and whether they have the interest of their communities at heart.

For the public relations practitioner, an organization's social media team can take a key role to 'reach out to community leaders' if they 'find genuine common ground' (Kane et al., 2009) to foster shared objectives for community growth.

The potential for social media is substantial but the need to also communicate through meetings and traditional communication is critical to the success of that communication. Blanchard and Horan (1998) refer to this as facilitating 'physically based virtual communities' to establish community ties and meaningful exchange and dialogue. The synergy between the virtual and the personalized contacts is possible. At the same time, the Australian-Canadian study found that regional media, including radio, television and local newspapers, have an important role in telling the stories about organizations' collaboration with their communities. The public needs to know what is happening. Fleming and Thorson (2008, p.414) found that 'local media coverage of community affairs and activities is an important force for building relationships and developing social norms amongst individuals'. They also found that new media were connecting, developing social capital and providing information sharing so that community members could be 'socially connected' (p.416). The focus on interactive, shared communication, be it traditional or through social media, ensures that reciprocal benefits are possible for all parties as social capital fosters engaged communities that collaborate for sustainable outcomes.

A MODEL FOR ENGAGED, SUSTAINABLE COMMUNITIES

One of the findings of Eversole (2011), in her study of regional community engagement in three Australian communities, was that they adopted a 'bureaucratic way of doing things' especially when government agencies engaged with communities on their terms. If engagement is to be inclusive, and if the end result is that business and communities can be sustainable, then several Australian-Canadian models of community engagement command attention (Chia, 2011a, 2011b). In these models the role of government is part of community engagement, but it is not prominent: rather community councils work with community leaders and members from the not-for-profit sector, media, government, business and academic institutions, with a strong focus on research to guide their planning. Universities become active community members where higher degree research frames better understanding of sustainability, and where the university becomes a meeting point, a point of engagement for business and the not-for-profit sector. The key to the Canadian model is that social capital is developed across the business, not-for-profit and government sectors as experts work together on core programs that aim to sustain communities, attract new business opportunities and develop meaningful networks for mutual, partner benefit.

Community engagement needs to be organized, researched and understood so that it is central to the community, whether that community is regional, or in a busy city. A visit by the research team (Chia, 2011b) to a cafe set up by a local community, supported the disadvantaged in downtown Victoria, Canada. A derelict space became a thriving meeting point, a connection, and a place that brought life into the community. Community members gained employment in the cafe and took pride in their business. A higher degree student at the University of Victoria (Canada, Vancouver Island) was leading the cafe development, and it was part of her research.

Credit union representatives were part of the Community Council that supported the cafe alongside media representatives, academics, local supermarket representatives, government agencies and not-for-profit representatives. All partners supported community projects and contributed to the over-arching goal to build thriving communities. The key to the success of the program was the combined effort, the focus on research, both academic and informal, to guide planning, and the funding of the business sector to make it possible.

Public relations and media council representatives facilitated constant communication to and from the community, about what was happening. This communication flow articulated how community ideas were incorporated and what long-term plans were being considered. The aim was socially responsible communication for community investment.

In Australia, the Roxby Downs community began a viable community plan and set up a Community Board to facilitate the process. In 2003 when it first began, based on 70 submissions and 130 written responses, the aim was that the Community Board would offer the highest possible level of participation, and responsibility to the community. It was interesting to see the active involvement of local media and public relations managers from the mining corporation on the Community Board, ensuring communication to community members (Chia, 2011b). A values based model was paramount as the Community Board emphasized the need to be caring, tolerant and inclusive, with interdependence of business and social partnerships. The focus on businesses and the community working together is critical in a town that is isolated in a remote part of Australia, but the Community Board model is one that could work in all communities. The Canadian and Roxby Downs models are rich in social capital contributing to economic and human capital.

SUSTAINABLE PRACTICE: ORGANIZATIONS AS ACTIVE COMMUNITY MEMBERS

There are many challenges for organizations. Social media are providing a point of connection and inclusion amidst an array of grass roots communication. From the community research in Australia and Canada, the critical components for sustainable business are to embed social capital development in organizational strategic plans, to facilitate networks, connections and relationships that are successful, and to add to the sound reputation of organizations. Diverse and meaningful communication is important to establish community trust. If organizations are trusted, that trust reinforces social capital initiatives that have the potential to make organizations more competitive within a socially responsible framework. The ability to communicate in an engaging way – to share, grow and bring the community with you so that everyone benefits – is a challenge but a worthwhile one for organizations' responsible social capital investment.

REFERENCES

Blanchard, A. and Horan, T. (1998), 'Virtual communities and social capital', *Social Science Computer Review*, **16**, 293–307.

Burt, R. (1997), 'The contingent value of social capital', *Administrative Science Quarterly*, **42**, 339–65.

Chia, J. (2011a), 'Making it possible: communicating, connecting and developing social capital for sustainable organizations and their communities', paper presented at the European Academy of Management Conference, Management Culture in the 21st Century, Tallinn, Estonia, 1–4 June.

Chia, J. (2011b), 'Communicating, connecting and developing social capital for sustainable organizations and their communities', *Australian Journal of Regional Studies*, **17** (3), 328–50.

Chia, J. and Peters, M. (2008), 'Employee engagement in organizations' social capital. Does public relations have a role?', *Asia Pacific Public Relations Journal*, **9**, 103–120.

Chia, J. and Peters, M. (2009), 'Making a difference. Employees as social capital investors', paper presented at the European Conference on Intellectual Capital, Holland University of Applied Sciences, The Netherlands, 28–29 April.

Coleman, J. (1988), 'Social capital in the creation of human capital', *The American Journal of Sociology*, **94**, 95–120.

Cunningham, I. (2002), 'Developing human and social capital in organizations', *Industrial and Commercial Training*, **34** (3), 89–94.

Doorley, J. and Garcia, H. (2011), *Reputation Management. The Key to Successful Public Relations and Corporate Communication*, 2nd edition, New York: Routledge, Taylor and Francis.

Eversole, R. (2011), 'Community agency and community engagement: re-theorising participation in governance', *Journal of Public Policy*, **31** (1), 51–71.

Ferragina, E. (2010), 'Social capital and equality: Tocqueville's legacy: rethinking social capital in relation with income inequalities', *The Tocqueville Review/la revue, Tocqueville*, **31** (1), 73–98.

Fleming, K. and Thorson, E. (2008), 'Assessing the role of information-processing strategies in learning from local news media about sources of social capital', *Mass Communication and Society*, **11**, 398–419.

Hart, S. (2008), 'Beyond greening: strategies for a sustainable world', in A. Crane, D. Matten and L. Spence (eds), *Corporate Social Responsibility: Readings and Cases in the Global Context*, New York, USA: Routledge, Taylor and Francis Group.

Hart, L. (2011), 'Social media', in J. Doorley and H. Garcia (eds), *Reputation Management. The Key to Successful Public Relations and Corporate Communication*, 2nd edition, New York: Routledge, Taylor and Francis, pp. 112–133.

Ihlen, Øyvind (2007), 'Building on Bourdieu: a sociological grasp of public relations', *Public Relations Review*, **33**, 269–74.

Ihlen, Øyvind, van Ruler, B. and Fredriksson, M. (2009), *Public Relations and Social Theory: Key Figures and Concepts*, New York and London: Routledge, Taylor and Francis Group.

Johnston, K.A. (2010), 'Community engagement: exploring a relational approach to consultation and collaborative practice in Australia', *Journal of Promotion Management*, **16**, 217–34.

Kane, G., Fichman, R., Gallaugher, J. and Glaser, J. (2009), 'Community Relations 2.0', *Harvard Business Review*, November, 45–50.

Lattimore, D., Baskin, O., Heiman, S. and Toth, E. (2012), *Public Relations: The Profession and the Practice*, 4th edition, New York, USA: McGraw Hill.

Luoma-aho, V. (2009), 'On Putnam: Bowling Together – applying Putnam's theories of community and social capital to public relations', in Ø. Ihlen, B. van Ruler, and M. Fredriksson (eds), *Public Relations and Social Theory: Key Figures and Concepts*, New York and London: Routledge, Taylor and Francis Group, pp. 231–51.

Lyon, A. (2008), 'The mis/recognition of Enron executives' competence as cultural and social capital', *Communication Studies*, **59** (4), 371–87.

Macnamara, J.R. (2010), *The 21st Century Media (R)evolution: Emergent Communication Practices*, New York: Peter Lang.

Putnam, R. (1995a), 'Turning in, turning out: the strange disappearance of social capital in America', *Political Science and Politics*, **28** (4), 664–83.

Putnam, R. (1995b), 'Bowling alone: America's declining social capital', *Journal of Democracy*, **6** (1) 65–78.

Sander, H. and Putnam, R. (2010), 'Still bowling alone? The post-9/11 split', *Journal of Democracy*, **21** (1), 9–16.

Svenden, L.H. (2006), 'Studying social capital in situ: a qualitative approach', *Theory and Society*, **35** (1), 39–70.

Tampere, K. (2011), 'A walk in the public relations field: theoretical discussions from a social media and network society perspective', *Central European Journal of Communication*, **4** (1).

Tsai, W. and Ghoshal, S. (1998), 'Social capital and value creation: the role of intrafirm networks', *Academy of Management Journal*, **41** (4), 464–76.

3. The sustainable firm as an ethical construct

Geoffrey Wells

INTRODUCTION

All analysis of business enterprise rests on ideas about the firm. These ideas can be explicitly developed, as in the traditional theory of the firm, or they can be a looser set of unstated assumptions. It is not always easy to discern the particular idea of the firm being advanced. However no systematic discussion of business, at any level, can proceed without it.

This observation is particularly relevant to the analysis of sustainable business. Historically the idea of sustainable business has emerged in large part from a questioning of the assumptions that underpin traditional theories of the firm. This chapter examines some of those assumptions. It does not attempt to make a contribution to the traditional theory of the firm (Kantarelis 2007; Ricketts 1994). Rather it explores the theoretical and conceptual categories that are required for any systematic discussion of the sustainable firm and its activities. In that sense, to employ a traditional term, it can be considered a prolegomenon to a formal theory of the sustainable firm.

'Sustainability' is one of those concepts which, submerged in modern public discourse, has almost lost clear referential meaning. When applied to business there is an obvious ambiguity between 'sustainable' as meaning, on the one hand, 'economically viable' and on the other, 'operating in accord with sustainability principles'; a sleight of hand not uncommon in the claims of some modern firms. It should be clear that the second sense of the term is the focus of this chapter.

Montiel (2008) identifies a confused contemporary conceptual landscape relating to sustainable business. It comprises a number of loosely linked ideas, drawn initially from the environment, aggregated with the social in parallel with the economic, and overlapping the umbrella concept of corporate social responsibility (CSR). Other approaches draw on the metaphor of capital, extending the original economic concept to notions of social capital and natural capital, with sustainability being any approach which preserves all three over time (Hawken et al. 1999; Dyllick and Hockerts 2002). With the advent of corporate sustainability reporting frameworks, such as the Dow Jones Sustainability Indexes (DJSI) (Dow Jones Indexes and Group 2011) and the Global Reporting Initiative (GRI) (Global Reporting Initiative 2011), the reach of the sustainability concept has extended into dealings of the firm with all its stakeholders, including its employees, its suppliers, its customers and the community at large. Faced with such a scope, there is a risk that sustainable business will be defined as a residual category. Google's concise motto is framed in just this way: 'Don't be evil.'

In this chapter it will be argued that the idea of the sustainable firm and its activities is fundamentally ethical. An ethical foundation allows for the systematic derivation of all the main elements of sustainable business identified in academic and common discourse. Such an approach not only unifies and simplifies the theories of its historical forebears – socially responsible business, corporate social responsibility, stakeholder theory, corporate social performance, corporate sustainability and so on – but provides normative guidelines for business practice. Although the interpretation of ethical frameworks remains complex and demanding, the principal sustainable business tasks are on this view clearly delineated. A program of research which builds on this foundational view is proposed.

PRINCIPLES AND CLASSIFICATION SCHEMES

The contemporary idea of the sustainable firm reaches back at least six decades (see the Introduction to this volume). In that historical trajectory there is a tension between principles and classifications. For example, Berle and Means (1932) and Drucker (1946) upheld a principle of social norms, which was given a quasi-democratic cast by Friedman (1970) in the service of shareholder returns. Bowen (1953) adopted a stewardship principle broadly based in common morality. Baumol (1970) and Wallich and McGowan (1970) explored the business case for social investment; a principle of financial performance.

Sethi (1975) however, introduced a tri-partite classification in dimensions of social responsibility. Carroll (1999) expanded it in legal and discretionary directions, generating a plethora of such classifications by those who followed him. Freeman (1984, 2009) developed the concept of the stakeholder as a principle of external claims on the firm but interpreted it in ways that are essentially classificatory.

The absence of an internal logic in modern classificatory approaches is, it would seem, fatal to their claims to form coherent theories of the broader responsibilities of business. A genuine theory must have explanatory power: its principles – or laws, or hypotheses – must be able to generate specific, logical consequences when applied to particular states of the world (Hempel 1966). The classificatory schemes discussed above are descriptive rather than normative (Jones and Wicks 1999): they identify attributes or characteristics of the sustainable firm, but largely fail to account for them systematically.

Consider for example, the most widely used of these frameworks, the 'triple-bottom line' (Elkington 1997). In formal terms this is a metaphor which implicitly urges firms to place social and environmental outcomes on the same level as economic outcomes; but it gives no guidance as to why these sectors have been chosen, what precisely they encompass, or how the framework constructed from them is to be put into practice. Accounting initiatives attempting to implement it have been unconvincing and have not found support in financial accounting standards (Unerman et al. 2007). Similarly in the DJSI and GRI the selection of representative elements has been directed by loose accretion; these indices therefore lack credibility with many in the business community who resist their implementation, and with critics who want them framed and applied more rigorously.

In response to the demand for more rigorous treatment we propose that the nature of the firm under sustainability principles is best approached normatively. The principles which embody this perspective both identify firms that are operating sustainably, and provide firms with clear directives for acting sustainably. Moreover we will argue that these normative principles are morally injunctive: they have their foundations in the theories of normative ethics, which are 'theories about how we should act from the standpoint of morality' (Kagan 1998, p. 11). That there is a business case for CSR and sustainable business will be accepted; but it will be proposed that the business case is not sufficient to guide sustainable action, and that a framework of normative ethics is required. Further, we argue that from these principles can be derived the central concepts associated with modern sustainable business.

The term 'principle' is used firstly, in the sense of a general proposition capable of being logically applied to individual cases. This has clear roots in the hypothetico-deductive school of the philosophy of science (Popper 1969; Nagel 1961; Lakatos et al. 1980). In human affairs it is found also in legal theory (Wacks 2009).

Secondly, the term is used in the sense of a general rule adopted as a guide to action. Such a guide can be injunctive without being ethically based, as in analytic philosophy of social science (Winch 1963). On the other hand such a guide can be ethically based: this idea has a long history in ethics (Macintyre 1998), and is found also in legal theory (Kennedy 2005).

It is clear that the two senses can be combined. A powerful principle is one that applies logically to a wide range of individual cases. If that general principle is also based in ethical theory, then its application to individual cases will provide an ethical guide to them. Just such principles, we now argue, are the foundations of sustainable business.

THE BUSINESS CASE AND BEYOND

Principles of the kind proposed are to be distinguished from arguments that present the business case for sustainability. That there is such a business case has been a constant theme of CSR commentary since its inception. For example, Baumol (1970, p. 8), in analyzing corporate philanthropy, proposes that '. . . corporations should provide funds only to causes that serve the firm's interests, broadly conceived.' He demurs against funding public goods, noting that it places the individual '. . . in the position of bearing all of the costs by himself while reaping only a portion of the benefits.' At the same time, the interests of the corporation are recognized to be wide: 'The company pays a high price for operating in a region where education is poor, where living conditions are deplorable, where health is poorly protected, where property is unsafe, and where cultural activity is all but dead' (p. 19).

When the costs of these factors to the firm are greater than the costs of corporate giving, Baumol concludes, funding public goods is economically rational.

The modern approach to the business case for sustainable practice is more firmly based in the day-to-day business realities. Kurucz et al. (2008) offer a four-dimensional justification which has been widely adopted in the literature (Carroll and Shabana 2010): cost and risk reduction; competitive advantage; reputation and legitimacy; and synergistic value creation (through networks). Drucker (1984, p. 62) provides a characteristically inverted view: '. . . the proper social responsibility of business is to . . . turn a social problem into economic opportunity and economic benefit, into productive capacity, into human competence, into well-paid jobs, and into wealth.'

There is however, a sense in which the elements of the business case presented in these schemas appear simply to be good business. That is, they are not different in kind from other accepted business functions, such as cost control, strategic management, and product innovation. For example, if competitive advantage can be obtained by sustainability positioning, a competent firm will adopt it, whether driven by sustainability imperatives or not. Energy, water and waste efficiencies, often cited as evidence of sustainable business, are difficult to see as anything other than competent operational management.

It can be argued then, that the business case for sustainable practice is not sufficient to define it in all the senses demanded by modern societies. Critical questions remain: value for whom, over what time period, and including or excluding what social and environmental costs? How have people been treated in the making of profit and the building of economic value?

The modern social 'license to operate' – the social contract between business and society – increasingly seems to move the firm into an area beyond standard business obligations. Carroll (1999) makes the widely accepted distinction between legal and economic obligations, which are 'required'; ethical obligations, which are 'expected'; and philanthropic obligations, which are 'discretionary'. Yet that schema raises more questions than it answers: it is precisely the boundaries and relationships between these categories of obligation that are at issue. For example, ethical obligations can override economic obligations, as, for example, in the recent controversy over Apple's Chinese labour conditions (Wingfield 2012), where ethical obligations become indeed 'required'.

ETHICAL FOUNDATIONS

We propose this alternative view: the foundational principles of sustainable business are ethical. The analytic task is then to locate ethical theory that is capable of playing such a role. Beauchamp et al. (2009, p. 2) place ethics within a general theory of morality, defined as 'social practices defining right and wrong . . . together with other kinds of customs, rules, and mores'. Ethical theory seeks '. . . to justify a system of standards or some moral point of views on the basis of carefully analyzed and defended concepts and principles such as respect for autonomy, distributive justice, equal treatment, human rights, beneficence, and truthfulness.'

Kagan (1998, pp. 1–8) observes that from the classical perspective ethics is delimited more simply by the range of answers to the question, 'How should one live?' Normative ethics is concerned with 'stating and defending the most basic moral principles.' Such principles can be presented as rules, but they can also be framed as rights, duties, virtues, beliefs and norms. The application of general ethical principles to particular cases, such as those which arise in business, is the domain of applied ethics. Here the analysis focuses on the question of how one should act and generates questions of this kind: Which acts are morally better or worse than others? Which acts are morally permissible, which ones morally required, and which ones morally forbidden – and what makes them so? The rational evaluation of moral claims is the business of ethics: it considers evidence and arguments for the rival theories of normative ethics, and assesses 'the reasons that can be offered for accepting or rejecting a given moral claim.'

A main difficulty in applying ethical principles to particular cases in business is the variety of ethical theories available. These include on one side, utilitarian ethics and its variants; and on the other side, Kantian ethics and its derivatives, including rights theory, virtue ethics and common morality theories. Sustainable business commentators have drawn loosely on most of these frameworks, in different business contexts. However a general preference for Kantian approaches, against utilitarian approaches, has characterized these discussions and will be employed here.

Traditional Kantian ethics is an ethics of duty. Kant distinguishes instrumental actions, undertaken in order to obtain some end, from actions that are morally 'required per se, with no ifs, ands or buts' (Bowie 2002, p. 62). This is the Kantian 'categorical imperative', formulated in three principles (here paraphrased): act only on principles that could be taken as universal rules; always treat humanity in a person as an end, never as a means (the respect for persons principle); and a community or organization should be so structured that each of its members can act as both 'subject and sovereign' (moral community).

The Kantian perspective has been influential in contemporary rights theory, embedded in key statements such as the United Nations Declaration of Human Rights (1949) and the European Charter of Fundamental Human Rights (2000). The rights perspective has been applied particularly to the working conditions of workers around the world, in industry codes of conduct, occupational health and safety regulations, collective bargaining, training and development, child labour prohibition and so on. Within modern firms rights approaches have been applied to issues such as work-life balance, privacy, discrimination by gender or age, whistle-blowing and hiring practices (Beauchamp et al. 2009, pp. 30–33).

A second Kantian perspective that has exercised considerable influence in modern ethics is the theory of justice articulated by John Rawls (1972), based on general rights to equity and social advancement. Of this analysis Sagoff (1988, p. 153) notes that 'since the rights secured by justice and equality are prior to goals like preference satisfaction and efficiency, they cannot be balanced against them.' It has been consistently argued in the traditional theory of the firm that the value of ethical actions is to be found in their contribution to economic outcomes: for example, in the contribution of trust and fairness to contractual relationships (Ricketts

1994). However the essence of the Kantian position is, as Sagoff notes, that whatever the indications for action of the business case, the moral imperative comes first. Thus Bowie (2002, pp. 70–71) argues that '. . . we should view profits as a consequence, or by-product, of ethical business practices, rather than as the sole goal of business, an end to which all means are subjugated.'

Attempts to apply broadly Kantian principles to firms have varied in strategy. For example, Dunfee (1998) sees the moral principles of firms as developed in a 'marketplace of morality (MOM)', in which individuals act under the influence of their conceived moral principles and which represents 'the aggregate acted-upon moral preferences of its participants.' The outputs of such a marketplace give guidance to firms on community moral preferences. There is a role for universal principles, which are derived from cross-cultural comparisons.

With moral preferences in hand, firms can then distinguish between three kinds of ethical problems and responses (Bowie and Dunfee 2002). *Benign* moral beliefs are unarguably consistent with universal principles, and direct mandatory action (for example, equity in employment). *Disputed* moral beliefs are contested issues within the community, and require action according to the core values of the firm (for example, affirmative action employment of minorities). *Problematic* moral beliefs are inconsistent with universal principles and require resistance to compliance (for example, a moral belief against hiring individuals who are in same sex relationships).

Bowie (2010, pp. 704–705) offers a set of seven principles as an application of Kantian theory to the question of what the business firm should be. These relate to the relevance, participation and equitable treatment of stakeholders; respect for persons; benefit to society; and rules of justice. They are linked to substantive and procedural norms of fairness.

Francis (2000, pp. 116–29) proposes a set of ethical principles to govern ethical corporate governance:

1. Preserve from harm.
2. Respect the dignity of all persons.
3. Be open and honest except in the exceptional cases where privacy and silence are clearly ethically preferable.
4. Act so as to preserve the equitability of relationships.

Seven subsidiary working principles of ethical governance are then outlined: dignity, equitability, prudence, honesty, openness, goodwill and alleviation of suffering. Francis notes that the application of any one principle may not be sufficient to resolve an issue of governance. Principles frequently conflict and rank differently according to the situational context.

Ultimately, it has been argued, all ethical theories have their basis in common morality theory, which asserts that most people understand and are broadly committed to the moral and ethical norms of their community. The legitimacy of these norms derives not from principle but from their proven success, in some cases over centuries, in promoting individual and social well-being. Common morality is thus viewed as foundational: '. . . there is no philosophical ethical theory that takes priority over the common morality; indeed, all philosophical theories find their grounding in the common morality' (Beauchamp et al. 2009, p. 36).

Such a position however, does not mean that ethical imperatives are necessarily either clear or simple. The process of ethical decision making by firms may well involve inspecting assumptions, testing logic, evaluating practical implications, revising positions, altering beliefs and so on, until a view is arrived at that seems to be the best available; an emergent, approach which has been termed processual (Watson 2009).

There are two further points to be made about applied ethics of this kind. Firstly, evaluation of the moral status of an act is, from the perspective of normative ethics, not limited in space and time:

> in saying that the moral status of an act is determined (at least in part) by its results, this is meant to include all of its results. It is not only the immediate, or short term, results that matter: long term results, side effects, indirect consequences – all these matter as well, and they count just as much as short term or immediate consequences. (Kagan 1998, p. 26)

Secondly, from an ethical point of view the important results of an act have to do with its effect on the well-being of people influenced by it. Well-being is a complex and widely debated concept (Eckersley 2004). In this context, however, the central question is who the people are whose well-being is to be considered? From the perspective of normative ethics, understood in terms of common morality, the answer is unequivocal:

> If an act will benefit me, this is certainly a good result; but if it will benefit others as well, this is an even better result, morally speaking . . . when we are considering goodness of outcomes as a factor that can help determine the moral status of an act, everyone's well-being counts. (Kagan 1998, p. 42)

To put it another way there is no ethical basis for excluding from consideration the well-being of any person who is affected by the actions of firms.

Finally in order to make our case three metaethical principles are needed, all of which, it is proposed, derive from common morality. They are as follows:

1. The acts of firms are governed by the same general principles of
    morality and ethics as acts undertaken in any other context by any
    individual or group. That is, we resist the idea that business firms are
    in some way, or at some times, exempt from the need to consider and
    act upon moral principles.
2. Ethical principles in business are foundational. That is, we resist the
    idea that business advantage can by its nature outweigh moral factors
    in the firm's decisions. On the contrary, we assert the priority of moral
    factors.
3. The implementation of actions determined by the firm to be ethical
    is mandatory. Embedded in the phrase 'determined by the firm' are
    important questions – how determined, and by whom? – but, that
    aside, this principle asserts that once determined ethical actions must
    be implemented.

SUSTAINABLE BUSINESS AS ETHICAL BUSINESS

We are now in a position to address the central proposition of this chapter:
that the foundational principles of sustainable business are ethical. This
thesis is approached in the first instance by considering four dimensions
of the sustainable firm and its activities as it is commonly conceived:
stakeholders; organization; the boundaries and responsibilities of the firm;
and future generations. These are not the only dimensions that need to
be considered in constructing the idea of the sustainable firm: ultimately
all areas of business practice need to be addressed. However these four
dimensions present a reasonable first test of our thesis. Our contention is
that they emerge systematically as sustainability principles for the firm and
its activities from the ethical and metaethical principles outlined above.

Stakeholders

It is evident that these ethical principles imply at least one version of
stakeholder theory. If it is accepted that there are people influenced by the
actions of firms, and to which, therefore, ethical principles apply, then we
may define these people as stakeholders of the firm.

Clarkson (1995) notes early definitions of stakeholder groups, from
General Electric in the 1930s, as 'shareholders, employees, customers and
the general public'; and from Johnson and Johnson in 1947, as 'customers, employees, managers, and shareholders.' Bowen proposed that the
directors of a firm are 'trustees, not alone for stockholders or owners, but
also for workers, suppliers, consumers, the immediate community, and

the general public', amongst whose interests they are required to mediate. In that task recourse will be taken to 'ethical connotations which extend far beyond the narrow principle of profit maximization' (Bowen 1953, pp. 48–50).

As recognition of these groups became formalized, Freeman framed stakeholder concept in terms of legitimate claims: the firm was required 'to give de facto standing to the claims of groups other than stockholders. It has in effect, required that the claims of customers, suppliers, local communities, and employees be taken into consideration' (Freeman 2009, p. 58). Following this line of thinking stakeholders were defined as 'persons or groups that have, or claim, ownership, rights, or interests in a corporation and its activities, past, present or future.' A distinction is often made between primary stakeholder groups, of the kind listed above, and secondary groups, such as media and special interest groups (Clarkson 1995, p. 106).

Dunfee (2008, p. 353) observes that, in addition to the legitimate claims principle, stakeholders have also been defined under a principle of power: '. . . the power that the putative stakeholder has to influence the ability of the firm to achieve its objectives.' This leads to a view of stakeholders as a part of the external business environment to be managed as an exercise in risk reduction (Kurucz et al. 2008).

In contrast to the 'legitimate claims' and 'power' definitions of stakeholders, Goodpaster (2010), like Bowen, proposes an ethical approach. Under this view, the move from shareholder to stakeholder models is not sufficient as an account of corporate responsibility: it may satisfy the demands of stakeholders and yet still not constitute social responsibility. Goodpaster looks to underpin stakeholder models with broader moral considerations: as one seeks a more satisfactory account of corporate responsibility, one discovers that it must be more comprehensive. Such comprehensiveness must eventually be anchored in (1) principles of human dignity and a just community and (2) a distinction between categorical responsibility and qualified (or conditional) responsibility (Goodpaster 2010, p. 130).

Although this statement is close to the position we have argued, we take a further step. We propose that people become stakeholders of the firm when they are affected by the firm's actions, because of the firm's moral and ethical obligations. There may also be legal or instrumental relationships between stakeholders and firms, but such relationships are not sufficient to define the complete class of stakeholders, nor the firm's responsibility to them. The defining principle, as well as the principle of action, is ethical. The class of stakeholders then includes the customary groups – customers, employees, managers, suppliers – but is not limited to those groups. It reaches into the near and distant communities affected by the firm's activities: 'everybody's well-being counts.' It then follows, according to our metaethical considerations, that the central principles of ethical behaviour – including principles of respect for persons, human dignity, justice, rights, fairness and social benefit, as we have outlined them above – apply with mandatory force to the actions of firms with respect to these stakeholders, so defined. This line of argument, we propose, presents the stakeholder character of the firm under sustainability principles.

One advantage of conceiving of stakeholder obligations in this way is that it can simplify what Dunfee (1998, p.353) sees as the inevitable need for triage between different sets of competing shareholder interests, particularly economic: 'Better terms for creditors and higher wages for employees often means lower returns for shareholders. Better terms for suppliers or distributors may mean higher prices for consumers.' However where stakeholder interests are conceived of in terms of ethical obligations, the process of establishing ethical grounds for action incorporates such claims, and points the way to an ethical resolution of them.

Organization

Consideration of the obligations to internal stakeholders leads to principles of sustainable organization. We have noted the implications of ethical principles developed by Francis (2000) for governance of organizations. Subsequently Dunphy et al. (2003), in a well-known account, applied standard organizational change models to the task of building a sustainable organization, termed here the 'sustaining' corporation. The sustaining corporation is said to be characterized by a shift in the values and behaviours of the corporation, collectively and individually, towards the role of business in creating a sustainable society. There is an interaction with other organizations within the sector, or in the supply chain, to promote the implementation of sustainability practice. High level communication with external parties, and continuing innovation in product and process redesign, and in customer education, are held to be central to the sustaining corporation.

The Dunphy model presents one conception of the sustainable firm. However little is offered on its conceptual foundations, or on how values and behaviours are to be moved in the desired direction. We argue that these values should primarily be framed ethically, and should be applied systematically to organizational tasks to promote change. On this view the sequence of stages the organization may move through is flexible, as is its final form: the overriding imperative is alignment at each point with ethical imperatives.

The direct relationship between ethical principles and sustainable organization is cogently argued by Solomon (2004) in applying the virtue ethics of Aristotle (1925) to business organizations. His interpretation of this framework is centred on community: 'What is worth defending in business is the sense of virtue that stresses cooperative joint effort and concern for consumers and colleagues alike.' The relevant principles of virtue are not abstractly but socially defined: 'A virtue has a place in a social context, in a human practice, and accordingly it is essentially part of a fabric that goes beyond the individual and binds him or her to a larger human network.' In business, this network is the corporation: 'Corporations are neither legal fictions nor financial juggernauts but communities, people working together for common goals.' With community and integrity at the centre of the business organization, the purposes of the firm become 'not only the fulfillment of obligations to stockholders (not all of them "fiduciary") but the production of quality and the earning of pride in one's products, providing good jobs and well-deserved rewards for employees and the enrichment of the whole community and not just a select group of (possibly short-term) contracted "owners".' Human well-being secured by ethical business practice, becomes as important an outcome of the firm's activities as its products and services.

On this view corporate culture moves to the centre: 'Cultures presuppose shared knowledge, experience and values and they are thus cooperative enterprises. A corporate culture is an essentially cooperative enterprise with public as well as private purposes.' Corporate cultures provide the continuity of corporate life, and determine its value structure: 'Among those essential structures are the various demands of ethics. It is, above all, shared values that hold a culture together.' These values are more than mechanisms of functional coherence: 'They also concern the sense of mission that the corporation embodies, its various stakeholder obligations and its sense of social responsibility and social (not just corporate) values.' For example, trust is both valuable in business and central to ethics. In this view, trust is developed within the exchanges of cooperation: it is 'a dynamic process, a function of communal practices and relationships, rather than a static cultural medium.' There are close links here to the processual approaches of modern human resources management (Watson 2009) and to Habermasian discourse ethics (Habermas 1990).

On this view the principles which are taken as defining modern sustainable organizations and firms – health, safety and welfare, flexibility in working hours, participation, equity, transparency, diversity, personal development, human rights and so on – have their foundations in ethical principles. These in turn are based on the shared norms of the firm, conceived of as a community. The sustainable firm is an ethical organization.

Boundaries and Responsibilities of Firms

Sustainability debates about business have centred historically on the boundaries of the firm. Traditional accounting frameworks avoid mention of boundaries in their user-based definitions of entities, but effectively construct boundaries in their definitions of the key elements of financial statements – assets, liabilities, income and expenses – where the focus is on economic benefits to the entity, and, in the case of assets, control by the entity (Picker et al. 2006, pp. 34, 45). The sustainability critique has been that such frameworks do not account for the full costs of products or services: for example, the costs of using natural resources or of handling environmental impacts, or both. Historically these have been regarded as social costs 'that are external to the firm but internal to society as a whole' (Field and Field 2009, p. 71). The sustainability requirement is to make firms accountable for all these costs, through full cost accounting. Proposals have been made for redefining accounting elements along these lines by, for example, including references to natural capital in the definitions of the elements of financial statements (Rubenstein 1994, p. 32).

Such accounting frameworks have close links to the traditional economic theory of externalities, which broadens the consideration of product and consumption impacts of firms' activities to include both environmental and social impacts (Perman et al. 2003, p. 134). Moreover the last two decades have seen a demand for firms to take responsibility for the impacts of their products and services across their life cycle, from beginning to end. That is, even though other firms may be responsible for the ways in which they generate inputs at earlier stages of the life cycle, and disseminate products at later stages, including disposal, the firm cannot excuse itself from a share of the responsibility for impacts at all stages in the life cycle of its products and services. This principle is incorporated in modern Life Cycle Assessment (LCA), as in the ISO standards 14040/44:

> Generic LCA method requires that all the main inputs to the processes that provide the service are taken into account, as well as the processes and materials that feed into those processes, and so on back 'up' the supply chains of the various materials in the product to the raw resource inputs. These raw inputs are invariably energy-based . . . rather than simply raw materials. (Horne 2009, p. 3)

Parallel principles govern the Social Impact Assessment (SIA) where the focus is on 'an assessment of the social impact and ethical behaviour of an organization, project, programme or policy in relation to its objectives and those of the people involved' (Barrow 2000, p. 8).

The requirement of sustainability principles that the firm be accountable for such impacts, broadly conceived, is clearly ethical. Social impacts are evaluated through ethical, human rights and social justice frameworks. For example, indigenous rights associated with mining and natural resource projects are now recognized as material. The degree to which such demands are respected is, however, a matter of controversy: monetary benefits from projects to indigenous peoples, for example, may not compensate for cultural losses.

The demand for environmental costs to be internalized also has ethical foundations. Beyond a biocentric position on environmental ethics (Attfield 2003), the modern view of ecosystems is that they provide critical services to society. These include provisioning services, such as food, water and genetic resources; regulating services, such as climate regulation and pollination; supporting services, such as soil formation; and cultural services, recreational, educational and spiritual; all explicitly linked to well-being (Sarukhan and Whyte 2003). Under such an analysis, therefore, the environmental impacts of firms are not taken as affecting only environmental systems, divorced from human populations: all such impacts have human effects. They are therefore governed unambiguously by mandatory ethical imperatives. Among the important implications which flow from this is an ethical requirement for use of the precautionary principle in management practice in order to avoid approaching or breaching biological thresholds that may lead to irreversible ecological collapse.

Future Generations

Sustainability has always been framed in terms of intergenerational ethics. The Brundtland Report's aspiration to 'meet the needs and aspirations of the present without compromising the ability to meet those of the future' was a radically new approach for its time, at least in western cultures. It has been noted that in Native American societies consideration of the impact of community decisions traditionally extended for seven generations (Rubenstein 1994, p.48); this principle has been systematically implemented in the modern indigenous forest business management (Berry 1995).

Prior to the Brundtland Report, Rawls (1972, pp.289–90) derived a just savings principle. According to this principle a society chooses a rate of capital accumulation which maintains just institutions and preserves their material base. Here justice is conceived in terms of intergenerational cooperation:

> ... all generations have their appropriate aims. They are not subordinate to one another any more than individuals are. The life of a people is conceived as

a scheme of cooperation spread out in historical time. It is to be governed by the same conception of justice that regulates the cooperation of contemporaries . . . Each generation makes a contribution to later generations and receives from its predecessors.

Solow (2003) applied this principle to macroeconomic theory, by defining the stock of capital that supports the well-being of human populations as including reproducible capital, renewable and non-renewable resources, and environmental capital, and by requiring that the capital stock, in aggregate, be maintained at a constant level over time. Substitutability between elements of capital – for example, between knowledge and resources – was, however, permitted; a 'weak sustainability' principle that contemporary ecological economists want to see replaced by a 'strong sustainability' principle of non-substitution, so that the integrity of environmental systems is guaranteed (Common and Stagl 2005, p. 378).

Such sustainability principles require firms to include future generations in their stakeholders, defined, as we have argued, by ethical obligations. As with present-day stakeholders there will always be a negotiation between interests, in this case current and future interests. The intergenerational principle simply requires that future generations be included in the ethical dialogue. It is not argued that the present generation can make judgements about the preferences of future generations. However, the base of environmental services can be secured, with options (new medicines, for example) kept intact. It may be thought somewhat fanciful that firms can make decisions with such long-range consequences, given the short-term imperatives of modern business; but it is worth recalling that in 1989 international firms did make such decisions with respect to the ozone layer, through the Montreal Protocol. Moreover globally firms are now facing similar decisions concerning their impacts on climate change, where projections reach to 100 years or more; if not for seven generations, then at least five.

CONCLUSION

This chapter has argued that the concepts which historically have come to characterize the sustainable firm have at their foundations ethical and moral principles. Once that proposition is accepted, the idea of the sustainable firm and its activities emerges as a set of logical consequences. We have reviewed four central concepts of the sustainable firm from that perspective. We have noted that the modern sustainability trivium – economic, social and environmental – finds a unified theoretical foundation in this approach.

We have further argued for the necessity and the power of such principles in conceiving the shape of sustainable business. It was noted that the historical development of sustainability in the business literature has centred primarily on classificatory schemes, which have been added to, or subtracted from, or changed on unsystematic grounds. In contrast, the higher-order principle of an ethical foundation appears to offer a coherent basis on which the theory and practice of the sustainable firm can systematically be generated.

The difficulties of establishing an ethical foundation of this kind for the firm have not, however, been minimized. The range of modern ethical theories is wide. We have taken a Kantian approach to common morality theories as the best-established and most intuitively acceptable of them. However modern ethical theory and its applications to sustainability themes are in active development – see, for example, Perpich (2008) and Smith (2001 – and research into the implications for firms of these new theoretical developments is clearly warranted. Building on the thesis outlined here, a comprehensive research program would apply these ethical theories systematically to the full range of business activities, such as strategy, accounting and finance, operations, knowledge and information, marketing, and human resourcing, with a view to constructing an integrated view of the sustainable firm. Crucially the process of ethical decision making in firms and organizations would be systematically investigated.

Our approach may offer further theoretical simplification. There is a sense in which, from this perspective, the historical distinctions between the socially responsible firm, the sustainable firm and the stakeholder firm – or indeed between sustainable business and business as usual – may cease to be useful. If Solomon is right in seeing the firm first as a community of people working for common goals then the central question is by what principles they will act; and as Solomon points out, 'Meaningful human activity is that which intends the good rather than stumbling over it on the way to merely competitive or selfish goals' (2004, p. 1026). On that reading the firm and its business, whatever it is to be called, is like any other cooperative human activity, and will principally be framed by its response to the great traditional question of ethics: 'How should one live?'

REFERENCES

Aristotle (1925), *The Nicomachaen Ethics*, Oxford, UK: Oxford University Press.
Attfield, R. (2003), *Environmental Ethics*, Cambridge, UK: Polity Press.
Barrow, C. (2000), *Social Impact Assessment: An Introduction*, New York: Oxford University Press.

Baumol, W. (1970), 'Enlightened self-interest and corporate philanthropy', in W. Baumol, R. Likert, H. Wallich and J. McGowan (eds), *A New Rationale for Corporate Social Policy*, New York: Committee for Economic Development.

Beauchamp, T., Bowie, N. and Arnold, D. (2009), *Ethical Theory and Business*, Upper Saddle River, NJ: Pearson Education.

Berle, A. and Means, G. (1932), *The Modern Corporation and Private Property*, New York: Harcourt Brace and World Inc.

Berry, W. (1995), *Another Turn of the Crank*, Berkeley, CA: Counterpoint Press.

Bowen, H. (1953), *Social Responsibilities of the Businessman*, New York: Harper & Brothers.

Bowie, N. (2002), 'A Kantian approach to business ethics', in T. Donaldson, P. Werhane and M. Cording (eds), *Ethical Issues in Business: A Philosophical Approach*, Upper Saddle River, NJ: Pearson Education.

Bowie, N. (2010), 'Organizational integrity and moral climates', in G. Brenkert and T. Beauchamp (eds), *The Oxford Handbook of Business Ethics*, Oxford, UK: Oxford University Press.

Bowie, N. and Dunfee, T. (2002), 'Confronting morality in markets', *Journal of Business Ethics*, **38** (4), 381–93.

Carroll, A. (1999), 'Corporate social responsibility: evolution of a definitional construct', *Business & Society*, **38** (3), 268–95.

Carroll, A. and Shabana, K. (2010), 'The business case for corporate social responsibility: a review of concepts, research and practice', *International Journal of Management Reviews*, 85–105. DOI: 10.1111/j.1468-2370.2009.00275.x

Clarkson, M. (1995), 'A stakeholder framework for analyzing and evaluating corporate social performance', *Academy of Management Review*, **20** (1), 92–117.

Common, M. and Stagl, S. (2005), *Ecological Economics: An Introduction*, Cambridge, UK: Cambridge University Press.

Dow Jones Indexes, S.L. & Group, S.A.M. (2011), 'Dow Jones Sustainability World Indexes Guide Version 9.0', Available at http://www.sustainability-indexes.com/dow-jones-sustainability-indexes/index.jsp (accessed 22 June 2012).

Drucker, P. (1946), *The Concept of the Corporation*, New Jersey: Transaction Publishers Rutgers University.

Drucker, P. (1984), 'The new meaning of corporate social responsibility', *California Management Review*, **26**, 53–63.

Dunfee, T. (1998), 'The marketplace of morality: first steps towards a theory of moral choice', *Business Ethics Quarterly*, **8** (1), 127–45.

Dunfee, T. (2008), 'Stakeholder theory: managing corporate social responsibility in a multiple actor context', in A. Crane, A. McWilliams, D. Matten, J. Moon and D. Siegel (eds), *The Oxford Handbook of Corporate Social Responsibility*, Oxford, UK: Oxford University Press.

Dunphy, D., Griffiths, A. and Benn, S. (2003), *Organizational Change for Corporate Sustainability*, London: Routledge.

Dyllick, T. and Hockerts, K. (2002), 'Beyond the business case for corporate sustainability', *Business Strategy and the Environment*, **11**, 130–41.

Eckersley, R. (2004), *Well & Good*, Melbourne, Australia: The Text Publishing Company.

Elkington, J. (1997), *Cannibals with Forks: The Triple Bottom Line of 21st Century Business*, Oxford: Capstone.

Field, B. and Field, M. (2009), *Environmental Economics: An Introduction*, New York: McGraw-Hill/Irwin.

Francis, R. (2000), *Ethics and Corporate Governance: An Australian Handbook*, Sydney: University of New South Wales Press.

Freeman, R. (1984), *Strategic Management: A Stakeholder Approach*, Boston: Pitman.

Freeman, R. (2009), 'Managing for stakeholders', in T. Beauchamp, N. Bowie and D. Arnold (eds), *Ethical Theory and Business*, London: Pearson Education.

Friedman, M. (1970), 'The social responsibility of business is to increase its profits', *The New York Times Magazine*, 13 September 1970, available at http://graphics8.nytimes.com/packages/pdf/business/miltonfriedman1970.pdf (accessed 22 June 2012).

Global Reporting Initiative (2011), *Global Reporting Initative Sustainability Reporting Guidelines: G3.1 Version*, available at https://www.globalreporting.org/reporting/latest-guidelines/g3-1-guidelines/Pages/default.aspx (accessed 22 June 2012).

Goodpaster, K. (2010), 'Corporate responsibility and its constituents', in G. Brenkert and T. Beauchamp (eds), *The Oxford Handbook of Business Ethics*, Oxford, UK: Oxford University Press.

Habermas, J. (1990), *Moral Consciousness and Communicative Action*, Cambridge, MA: The MIT Press.

Hawken, P., Lovins, A. and Hunter Lovins, L. (1999), *Natural Capitalism: Creating the Next Industrial Revolution*, Boston: Little Brown and Company.

Hempel, C. (1966) *Philosophy of Natural Science*, Englewood Cliffs, NJ: Prentice-Hall.

Horne, R. (2009), 'Life cycle assessment: origins, principles and context', in R. Horne, T. Grant and K. Verghese (eds), *Life Cycle Assessment: Principles, Practice and Prospects*, Collingwood, Australia: CSIRO Publishing.

Jones, T. and Wicks, A. C. (1999), 'Convergent stakeholder theory', *Academy of Management Review*, **24** (2), 206–21.

Kagan, S. (1998), *Normative Ethics*, Oxford: Westview Press.

Kantarelis, D. (2007), *Theories of the Firm*, Geneva, Switzerland: Inderscience.

Kennedy, H. (2005), *Just Law*, London: Random House.

Kurucz, E., Colbert, B. and Wheeler, D. (2008), 'The business case for corporate social responsibility', in A. Crane, A. McWilliams, D. Matten, J. Moon and D. Siegel (eds), *The Oxford Handbook of Corporate Social Responsibility*, Oxford, UK: Oxford University Press.

Lakatos, I., Worrall, J. and Currie, G. (1980), *The Methodology of Scientific Research Programmes*, Cambridge: Cambridge University Press.

MacIntyre, A. (1998), *A Short History of Ethics*, Notre Dame: University of Notre Dame Press.

Montiel, I. (2008), 'Corporate social responsibility and corporate sustainability: separate pasts, common futures', *Organization & Environment*, **21** (3), 245–69.

Nagel, E. (1961), *The Structure of Science; Problems in the Logic of Scientific Explanation*, London: Routledge & Kegan Paul.

Perman, R., Ma, Y., McGilvray, J. and Common, M. (2003), *Natural Resource and Environmental Economics*, Harlow, Essex, UK: Pearson Education Limited.

Perpich, D. (2008), *The Ethics of Emmanuel Levinas*, Stanford, CA: Stanford University Press.

Picker, R., Leo, K., Alfredson, K., Radford, J., Pacter, P. and Wise, V. (2006), *Australian Accounting Standards*, Milton, Australia: John Wiley & Sons Australia, Ltd.

Popper, K.R. (1969), *Conjectures and Refutations: the Growth of Scientific Knowledge*, London: Routledge & Kegan Paul.

Rawls, J. (1972), *A Theory of Justice*, Oxford, UK: Oxford University Press.

Ricketts, M. (1994), *The Economics of Business Enterprise: An Introduction to Economic Organisation and the Theory of the Firm*, Hertfordshire, UK: Harvester Wheatsheaf.

Rubenstein, D. (1994), *Environmental Accounting for the Sustainable Corporation*, Westport, CT: Quorum Books.

Sagoff, M. (1988), *The Economy of the Earth*, New York: Cambridge University Press.

Sarukhan, J. and Whyte, A. (2003), 'Ecosystems and well-being: a framework for assessment', *Millennium Ecosystem Assessment*, Washington DC: Island Press.

Sethi, P. (1975), 'Dimensions of corporate social performance: an analytic framework', *California Management Review*, **17**, Spring, 58–64.

Smith, M. (2001), *An Ethics of Place*, Albany, NY: SUNY Press.

Solomon, R. (2004), 'Aristotle, ethics and business organizations', *Organization Studies*, **25** (6), 1021–43.

Solow, R. (2003), 'An almost practical step toward sustainability', *Resources Policy*, **19** (3), 162–72.

Unerman, J., Bebbington, J. and O'Dwyer, B. (2007), *Sustainability Accounting and Accountability*, London: Routledge.

Wacks, R. (2009), *Understanding Jurisprudence: An Introduction to Legal Theory*, New York: Oxford University Press.

Wallich, H. and McGowan, J. (1970), 'Stockholder interest and the corporation's role in social policy', in W. Baumol, R. Likert, H. Wallich and J. McGowan (eds), *A New Rationale for Corporate Social Policy*, New York: Committee for Economic Development.

Watson, T. (2009), 'Organisations, strategies and human resourcing', in J. Leopold and L. Harris (eds), *The Strategic Managing of Human Resources*, Harlow, Essex, UK: Pearson Education Limited.

Winch, P. (1963), *The Idea of a Social Science and Its Relation to Philosophy*, London: Routledge and Kegan Paul.

Wingfield, N. (2012), 'Apple's chief puts stamp on labor issues', New York: The New York Times, available at http://www.nytimes.com/2012/04/02/technology/apple-presses-its-suppliers-to-improve-conditions.html?_r=3&hp (accessed 22 June 2012).

PART II

Sustainable Business Management

4. Sustainability accounting and reporting: an overview, contemporary developments and research possibilities

Sumit Lodhia

INTRODUCTION

This chapter focuses on sustainability accounting and reporting. Initially the notion of sustainability accounting and reporting is discussed with attention given to the internal (sustainability management) and external (sustainability reporting) aspects. These components of sustainability accounting have parallels to the accounting process where management accounting and financial reporting are prominent. However it is highlighted that sustainability issues are much broader and provide unique challenges for the accounting process.

The chapter then proceeds to contemporary developments in sustainability accounting in order to highlight the 'state of the art' in this discipline. There are two aspects that warrant specific discussion. Carbon accounting is an area receiving increased attention, driven by the global concern over climate change. Its subcomponents, carbon management accounting and carbon reporting, are derived from sustainability accounting, and provide the means to account for climate change.

Another critical development in sustainability accounting and reporting has the potential to transform business practices. Integrated reporting is an attempt to integrate financial information with social and environmental issues and requires integrated thinking to be embedded throughout an organization through its planning, systems and processes and decision making.

Finally the chapter addresses some of the current areas of research in sustainability accounting and reporting and suggests that research possibilities in this area are abundant and could contribute to the literature as well as practice and policy.

WHAT IS SUSTAINABILITY ACCOUNTING AND REPORTING?

The link between social and environmental issues and accounting has developed due to the need for corporations to extend accountability to their stakeholders. Accounting is a practice that has traditionally enabled managers to be accountable to shareholders in relation to the financial management of a corporation. Given the increasing emphasis on social and environmental issues in recent times, a need arises for the accounting process to be extended to include social and environmental issues.

The importance of social and environmental issues was brought to prominence in the 1990s by the emergence of the notion of triple bottom line. Elkington (1997) coined the triple bottom line concept whereby economic, social and environmental issues are considered to be vital issues for businesses. According to Elkington, corporations have a critical role in addressing social and environmental issues, and for them to survive in the long term, accounting for such issues is important. The triple bottom line concept has developed in response to the sustainable development debate and emphasizes the role corporations have in striving for sustainability. More recently the term sustainability accounting and reporting (Schaltegger et al., 2006; Unerman et al., 2007) has replaced the notion of triple bottom line accounting as an increasing global emphasis is placed on sustainability.

There are similarities and differences between accounting and the sustainability function. Both these areas affect the entire organization and are not simply distinct functions of a business (Gray and Bebbington, 2001; Unerman et al., 2007). There is an increasing emphasis on provision of information to stakeholders in order to demonstrate accountability (Gray, 1992; Gray et al., 1996). Similarly both functions require information for managerial purposes (Gray and Bebbington, 2001; Burritt et al., 2002; Schaltegger et al., 2006). However there are critical differences. The primary distinction is that the information produced for each function is quite different, as social and environmental information cannot always be expressed in financial terms (Burritt et al., 2002; Schaltegger et al., 2006). Legal requirements also differ with legislation existing for specific social and environmental issues and not disclosure, whilst accounting mandatory requirements are focused entirely on disclosure in annual reports (Gray and Bebbington, 2001; Unerman et al., 2007). The final fundamental difference is the purposes of each function, with the accounting goal of profit and shareholder value maximization being often at odds with the goals of sustainability (Gray, 1992, 2001).

The development of sustainability accounting and reporting draws upon the basic elements of accounting: management accounting and financial reporting. Accounting for sustainability has focused on the internal component, sustainability management, and the external reporting element, sustainability reporting. It is the managerial, measurement, reporting and auditing skills that accounting provides that supply the foundations of sustainability accounting and reporting.

Management accounting involves a focus on the internal operations of a corporation with the intention of providing information to managers for planning, control and decision making purposes. This information can range from hourly to multi-year time spans and is for management use only. Management accounting focuses on managing the organization so that the goals of senior management are achieved. It also emphasizes measurement with emphasis being on both monetary (dollars and cents) as well as physical measurement (for example, kilograms of raw materials). These skills are transferable to management of sustainability issues within an organization.

Financial reporting involves preparing financial accounts in accordance with corporate law, accounting standards and stock exchange listing requirements. An annual report with financial accounts and associated notes as well as limited narrative information is produced on an annual basis and is verified by auditors, thereby presenting an account of the corporation's financial position and performance for a particular year. This information is accessible to shareholders and anyone with a financial interest in a business. The reporting skills provided by accounting enable sustainability reporting to be undertaken through a range of different media that extend beyond the use of an annual report. The internal and external auditing aspects of accounting can also be applied to sustainability issues. However sustainability assurance is currently lagging behind the financial auditing process, largely due to the voluntary nature of sustainability reporting (Deegan et al., 2006).

The focus on sustainability management has primarily been on environmental management. This is an internal process with an emphasis on environmental performance. Environmental management systems such as ISO14001 can exist within organizations which attempt to manage their environmental impacts. This can include establishment of environmental policies, environmental audit and management systems, accounting for energy, waste packaging and recycling, investment appraisal and budgeting, as well as life cycle assessment and mass balance activities (Gray and Bebbington, 2001).

More recent developments have seen the emergence of Environmental Management Accounting (EMA) (Schaltegger and Burritt, 2000; Burritt et al., 2002; Schaltegger et al., 2003). The basic idea behind EMA is that organizations should internalize environmental costs. Currently, these costs are externalized as society bears the impact of organizational social and environmental impacts. EMA mechanisms attempt to trace costs of the organization's activities to the environment. It is considered that once organizations are made accountable for these costs, they would be compelled to minimize their environmental impacts.

Burritt et al. (2002) divide EMA into Monetary Environmental Management Accounting (MEMA) and Physical Environmental Management Accounting (PEMA). The former involves accounting for the environment in terms of financial measures while the latter focuses on the physical measurement of environmental issues. The EMA framework also considers the timeframe for decision making (past, present, future), the length of the time frame (short or long run) and the routineness of the information supplied (regular or ad-hoc).

Whilst there has been considerable progress in environmental management, social issues management has lagged behind these developments. It is not clear whether organizations devote as much time and effort to management of social matters when compared to environmental management. Occupational health and safety, product safety and responsibility systems provide the major evidence of social issues management in organizations. Thus the concept of sustainability management has to move beyond its exclusive environmental focus and provide guidance on the management of other social issues.

Sustainability reporting is the disclosure of social, environmental and economic performance of an organization to relevant stakeholders (GRI, 2011). This reporting is usually within the domain of the environmental/ sustainable development as well as communications/public relations staff. Sustainability reporting attempts to provide a balanced and reasonable representation of organizational performance (positive as well as negative) in relation to social and environmental issues.

Sustainability reporting enables an organization to extend its accountability to external stakeholders (Gray et al., 1996). It allows an organization to enhance its reputation, and gain the confidence of stakeholders (Gray and Bebbington, 2001; Unerman et al., 2007). Operational and managerial improvements, performance benchmarking and better management of social and environmental risks are the internal changes that can be brought about by sustainability reporting (Burritt et al., 2002; Schaltegger et al., 2006). All these benefits can enable a corporation to differentiate itself from its competitors in regard to its social and environmental credentials (Gray and Bebbington, 2001).

The annual report is the primary communication tool for disseminating information to stakeholders in relation to a company's financial position and performance. It was extensively used as a medium of communication for portraying social and environmental information in the early 1990s (Gray and Bebbington, 2001; Unerman et al., 2007; KPMG, 2011). However, recently, sustainability reports have gained prominence (ACCA, 2001; Unerman et al., 2007; KPMG, 2011). Advertisements and brochures may also be useful in disclosing sustainability information (Zeghal and Ahmed, 1990) while media releases can be used to disseminate information on a company's social and environmental performance or to report specific issues (Brown and Deegan, 1998; Deegan et al., 2002). In contemporary times, sustainability reporting on the web has emerged as a critical component of corporate communications (Adams and Frost, 2004; Lodhia, 2004, 2012; KPMG, 2011).

The Global Reporting Initiative (GRI) is a global set of guidelines that aim to provide a consistent basis for disclosing sustainability information (GRI, 2002, 2011). The GRI, which was conceived in 1997 by the Coalition for Environmentally Responsible Economies (CERES) and the United Nations Environmental Program (UNEP), is an international multi stakeholder effort towards developing globally applicable guidelines for reporting on the economic, social and environmental performance of corporations, governments and non-governmental organizations (GRI, 2002). These guidelines were developed in 2000 and subsequently updated in 2002 and 2006. A fourth version is in process of development (GRI homepage). The GRI provides guidelines to all companies for general reporting, report structure and core content. A range of indicators has been developed to assess environmental, social and economic performance of organizations. Supplements for different industry sectors and specific issues, and technical protocols for measurement of performance indicators are also being developed. Engagement processes continue to take place regularly in order to receive feedback to aid in refining these criteria and to seek different views on sustainability reporting.

The accountancy firm KPMG has undertaken a triennial survey of global sustainability reporting since 1993. Its recent survey (KPMG, 2011) suggests that corporations are now recognizing that sustainability reporting is more than just good corporate citizenship, it is part of organizational learning and innovation. This is exemplified by the fact that 95 per cent of the largest 250 global corporations (G250) currently engage in sustainability reporting.

CONTEMPORARY DEVELOPMENTS IN SUSTAINABILITY ACCOUNTING AND REPORTING

Two major developments in sustainability accounting and reporting attempt to ensure that sustainability issues remain a vital part of the corporate agenda. These include carbon accounting and integrated reporting.

Carbon accounting is a subset of sustainability accounting which emphasizes the management and reporting of carbon emissions. Carbon management accounting and carbon reporting have the same characteristics as sustainability management accounting and sustainability reporting but concentrate primarily on the critical problem of climate change.

Integrated reporting is a process that seeks to integrate traditional financial reporting with social and environmental issues. The intention is for integrated reporting to extend to strategic planning and decision making processes whereby integrated information is the basis for critical business decisions.

Carbon Accounting

The seriousness of climate change is highlighted by recent economic (Stern, 2006, 2009), scientific (IPCC, 2011), and political (Gore, 2006, 2009) evidence. This has led to an increasing concern about carbon emissions and associated greenhouse gases, often expressed as carbon equivalents, as these contribute to climate change (Garnaut, 2010). There is a need to extend management and reporting systems in order to incorporate carbon-related issues into mainstream business practices.

The increasing emphasis on climate change has led to the development of carbon accounting as a corporate tool that would incorporate climate change considerations into mainstream business practices (see also chapter by Ratnatunga in this book). Carbon Management Accounting (CMA) has emerged as a mechanism for businesses to manage their carbon dioxide and other greenhouse gas (carbon dioxide equivalents) emissions. Similarly carbon reporting is an area that has received significant academic attention recently.

There are varying interpretations of CMA within the social and environmental accounting literature. Ratnatunga and Balachandran (2009) perceive CMA as a combination of strategic cost management and strategic management accounting principles that could be related to carbon management. These include conventional cost accounting techniques such as life cycle costing, target costing, activity based management, and strategic management issues such as marketing and promotional strategies, and performance evaluation. Conversely Burritt et al. (2011) take a broader view by drawing upon prior EMA literature (Burritt et al., 2002) discussed earlier in this chapter to develop a CMA framework. This framework distinguishes between monetary and physical carbon accounting in a similar manner to MEMA and PEMA, and represents the difference between the work of Burritt et al. (2011) and that of Ratnatunga and Balachandran (2009). The latter focus primarily on the costing aspects of CMA while the former perceive that in addition to costing (monetary) aspects, CMA also includes physical information such as kilograms, hours, and so forth.

Bebbington and Larrinaga-Gonzalez (2008) have developed the concept of carbon reporting. The authors suggest that in addition to the standard reporting of carbon emissions levels, the risk and uncertainty associated with climate change should also be disclosed by organizations. Current practices in carbon reporting currently do not incorporate these critical aspects. Moreover carbon disclosure is often part of sustainability reports rather than being a standalone activity. Organizations may provide carbon information separately but these are not in the form of corporate reporting to stakeholders. Voluntary mechanisms such as the carbon disclosure project (CDP, 2009) or mandatory requirements such as the National Greenhouse and Energy Reporting Act in Australia (Lodhia, 2011a; Lodhia and Martin, 2012) lead to third parties making aggregate carbon-related information available to the general public.

Current literature has concentrated on CMA and carbon reporting in isolation and provides limited attention to the linkages between these areas. Carbon accounting is taken to include either CMA or reporting of carbon emissions, rather than an integrated process of carbon management and reporting. Integration is essential in order to consider the entire process that leads to the accounting for carbon emissions.

Integrated Reporting

Whilst the development of sustainability reporting has over the years been phenomenal, it is argued that its development has been largely in isolation from financial reporting. Sustainability information is not integrated with financial information, leading to sustainability reporting being a voluntary practice that is not always linked to strategic organizational objectives. The recent global financial crisis has highlighted the reliance on an outdated financial reporting model (developed in the 1930s as a response to the Great Depression) which was inadequate to address the increasing complexities of modern day organizational activity (IIRC South Africa, 2011). There have been increasing calls for new forms of reporting that can integrate financial information with social and environmental/sustainability information. It is in this regard that the notion of integrated reporting has gained prominence recently.

Integrated reporting brings together the material information about an organization's strategy, governance, performance and prospects in a way that reflects the commercial, social and environmental context within which it operates (IIRC, 2011, p. 6). It integrates financial information (available in annual reports) with social and environmental information (in sustainability reports) so that all stakeholders (including financial and other stakeholders) can gain an understanding of the underlying health of the organization over the short, medium and long-term (ICAA, 2011). An integrated report is more than just a combination of different reports, it a critical tool in embedding integrated thinking through an organization (IIRC, 2011).

The International Integrated Reporting Committee (IIRC) has been established to develop an integrated reporting framework. Its recent discussion paper outlines the potential components of such a framework. These include:

- Organizational overview and business model
- Operating context, including risks and opportunities
- Strategic objectives
- Governance and remuneration
- Performance
- Future outlook.

According to the IIRC (2011), an integrated report is a single document reporting the company's financial and environmental, social and governance information (ESG) in a clear, concise, consistent and comparable format. It is more than a mere combination of various reports and requires explanations of the relationship between financial and nonfinancial performance. Ideally an integrated report should be precise and be limited to about 20 pages (IIRC, 2011).

There are several advantages to an organization in undertaking integrated reporting. Foremost, it signals a desire to embed sustainability into business practices and enables the organization to inform and gain the trust of its numerous stakeholders (ICAA, 2011). The reporting process not only becomes simpler but is also relevant and transparent (IIRC, 2011). Internal improvements can also be made through this external reporting process. Through integrated reporting, internal awareness and improvements are feasible, sustainability can be integrated into strategy as well as operations, and performance management can be extended to include social and environmental issues (ICAA, 2011).

Integrated reporting does bring along with it numerous challenges. Whilst the focus with this form of reporting is on integration, in the absence of a comprehensively developed framework, it is unclear how and the extent to which integration of sustainability with financial issues is possible. As discussed earlier in the chapter, financial and social and environmental issues could be conflicting, and therefore it is difficult to expect sustainability matters to take precedence over economic issues. This could then raise questions about the effectiveness of integrated reporting. There will also be challenges in relation to the preparedness of personnel to cope with a fundamental change to reporting especially in relation to their existing skills and capacities (IIRC, 2011; IIRC South Africa, 2011). The robustness of existing systems and processes will be stretched, and smaller to medium sized enterprises could struggle with making significant investments in new systems and personnel (IIRC South Africa, 2011). Getting the attention of stakeholders in relation to integrated reporting could also be difficult. Current reporting systems are geared towards producing an annual report for financial stakeholders and sustainability reports for other stakeholders, and changes to existing reporting structures are not matched by an integrated set of users of reports (integrated stakeholders).

Integrated reporting is currently in its infancy but it is hoped that this new form of reporting will lead to consideration of sustainability issues as part of business strategy and decision making. Already South African listed companies are mandated to produce integrated reports, suggesting that the prospects of integrated reporting as part of mainstream business practice look good.

The goal of integrated reporting will be achieved not merely through disclosure but through internal changes to management systems and processes. These need to be expanded to ensure that integrated economic, social and environmental considerations are embedded in strategic planning and decision making. Performance should follow the strategy and targets set (IIRC, 2011).

RESEARCH POSSIBILITIES

Having discussed the notion of sustainability accounting and reporting in detail and identified contemporary developments in this area, this chapter proceeds to identify the extensive research possibilities that can be undertaken in this area.

The early research on sustainability accounting and reporting was focussed on environmental reporting (1990s) and emphasis was on descriptive studies of environmental disclosure (for example, Harte and Owen, 1991; Roberts, 1991). These studies analysed what companies were reporting and emphasis was primarily on annual report disclosures. Over the years the focus has moved to social and environmental disclosure in a range of additional media such as sustainability reports and the World Wide Web (for example, Frost et al., 2005; Lodhia, 2004, 2006, 2012).

Such studies have value because one must be aware of the current status of the practice before undertaking more in-depth investigations. Developing country literature on incidence of reporting is still a major contribution to the literature (for example, Belal, 2000, 2001; Cahaya et al., 2008) but studies of a similar nature in the developed world are often restricted to specific issues (for example, carbon reporting, disclosure of human rights) and are often an initial and minor part of a more focused and in depth study.

Another area of research in sustainability accounting and reporting is the investigation of the motivations for reporting by corporations. Whilst the majority of the literature points to legitimacy theory as an explanatory theory for sustainability disclosures (Deegan, 2002), recent work has advanced the theorization for sustainability reporting by using more extensive theoretical frameworks such as reputation risk management (Bebbington et al., 2008; Hogan and Lodhia, 2011) and new institutional theory (Bebbington et al., 2009). The earlier literature relied on the content analysis of reports, while more recently researchers have carried out field studies in corporations and addressed motives for reporting by key decision makers (see for example, Adams, 2002; Islam and Deegan, 2008; Bebbington et al., 2009). There is scope for extending theoretical perspectives in order to explain corporate sustainability disclosure in different contexts. Theories from other disciplines have the potential to explain motivations or influences on sustainability reporting, given that this area is multi-disciplinary.

Recent sustainability accounting and reporting research has moved from a primary emphasis on the reporters and focused on the stakeholders of an organization. Studies have addressed the demand of stakeholders for sustainability information (see for example, O'Dwyer et al., 2005a; Lodhia and Martin, 2012) and researched the use of counter accounts by stakeholders whereby an alternative to corporate accounts of sustainability performance is provided (for example, Gallhofer et al., 2006). Research has also looked at the accountability of critical stakeholders such as non-governmental organizations (NGOs) (for example, O'Dwyer et al., 2005b), suggesting that even these organizations are not exempt from scrutiny. Another emerging area of research is the social and environmental partnerships/collaborations between a corporation and its stakeholders such as NGOs, industry associations, suppliers, and even the local community (for example, Fiedler and Deegan, 2007). Insights have been provided on the formation, ongoing operations and the motives of partnerships as well as the assessment of the outcomes of the partnership.

Studies have also started to address the sustainability accounting and reporting practices in the public sector (Ball and Grubnic, 2007). This sector is different from the private sector as the profitability motive is replaced by public service intentions, leading to accountability being extended to citizens rather than just powerful stakeholders. However research findings indicate that the public sector accounting and reporting practices lag behind those of companies (for example, Gibson and Guthrie, 1995; Dickinson et al., 2005), representing a major roadblock to the aspirational goal of sustainable development. There is a need for research to explore public sector practices through methods such as field studies and to understand the drivers of, and impediments to, current practices.

Sustainability accounting and reporting research has not only focused on reporting aspects but has also looked at the use of management accounting tools in organizations as a means of managing sustainability issues. As discussed earlier the work of Burritt and Schaltegger is prominent in this regard (for example, Burritt et al., 2002; Schaltegger et al., 2003). Recent research has applied such work to critical environmental issues such as environmental costing (Deegan, 2008) and accounting for climate change (Milne and Grubnic, 2011), whilst techniques such as full cost accounting encourage organizations to take a cradle to grave approach whereby social and environmental costs are measured throughout the life of a product or service, from creation to eventual disposal as scrap (Bebbington et al., 2001). Field studies have also looked at the internal factors that drive sustainability accounting and reporting (Adams, 2002) and described the multi-disciplinary focus of this discipline with sustainability managers, accountants and communication managers playing a critical role.

Sustainability accounting and reporting education research is an area that requires further development, especially with the potential move towards extended reporting frameworks such as integrated reporting in the future. Existing research has looked at the incorporation of sustainability into the accounting curricula and the role of professional accounting bodies in facilitating sustainability accounting education (for example, Nowak et al., 2008; Lodhia, 2010). Future research is needed to investigate issues such as the background of staff involved in sustainability accounting teaching, the student demand for sustainability accounting skills, the skills that need to be developed for accounting students in order for them to contribute to corporate sustainability, and whether potential conflicts between financial and sustainability issues are covered in the accounting curriculum.

Carbon pricing is another area where accounting can contribute extensively (Lodhia, 2011b). However research in this regard is limited, largely due to the slow adoption of emissions trading schemes or carbon tax in a number of countries. Future research could explore the management and reporting changes that carbon pricing requires so that externalities can be incorporated into mainstream business practices. The accounting for carbon pricing as well as carbon offsets is another area that requires immediate research given that international accounting bodies have failed in their attempts to develop guidance on these matters. For instance, Cook (2009) states that the international accounting standards board failed in their attempt to develop an accounting standard for emissions trading.

Carbon accounting research requires studies that consider the entire CMA and carbon reporting process in order to understand how organizations account for climate change. Such studies will be comprehensive and involve longer time spans but will make a very useful contribution to literature as well as practice and policy.

As discussed earlier, integrated reporting is expected to be a major change in corporate reporting that has implications for sustainability. Both the practice as well as academic research will be grappling with integrated reporting for years to come. Critical issues do need to be addressed before integrated reporting replaces existing forms of reporting, and these matters are posed as researchable questions:

- How to integrate financial and sustainability information in a meaningful manner?
- Could sustainability reporting be swallowed up by financial reporting as a result of integrated reporting and how can we prevent this?
- What is the role of accountants and the accounting profession in relation to integrated reporting? How can their skills and competencies be enhanced so that they are prepared to play an instrumental role in integrated reporting?

SUMMARY AND CONCLUSIONS

This chapter has introduced the notion of sustainability accounting and reporting which is a vital element in a corporation's response to sustainability issues. Sustainability accounting and reporting is more than simply a moral responsibility; it is a major component of a modern day corporation's quest for survival in the global economy. Corporations are accountable to stakeholders for their social and environmental impacts and have the power and influence to be major players in addressing critical issues such as climate change.

Contemporary developments such as carbon accounting and integrated reporting are reflective of the shift in focus of accounting from a mere management of economic issues to a broader sustainability agenda encompassing economic, social and environmental responsibilities. Climate change related issues and broader social and environmental matters need to be integrated into business processes and systems so that the three pillars of sustainable development (economic, social and environmental) are addressed. Integrated reporting is an ambitious agenda but its potential success provides the opportunity to transform business practices and create a fair and equitable society.

Sustainability accounting and reporting research is an emerging and expanding area of research where academics can play a vital role in contributing to sustainable business practices. There are a range of areas that can be explored through various theoretical perspectives and methods.

The challenge for sustainability accounting researchers and practitioners is to ensure that business as usual attitudes are replaced by a more eclectic focus on economic, social and environmental responsibilities. Sustainability issues are critical and can no longer be a fringe aspect of corporate goals, and sustainability accounting and reporting is a way forward for broadening the simplistic focus on profitability alone as a measure of business success.

REFERENCES

ACCA (2001), *Environmental, Social and Sustainability Reporting on the World Wide Web: A Guide To Best Practice*, London: The Certified Accountants Educational Trust.

Adams, C. (2002), 'Internal organisational factors influencing corporate social and ethical reporting', *Accounting, Auditing & Accountability Journal*, **15** (2), 223–50.

Adams, C.A., and Frost, G.R. (2004), *The Development of the Corporate Website and Implications for Ethical, Social and Environmental Reporting Through These Media*, Edinburgh: The Institute of Chartered Accountants of Scotland.

Ball, A., and Grubnic, S. (2007), 'Sustainability acounting and accountability in the public sector', in Unerman, J., O'Dwyer, C., and Bebbington, J. (eds), *Sustainability Accounting and Accountability*, London: Routledge, pp. 243–65.

Bebbington, J., and Larrinaga-Gonzalez, C. (2008), 'Carbon trading: accounting and reporting issues', *European Accounting Review*, **17** (4), 697–717.

Bebbington, J., Gray, R., Hibbitt, C., and Kirk, E. (2001), *Full Cost Accounting: An Agenda for Action*, London: Association of Chartered Certified Accountants.

Bebbington, J., Larrinaga-Gonzalez, C., and Moneva, J. (2008), 'Corporate social reporting and reputation risk management', *Accounting, Auditing & Accountability Journal*, **21** (3), 337–61.

Bebbington, J., Higgins, C., and Frame, B. (2009), 'Initiating sustainable development reporting: evidence from New Zealand', *Accounting, Auditing & Accountability Journal*, **22** (4), 588–625.

Belal, A. (2000), 'Environmental reporting in developing countries: empirical evidence from Bangladesh', *Eco-Management and Auditing*, **7** (3), 114–21.

Belal, A. (2001), 'A study of corporate social disclosures in Bangladesh', *Managerial Auditing Journal*, **16** (5), 274–89.

Brown, N., and Deegan, C. (1998), 'The public disclosure of environmental performance information – a dual test of media agenda setting theory and legitimacy theory', *Accounting and Business Research*, **29** (1), 21–41.

Burritt, R.L., Hahn, T., and Schaltegger, S. (2002), 'Towards a comprehensive framework for environmental management accounting – links between business actors and Environmental Management Accounting tools', *Australian Accounting Review*, **12** (2), 39–50.

Burritt, R.L., Schaltegger, S., and Zvezdov, D. (2011), 'Carbon management accounting – practice in leading German companies', *Australian Accounting Review*, **21** (1), 80–98.

Cahaya, F., Porter, S., and Brown, A. (2008), 'Social disclosure practices by Jakarta stock exchange listed entities', *Journal of the Asia-Pacific Centre for Environmental Accountability*, **14** (1), 2–11.

Carbon Disclosure Project (CDP) (2009), *CDP report 2009*, Australia and New Zealand: CDP.

Cook, A. (2009), 'Emission rights: from costless activity to market operations', *Accounting, Organizations and Society*, **34**, 456–68.

Deegan, C. (2002), 'The legitimizing effect of social and environmental disclosures: a theoretical foundation', *Accounting, Auditing & Accountability Journal*, **15** (3), 282–311.

Deegan, C. (2008), 'Environmental costing in capital investment decisions: electricity distributors and the choice of power poles', *Australian Accounting Review*, **18** (1), 2–15.

Deegan, C., and Rankin, M. (1999), 'The environmental reporting expectations gap: Australian evidence', *British Accounting Review*, **31**, 313–46.

Deegan, C., Rankin, M., and Tobin, J. (2002), 'An examination of the corporate social and environmental disclosures of BHP from 1983–1997: a test of legitimacy theory', *Accounting, Auditing, and Accountability Journal*, **15** (3), 312–43.

Deegan, C., Cooper, B.J., and Shelly, M. (2006), 'An investigation of TBL report assurance statements: Australian evidence', *Australian Accounting Review*, **16** (2), 2–18.

Dickinson, D., Leeson, R., Ivers, J. and Karic, J. (2005), *Sustainability Reporting By Public Agencies: International Uptake, Forms and Practice*, Victoria, Australia: The Centre for Public Agency Sustainability Reporting.

Elkington, J. (1997), *Cannibals with Forks: The Triple Bottom Line of 21st Century Business*, Oxford: Capstone Publishing.

Fiedler, T., and Deegan, C. (2007), 'Environmental collaborations within the building and construction industry: a consideration of the motivations to collaborate', *Managerial Auditing Journal*, **22** (4), 410–41.

Frost, G., Jones, S., Loftus, J., and Van Der Laan, S. (2005), 'A survey of sustainability reporting practices of Australian reporting entities', *Australian Accounting Review*, **15** (1), 89–97.

Gallhofer, S., Haslam, J., Monk, E., and Roberts, C. (2006), 'The emancipatory potential of online reporting: the case of counter accounting', *Accounting, Auditing and Accountability Journal*, **19** (5), 681–718.

Garnaut, R. (2010), *The Garnaut Climate Change Review: Final Report*, Melbourne: Cambridge University Press.

Gibson, R., and Guthrie, J. (1995), 'Recent environmental disclosures in annual reports of Australian public and private sector organisations', *Accounting Forum*, **19** (2/3), 111–27.

Global Reporting Initiative (GRI) (2002), *Sustainability Reporting Guidelines on Economic, Environmental and Social Performance*, Boston, MA, US: Interim Secretariat, GRI.

Global Reporting Initiative (GRI) (2011), *Sustainability Reporting Guidelines: Version 3.1*, Amsterdam, Netherlands: GRI.

Gore, A. (2006), *An Inconvenient Truth: The Planetary Emergency of Global Warming and What We Can Do About It*, London: Bloomsbury Publishing.

Gore, A. (2009), *Our Choice: A Plan to Solve the Climate Crisis*, London: Bloomsbury.

Gray, R.H. (1992), 'Accounting and environmentalism: an exploration of the challenge of gently accounting for accountability, transparency and sustainability', *Accounting Organisations and Society*, **17** (5), 399–426.

Gray, R.H. (2001), 'Social and environmental responsibility, sustainability and accountability: can the corporate sector deliver?', *The Corporate Citizen*, **2** (3), 9–16.

Gray, R.H., and Bebbington, K.J. (2001), *Accounting for the Environment*, 2nd edition, London: Sage.

Gray, R.H., Owen, D.L., and Adams, C. (1996), *Accounting and Accountability: Social and Environmental Accounting in a Changing World*, Hemel Hempstead: Prentice Hall.

Harte, G., and Owen, D.L. (1991), 'Environmental disclosure in the annual reports of British companies: a research note', *Accounting, Auditing & Accountability Journal*, **4** (3), 51–61.

Hogan, J., and Lodhia, S. (2011), 'Sustainability reporting and reputation risk management: an Australian case study', *International Journal of Accounting and Information Management*, **19** (3), 267–87.

Institute of Chartered Accountants in Australia (ICAA) (2011), *Integrating Sustainability Into Business Practices: A Case Study Approach*, ICAA.

International Integrated Reporting Committee (IIRC) (2011), *Towards Integrated Reporting: Communicating Value in the 21st Century*, IIRC.

International Integrated Reporting Committee South Africa (IIRC South Africa) (2011), 'Framework for integrated reporting and the integrated report: discussion paper', IIRC South Africa.

IPCC (2011), available at http://www.ipcc.ch/ (accessed 10 February 2011).

Islam, M., and Deegan, C. (2008), 'Motivations for an organisation within a developing country to report social responsibility information: evidence from Bangladesh', *Accounting, Auditing & Accountability Journal*, **21** (6), 850–74.

KPMG (2011), *International Survey of Corporate Responsibility Reporting*, KPMG.

Lodhia, S. (2004), 'Corporate environmental reporting media: a case for the World Wide Web', *Electronic Green Journal*, 20.

Lodhia, S. (2006), 'The World Wide Web and its potential for corporate environmental communication: a study into present practices in the Australian minerals industry', *International Journal of Digital Accounting Research*, **6** (11), 65–94.

Lodhia, S. (2010), 'Teaching a sustainability accounting course in an Australian University: insights for sustainability accounting education', *Asia Pacific Centre for Environmental Accountability Journal*, **16** (1), 15–22.

Lodhia, S. (2011a), 'The National Greenhouse and Energy Reporting Act and its implications for accounting practice and research: a mini-review', *Journal of Accounting and Organizational Change*, **7** (2), 190–98.

Lodhia, S. (2011b), 'Why we need carbon pricing: a social and environmental accounting research perspective', *Journal of Law and Financial Management*, **10** (1), 15–18.

Lodhia, S. (2012), 'Web based social and environmental communication in the Australian minerals industry: an application of media richness framework', *Journal of Cleaner Production*, 25.

Lodhia, S., and Martin, N. (2012) 'Stakeholder responses to the national greenhouse and energy reporting act: an agenda setting perspective', *Accounting, Auditing and Accountability Journal*, **25** (1), 126–45.

Milne, M., and Grubnic, S. (2011), 'Climate change accounting research: keeping it interesting and different', *Accounting, Auditing and Accountability Journal*, **24** (8), 948–77.

Nowak, M., Rowe, A.L., Thomas, G., and Klass, D. (2008), 'Weaving sustainability into business education', *Asia Pacific Centre for Environmental Accountability Journal*, **14** (2), 19–34.

O'Dwyer, B., Unerman, J., and Hession, E. (2005a), 'User needs in sustainability accounting: perspectives of stakeholders in Ireland', *European Accounting Review*, **14** (4), 759–87.

O'Dwyer, B., Unerman, J., and Bradley, J. (2005b), 'Perceptions on the emergence and future development of corporate social disclosure in Ireland: engaging the voices of non-governmental organisations', *Accounting, Auditing & Accountability Journal*, **18** (1), 14–43.

Ratnatunga, J., and Balachandran, K. (2009), 'Carbon business accounting: the impact of global warming on the cost and management accounting profession', *Journal of Accounting, Auditing and Finance*, **24** (2), 333–55.

Roberts, C.B. (1991), 'Environmental disclosures: a note on reporting practices in Europe', *Accounting, Auditing and Accountability Journal*, **4** (3), 62–71.

Schaltegger, S., and Burritt, R. (2000), *Contemporary Environmental Accounting: Issues, Concepts and Practice*, UK: Greenleaf.

Schaltegger, S., Burritt, R., and Petersen, H. (2003), *An Introduction to Corporate Environmental Management: Striving for Sustainability*, Sheffield, United Kingdom: Greenleaf.

Schaltegger, S., Bennett, M., and Burritt, R. (2006), *Sustainability Accounting and Reporting*, Dordrecht: Springer.

Stern, N. (2006), *The Economics of Climate Change: The Stern Review*, United Kingdom: Cambridge University Press.

Stern, N. (2009), *A Blueprint for a Safer Planet: How to Manage Climate Change and Create a New Era of Progress and Prosperity*, London: Random House.

Unerman, J., O'Dwyer, C., and Bebbington, J. (eds) (2007), *Sustainability Accounting and Accountability*, London: Routledge.

Zeghal, D., and Ahmed, S.A. (1990), 'Comparison of social responsibility information disclosure media used by Canadian firms', *Accounting, Auditing, and Accountability Journal*, **3** (1), 38–53.

5. Carbon accounting and carbon auditing for business

Janek Ratnatunga

CARBON EMISSIONS MANAGEMENT ISSUES

The United Nations Framework Convention on Climate Change (UNFCCC) was first agreed in 1992 by most developed countries and was designed to impose limits on greenhouse gas emissions and thus minimize the adverse effects of climate change. The third session of the Conference of the Parties to the UNFCCC took place in Kyoto, Japan in December 1997, resulting in the Kyoto Protocol. This working agreement of the signatories committed developed countries to reduce their collective emissions of six greenhouse gases by at least 5 per cent of 1990 levels by 2012. The Kyoto Agreement became legally binding on 16 February 2005 when 132 signatories agreed to strive to decrease CO_2 emissions accounting for an estimated 55 per cent of global greenhouse gas emissions (Dunn, 2007).[1] The USA and Australia were the only two major carbon emitting countries that did not initially ratify the Kyoto Protocol.[2] Some developing countries, such as China, India, Indonesia and Brazil have ratified the protocol but are not required to reduce CO_2 emissions under the present agreement despite their large populations.

The Kyoto Protocol provided no model framework to be mandatorily applied by its participating countries. Instead it prescribed three market mechanisms for ratifying countries to use in meeting their emissions reduction targets. First the Protocol proposed to conduct an international emissions trading scheme (ETS) which allows the participating countries to multilaterally exchange carbon credits to meet their Kyoto Protocol obligations.[3] Those countries with emissions reduction targets can engage business entities within their carbon-rationing jurisdictions, by passing on these pollution limits. Here by applying an ETS with a cap-and-trade system, a country may allocate permits to companies to emit a certain quantity of GHGs (the cap). An enterprise that emits less than its cap is allowed to trade its excess permits to a company that pollutes more than its cap.

The other two mechanisms are project-based instruments: Joint

Implementation (JI) projects between industrialized (developed) countries and Clean Development Mechanism (CDM) investment projects undertaken by industrialized countries to lessen GHG emissions in developing countries. The former project generates an Emission Reduction Unit (ERU) whereas the latter generates a Certified Emission Reduction (CER). Both can be traded in the carbon market.

In all these three Kyoto mechanisms the concept of a carbon credit as a measurable and tradable instrument that is acceptable across nations is required. As per the Kyoto Protocol, each carbon credit represents one metric tonne of CO_2 either removed from the atmosphere or saved from being emitted.

CARBON EMISSIONS AND SEQUESTRATION (CES) ACCOUNTING

The mechanism for calculating the quantum of CO_2 either emitted by a source or sequestered in a biomass sink is referred to as carbon accounting. This has very little to do with monetary values usually associated with the term accounting. Therefore in this chapter it will be referred to as carbon emission and sequestration (CES) accounting.[4] Any CES accounting mechanism must be sufficiently robust that the carbon trading market has confidence that the amount of carbon sequestered can be both measured and considered to be equivalent in its impact on global warming potential to the CO_2 released to the atmosphere from activities producing greenhouse gases.

As can be appreciated the detailed requirements for a CES accounting system are continually being developed by organizations such as the Intergovernmental Panel on Climate Change[5] (IPCC, 2007). Any CES accounting standard developed by a country or NGO will need to be consistent with the IPCC principles before credits generated from carbon sinks can be used in an emissions trading regime under the Kyoto Protocol.

Unfortunately the current situation is that although the interest in the carbon trading market is high, the new market is largely unregulated and lacks transparency (Ratnatunga and Balachandran, 2009). Government policy in countries such as the USA and Australia is in a constant state of change and questions of measurement and pricing required for an efficient trading system are far from settled. In essence business organizations and individual customers[6] have no way of discriminating between the providers who claim that their scheme is better able to measure, for example, that (Tandukar, 2007):

X trees = the sequestration of Y tons of CO_2 emissions = $\$Z$

Whilst CES accounting is required to calculate the first two variables, the introduction/existence of a carbon price or emissions trading market is needed to enable the third variable, a monetary value ($\$Z$) to be determined. In turn, as there will be real dollar transactions involved, these monetary values will need to be reported in organizational financial statements under current Generally Accepted Accounting Principles (GAAP) of most countries.

As yet no reporting standard has been issued by the accounting profession for suitable criteria for GHG emissions disclosure. Many large corporations use the Greenhouse Gas Protocol of the World Business Council for Sustainable Development and the World Resources Institute.[7] It is currently the most widely used international accounting tool for government and business leaders to understand, quantify and manage emissions. For the global top 500 companies, research from the Ethical Corporation Institute in 2008 shows that 262 noted a specific emissions measurement and disclosure methodology and 176 used the Greenhouse Gas Protocol (King and Simnett, 2010).

Despite the wide use of the GHG Protocol, there is still no agreed CES measurement framework and without this the variation possible in the middle section of the equation could lead to gross distortions of whatever dollar value was offered in a carbon trading exchange; that is, as the sequestration or emissions measured could be a range of values (rather than a deterministic agreed value) so would the dollars received or paid for such.

Whatever the methodology or approach that is ultimately agreed in terms of CES measures, the issue for the accounting profession is the reporting of the monetary value ($\$Z$) of the CO_2 that these CES accounting measurements say has been either removed from the atmosphere or saved from being emitted by an organization's products, services, equipment and processors. The existence of an efficient carbon trading market would be able to put a price on this in terms of a carbon credit (or allowance). In addition the traditional accounting reports would need to recognize that certain non-current assets (or liabilities) could also give rise to future carbon related revenues and expenses. Such balance sheet items may have a market for the tangible asset, for example a power plant or forest, but not for its related intangible asset or liability, that is the CO_2 sequestration or emissions ability of such CO_2 sinks and sources. If you buy or sell the tangible you would need to consider the value of the related intangible (see Ratnatunga et al., 2011 for a detailed discussion of this issue).

In such instances the accounting profession would need to obtain the services of outside consultants, such as environmental scientists and biologists to undertake CES accounting projects. The use of such external experts is not uncommon. The accounting profession often incorporates reports from company directors, actuaries, business analysts, engineers, quantity surveyors, lawyers, etc., especially in the area of balance sheet asset valuation and fair-value accounting. Using expert opinions in accounting for CO_2 flows would be no different. However accounting standard setters have been reticent in accepting expert opinions as balance sheet values of intangible assets and one could envisage them having concerns with values generated via CES accounting.

CARBON AUDITING FOR ASSURANCE AND VERIFICATION

An important issue in the discourse on CES accounting is that of assurance and verification. An entity's carbon accounts will need to be independently verified (audited) by qualified assurors before they are accepted for use in an emissions trading regime. There needs to be accountability, transparency and integrity in relation to compliance arrangements, especially in relation to the inputs that are going into such a trading scheme. If such assurance is not present, then business organizations are not going to have comfort or certainty in investing in such a market.

Before any assurance can be given, however, the framework for reporting must be first agreed upon; that is, a necessary condition for an assurance engagement is that first the reporting framework is accepted as suitable criteria for CES accounting. We have already discussed the confusion in the plethora of measurement protocols available for CES accounting (Ratnatunga, 2007; Simnett et al., 2009).

Currently the global assurance community maintains a generic standard, an International Standard on Assurance Engagements (ISAE 3000), for the assurance of non-financial information. This permits two levels of assurance: the first, providing a reasonable assurance, is the most comprehensive and offers minimal risk; the second provides limited assurance, and mandates less information and security. Under the first method assurors collect enough data to state in their reports whether in their opinion, information is materially mis-stated. The second engagement requires less evidence and thus carries more risk (King and Simnett, 2010).

Until early 2011 the auditing profession's own input to the discourse has been very limited with significant contradictions and resistances engendered by environmental accounting techniques resulting in incomplete efforts of accountants and their allies to overcome them (Lohmann, 2009).

The International Auditing and Assurance Standards Board (IAASB) has issued IASE 3000 – Assurance Engagements other than Audits and Reviews of Historical Financial Information (IAASB, 2004) to cover the assurance on sustainability reports. It is a framework that applies equally to assurance engagements on historical financial information and on other information. In a country that has adopted ISAE 3000, any assurance engagement on other than historical financial information is to be undertaken by the auditing firms in accordance with ISAE 3000. The American Institute of Certified Public Accountants (AICPA, 2005) also put out Statement of Position 03-2: Attest Engagements on Greenhouse Gas Emissions Information, but this provides very little in terms of detail.

It must be pointed out that ISAE 3000 is a very general standard for assurance engagements that covers a wide range of possible subject matter with sustainability being just one. Due to the broad scope of sustainability, numerous challenges exist regarding the suitable criteria required to fulfil the assurance requirements of relevance, completeness, reliability, neutrality and understandability. The IAASB approved a project in December 2007 to address professional accountants' responsibilities with respect to assurance engagements on carbon emissions information. The project explored the need for guidance regarding assurance about carbon offsets. While this was not a primary focus of the project, the IAASB was of the view that an ISAE on this topic will likely be of assistance to financial statement auditors when considering the carrying value of emission trading rights. The final output of this project was to be a new ISAE. In January 2011, a proposed IASE 3410 – Assurance Engagements on Greenhouse Gas Statements was released for comment (IAASB, 2011).

The most significant issue arising in the proposed ISAE 3410 is the concept of Limited Assurance Engagements (LEA) in addition to Reasonable Assurance GHG Engagements (REA). The main issue relates to whether ISAE 3410 should require certain types of procedures (such as inquiry and analytical procedures) as the primary means of obtaining evidence, or whether it should acknowledge a broader range of procedures selected by the practitioner based on an assessment of risks of material misstatement in the circumstances of the engagement.

After careful deliberation, the IAASB has concluded that in order to obtain a meaningful level of assurance, an explicit risk assessment is necessary and that mandating certain types of procedures (such as inquiry and analytical procedures) as the primary means of obtaining evidence is not appropriate. The IAASB is aware that this approach is different from that for LEA on historical financial information. The IAASB reached this decision based on a number of factors, including: (1) that the nature of GHG information is quite different from historical financial information; (2)

the nature of assurance engagements on GHG statements, which can vary greatly; (3) the approach incorporated in the proposed ISAE is consistent with the advice of the GHG assurance experts with whom the IAASB has consulted; and (4) it is also consistent with current practice as evidenced by publicly available limited assurance reports on GHG statements. As such the approach taken in the proposed ISAE 3410 requires the practitioner to select procedures appropriate to the circumstances of the engagement based on an assessment of risks of material misstatement.

One of the differences regarding further procedures differentiating LEA from REA relates to when and how the practitioner determines whether it is necessary to perform additional procedures, and the nature and extent of those procedures, if the practitioner becomes aware of a matter(s) that causes the practitioner to believe the GHG statement may be materially misstated. In addition differences exist in the practitioner's objectives, in the requirements for forming and expressing the practitioner's conclusion and in the requirement to include a summary of the practitioner's procedures in the assurance report.

It is also important to note, however, that the proposed ISAE 3410 requires that the skills, knowledge and experience required for a LEA on a GHG statement are identical to those required for a REA on a GHG statement. Another requirement is that the preconditions for the engagement are identical for both LEA on a GHG statement and REA on a GHG statement. These requirements are debatable as to be implementable in practice.

Note that the proposed ISAE specifically states that the suitability of the applicable criteria should not be affected by the level of assurance; that is, if criteria are not suitable for a REA, they are also not suitable for LEA, and vice versa. The proposed ISAE 3410 specifically states that decisions regarding materiality should not be affected by the level of assurance; that is, materiality for a REA is the same as for a LEA.

For both reasonable assurance and limited assurance engagement on GHG statements, the practitioner's report is required to include a summary of the practitioner's procedures. In the case of a LEA the report must also include a statement that the extent of procedures is substantially less than a REA and consequently does not enable the practitioner to obtain the assurance necessary to become aware of all significant matters that might be identified in a reasonable assurance engagement.

The practitioner's report in a REA is ordinarily in the short-form; that is, it follows a standard wording and only briefly describes procedures performed. This is because describing in detail the specific procedures performed would not assist users to understand that in all REAs where an unmodified report is issued, sufficient appropriate evidence has been obtained to enable the practitioner to express a conclusion in the positive form.

In a LEA, however, the level of assurance that the practitioner obtains can vary significantly depending on the procedures performed in the individual circumstances of the engagement. It is important therefore that the summary be written in an objective way that allows intended users to understand the work done as the basis for the practitioner's conclusion. While the proposed ISAE 3410 states that it is difficult to describe the appropriate level of summation in a general way, in most cases it will not involve detailing the entire work plan. Nevertheless it is important for it not to be so summarized as to be ambiguous, nor written in a way that is overstated or embellished.

ISAE 3410 also states that if the practitioner becomes aware of a matter(s) that causes the practitioner to believe the GHG statement may be materially misstated, the practitioner shall design and perform additional procedures sufficient to enable the practitioner to: (a) conclude that the matter(s) is not likely to cause the GHG statement to be materially misstated; or (b) determine that the matter(s) causes the GHG statement to be materially misstated.

The comments from the professional bodies were due by June 2011 and can be viewed at http://www.ifac.org. At the time of writing the IAASB's response to the comments has still not been released. In general the proposed ISAE 3410 is based on the earlier ISAE 3000, and is a much simplified proposal to what IAASB was proposing in its earlier Exposure Drafts. Academic comment on this proposal has been muted to date.

CARBON FINANCIAL STATEMENT ACCOUNTING AND REPORTING

The conventional means by which economic activity is reported is via financial accounting and the resultant financial statements. Interesting financial accounting issues and controversies arise in the suggested conventional treatments of accounting for credits depending on if an allowance or credit is: (a) granted free to a business entity by a government; (b) purchased in an auction run by a government; (c) purchased in a free market; or (d) created by an organization allowed by an international or state authority to issue it.

Some in the accounting profession have argued that a rationed carbon allowance is an *intangible asset*; that is, a right to pollute. For instance International Financial Reporting and Interpretations Committee

(IFRIC) issued IFRIC 3 Emission Rights in March 2004 which proposed measurement and disclosure rules for ETSs. IFRIC 3 required that:

1. Rights (allowances) are intangible assets that should be recognized in the financial statements in accordance with IAS 38 *Intangible Assets*.
2. When allowances are issued to a participant by government (or government agency) for less than their fair value, the difference between the amount paid (if any) and their fair value is a government grant that is accounted for in accordance with IAS 20.
3. As a participant produces emissions, it recognizes a provision for its obligation to deliver allowances in accordance with IAS 37 Provisions, Contingent Liabilities and Contingent Assets. This provision is normally measured at the market value of the allowances needed to settle it.[8]

Depending on the business, it could be argued that this category of intangible assets can be accounted in three ways: as items of *inventory* if the organization is set up to trade in allowances; as *financial assets*; and as *derivatives* by accounting for them as a cash flow hedge. If it is considered a financial asset, the allowance could be reported as a new category of intangible asset, that is, one that could be measured at fair value with changes in value recognized in profit or loss.[9]

The counter-argument is that for many organizations, the existence of government and other controls (rationing) in the carbon emissions area would more likely result in a *liability* situation, if the entity's CO_2 emissions are greater than the allowable ration granted (or purchased).

Following these different viewpoints, the profession has recognized at least three treatments of carbon allowances even within the traditional accounting framework as follows:

1. If the allowance is obtained as a government grant (when allowances are allocated by governments for less than fair value) then it is first recognized as an intangible asset at cost (debit: intangible asset; credit: cash). Then the intangible asset is increased to fair value with the difference between cost and fair value recognized as revenue on a systematic basis over the compliance period (debit: intangible asset; credit: revenue).[10] As an organization emits carbon the intangible asset is used up at market value (debit: expense; credit: intangible asset). Any gains or losses that result in disposing of the intangible asset are recognized in the income statement.
2. If the allowance is purchased as an asset, then it is recorded at fair value pertaining to the carbon allowances held (debit: intangible asset;

credit: equity reserves).[11] Again, as an organization emits carbon the intangible asset is used up at market value (debit: expense; credit intangible asset).

3. If under a carbon rationing scheme a liability arises for the obligation to deliver carbon allowances equal to emissions that have been made, then it is recorded at fair value (debit: expense; credit: liability), and ultimately purchasing in an open market carbon credits equal to the shortfall (debit: liability; credit: cash) at market value.[12]

To account for such treatments in a carbon rationing scheme, a *net model* has been proposed whereby an entity does not recognize allocated allowances (they remain off-balance sheet), and accounts for actual emissions only when it holds insufficient allowances to cover those emissions by buying carbon credits (debit: expenses; credit: cash) at market price.

Traditionally, however, the accounting profession prefers the separate recognition of assets and the liabilities and the different treatment of such; that is, to treat carbon assets (allowances) independent of the liabilities (obligations). Accordingly, netting off (offsetting) of the assets and liabilities in such cases will not be permitted.

Thus an *amortizing model* has been proposed whereby an entity recognizes allocated allowances as an asset (debit: asset; credit: equity reserves as deferred income) at cost price, but then amortizes the allowances as it pollutes (debit: expense; credit: asset) and simultaneously releases the deferred income to revenue (debit: equity reserves; credit: revenue). In this method the entity recognizes a liability for actual emissions only when it holds insufficient allowances to cover those emissions (debit: expense; credit: liability). The liability that the entity incurs as it emits is measured at the cost of the allowances held by the entity. However, ultimately the entity has to purchase carbon credits in an open market equal to the shortfall (debit: liability; credit: cash), and there would be an over/under provision of this liability depending on market price. Clearly pricing and the valuation of carbon allowances (permits) is a key to this method of accounting.

In the United States the guidance contained in the Federal Energy Regulatory Commission's (FERC) Uniform System of Accounts is the only accounting guidance currently available that explicitly addresses emission allowances. FERC requires business entities to recognize emission allowances on a historical cost basis. The Financial Accounting Standards Board (FASB) has researched the actual practices of business entities and reports that whilst there is a diversity of practices, most follow the FERC guidelines. The FASB also reports that some business entities follow an intangible asset model for emission allowances and that there is no authoritative guidance that addresses the accounting for carbon credits.[13]

There are numerous examples of the financial accounting profession's inability to deal with the issue of accounting for carbon credits. Guidelines such as the Financial Reporting Interpretations Committee's IFRIC 3: Emission Rights have been issued and subsequently withdrawn, comprehensive models such as the Emerging Issues Task Force (EITF) Issue No. 03-14 Participants' Accounting for Emissions Allowances under a 'Cap and Trade' Program have been proposed and removed, and committees such as that set up by the IASB to provide a comprehensive model for emission allowances similar to issues discussed in IFRIC 3 have been set up that have not had their reports released. Thus, in a recent paper Cook (2009) states that one such solution for the IFRIC to consider is to maintain the status quo.

A further example of the financial accounting profession's inability to deal with the issue is that after the FASB Statement No. 153 Exchanges of Nonmonetary Assets was issued in December 2004, questions arose in practice related to its scope and, specifically, whether exchanges of emission allowances (vintage year swaps) should be accounted for at fair value or on a carryover basis. In August 2006, the Technical Application and Implementation Activities (TA&I) Committee approved a recommendation for the Board to add a project to its agenda to address the nature of emission allowances and clarify the accounting for vintage year swaps of emission allowances by participants in emission trading schemes. This project also is yet to report.

In countries where carbon allowances are to be obtained via a rationing system they would probably be seen as government grants and thus fall under the International Accounting Standards Board's IAS 20 Accounting for Government Grants and Disclosure of Government Assistance standard, which states that such grants are intangible assets and must be recognized as income over the periods necessary to match them with the costs for which they are intended to compensate. This in effect is the *amortizing model,* but there is some debate as to the recognition of deferred income. As the IASB has stated that only assets and liabilities may be shown on the balance sheet, then revenue received but not yet recognized as income (that is, deferred income) is not a liability and thus cannot be shown on the balance sheet. But it cannot be shown as an Equity Reserve either, as IAS 20 states that government grants cannot be credited directly to shareholders' interests. There is clearly contradiction and confusion here.

Even if the IASB decides to recognize deferred income as a balance sheet item, the release of the government grant to revenue by reference to the initial value of the allowances can also cause volatility as the liability that arises as the entity emits is measured by reference to the current market value of the allowances. Even if the entity elects to measure the allowances subsequently at market value, a mismatch arises because some gains and losses are reported in the income statement and others in equity.

Thus it can be seen that under the amortizing model, carbon allowances/liabilities could represent a significant figure that potentially could have an impact on the bottom line volatility of a company's reported financial statements. This perceived (artificial) volatility in the income statement would be a major concern for CFOs, as they would have to record a gain in the value of emission rights to equity, but the loss related to revaluing the liability as a profit or loss item. Further the current traditionalist thinking is that they would need to record a loss in the value of emission rights against previous gains recognized in equity, but the gain related to revaluing the liability would be recorded in profit or loss.

The accounting treatment is a little clearer for reporting unconditional government grants. This is covered by IAS 41 Agriculture. An unconditional government grant must be recognized as income on receipt. However a conditional government grant is recognized as income on receipt only when certain conditions are met. Further even if it could be argued that a carbon permit issued to offset increased future costs arising from a cap and trade scheme is a conditional government grant, the issue of recognizing deferred income remains. If the carbon permit is not recognized as even a conditional grant, all the income needs to be recognized (and taxed) in year of receipt, even though the related cost is in a future period, thus effectively negating the *matching principle* of GAAP.

Issues that are still to be considered by the accounting profession are on how to account for allowances and obligations if there is no *active market*,[14] and the accounting requirements of brokers and other position-taking institutions that are not subject to an emission limit or cap. The non-existence of a market price would be seen as not meeting the reliability and relevance test required in conventional accounting reporting.

The most concerning issue however stems from the failure of conventional GAAP to recognize and measure intangible assets that are *not acquired*. This failure presents a significant problem in accounting for carbon sources and sinks that are not acquired such as the internal development of assets with the potential to generate future carbon credits. In this area a shift in conventional thinking is required.

Here, business entities will also need to consider issues such as *fair value* accounting[15] and *impairment* of assets. As fair value accounting and asset impairment tests are still the subject of much debate in the profession with regards to even conventional tangible asset valuations, an inconvenient truth is that business entities to date have very little guidance from accounting and assurance standard setters as to the treatment of carbon related intangible assets (and intangible liabilities), especially those that are internally generated (that is, not acquired).

Finally the unique tangible/intangible nature of carbon related assets makes their accounting treatment under conventional accounting frameworks fraught with difficulty, especially in organizations such as forestry companies that have carbon sequestration assets (sinks). These entities may find these assets instantly becoming carbon emitting sources (liabilities) should their trees be destroyed in a forest fire. Whilst accepting that there are situations in business life that organizational assets contain elements of contingent liability, such that in the instant the asset is wiped off the books a liability arises, most of these contingent liabilities are litigious in nature. A plane (tangible asset) that crashes, or a dangerous side effect that is discovered in a drug patent (intangible asset) may not only wipe out the assets from the balance sheet, but also simultaneously give rise to a class action contingent liability.[16] However carbon sinks such as trees are simultaneously carbon sources as well, as they shed leaves etc., whilst growing. Thus any metric to value the carbon sequestration capabilities of these assets must simultaneously capture their carbon emission capabilities. Ratnatunga et al. (2011) suggest that such a valuation model should not value assets (what an organization 'has') but instead value capabilities (what an organization 'can do').

Cost and strategic management accounting also need to be considered in this new economy that the Kyoto Protocol has forced upon us. For example even if an entity can allocate the costs and revenues brought about by carbon trading, how would that affect the prices charged? How would the prices charged impact on an entity's competitive advantage and ultimately share price and value? Can the trading of carbon emissions form a line-of-business for companies? These and many more questions need to be asked as more and more countries grapple with the response to efficient carbon management to mitigate the effects of climate change.

To date, the focus (if any) has been mainly on financial statement accounting and taxation. Little if any work has been done in the accounting profession on cost management, management accounting and project evaluation.

'WHOLE OF LIFE' CARBON COST ACCOUNTING

Traditional cost management relates to accounting for direct and indirect costs[17] and the assignment of such costs to cost objects such as products, services, customers and organizational processes. A cost can be attached directly to a cost object if it is traceable solely to that cost object; and if not, it is allocated (see Sharma and Ratnatunga, 1997 for a comprehensive discussion of costing systems). Recent discussions in the cost accounting literature have been mainly to do with the allocation of indirect costs; that is, if using traditional allocation systems with a single cost driver (such as direct labor) or if using activity based costing systems (with multiple cost drivers) better describes the cause/effect relationships found in products, services, customers and organizational processes (Cooper and Kaplan, 1988). In product costing the cost is computed up to the stage that goods are available for sale. Costs incurred subsequent to the product being sold are usually not calculated, except in the case where a product carries a warranty or some other after-sales service component; then the expected cost (based on a probability estimate) of that service is incorporated into the cost (and therefore its price). Some cost calculations may also include the cost of money blocked in accounts receivable, that is, the credit period being treated as an after-sales service that has a cost associated with it.

Carbon cost management is a subset of the push towards environmental cost accounting (Mathews, 1997; Adams, 2004) that highlights the cost impacts beyond those related to a specific cost object such as a product. Let us take a product such as a computer printer as an example. Typical environmental costs (both prior and subsequent to the sale) are:

1. *Raw material* The environmental costs are simply the cost of the raw materials such as plastics, cartridges and steel in waste. Much of such raw material is brought into usable form for manufacturing using significant energy and thus has related CO_2 emissions.[18] Every time a raw material is used and does not become a product, it becomes waste. Even when such material becomes saleable products, when the product becomes obsolete it goes into landfills as waste.

2. *Labor* Labor requires energy to function, such as traveling time to a production facility and air conditioning etc. at the facility, and thus there are significant CO_2 emissions associated with its use. Prior to the sale of the product the typical labor environmental costs would be the labor component of an off-specification product that becomes waste. Post sale the labor costs that are required for recycling of parts is an environmental related cost, which also generates CO_2 emissions.

3. *Overhead* Utility costs such as water and energy are also often overlooked in determining the true cost of waste generation, both before and after a sale. These costs are a significant item in CO_2 emissions management.

4. *Waste management* The most obvious environmental expenses are the treatment and disposal costs of waste generated in the production

process. Again these require significant energy and thus have associated CO_2 emissions. Other waste management costs may include the
expenses to collect samples, paper work, permit fees, consulting fees,
and (potentially) fines for violations. The flip side of the hidden costs
and impacts of waste generation is the hidden benefits resulting from
actions taken to improve the environmental performance of a particular facility.

5. *Recycling*   This is a form of waste management at the obsolescence
    end of the product life cycle. This requires a three pronged approach:
    (a) the opportunity cost calculation (including the environmental
    impacts) of recycling components of existing hardware vis-à-vis
    using new components, (b) locking in recycling cost efficiencies at
    the design stage of new hardware, (c) using a cost-benefit analysis
    of the first two stages to influence government policy on tax credits,
    etc. for undertaking such environmentally sustainable programs. The
    US Environmental Protection Agency (EPA) has an Environmental
    Accounting Project which encourages business to understand the full
    spectrum of their environmental costs and integrate these costs into
    decision-making.[19]

Note that in undertaking a life-cycle costing exercise using carbon allowance costs, the issue of transaction costing vs opportunity costing needs to
be recognized. Some studies may take an opportunity cost approach and
determine that the freely allocated allowances are worth the same as purchased allowances. Others may take a more transactional environmental
compliance approach and treat as a hard cost only the cost of purchased
allowances over the year.

As pointed out before in discussing CES accounting and assurance, there
are many accreditation approaches in the environmental arena all having
different measurement metrics. These measurement approaches also have
a direct impact on carbon cost calculations. Whilst no study or approach
can be considered definitive, there is clearly a need for accurate carbon cost
accounting using life-cycle costing techniques that should not only consider
costs to bring to the point of sale a product or service, but also consider the
carbon costs prior and subsequent to the manufacture of the product or the
performance of the service. Such costs are elaborated in Table 5.1.

Once product costs are known the wider issues of strategic management
accounting need to be considered by organizations in managing their emissions liabilities. These include strategic marketing, pricing, demand modelling, capacity usage, risk management, cash flow, capital investment,
capital structure and financing issues (see Ratnatunga and Balachandran,
2009 for a comprehensive discussion of these).

Table 5.1 The whole-of-life impact of carbon emission efficiencies on costs and revenues

Areas of cost reduction or revenue generation via efficient carbon cost management	Pre-sale environmental impact	Post-sale environmental impact*
Raw materials	Production waste	Landfill waste
Human input	Wasted time on rejects and recovery	Time to separate recyclable components
Traditional Overhead Expenses		
Electricity Rental Marketing Transportation Administration Depreciation of machinery After sales service costs	All of these overhead items have carbon emissions that will affect whether the organization is a net-sequester or net-emitter. Techniques utilized to reduce CO_2 emissions via using alternative energy sources etc. will impact on the carbon credit cost item shown under the Environmental Overhead category	
Environmental Overhead		
Regulatory costs	Meeting emissions standards	Litigation costs of environmental pollution
Waste management	Production waste	Landfill waste
Recycling Amortization of design costs	These costs can be reduced via the proper design of components at pre-production stage. Such design costs should be amortized over life of product, via life-cycle costing.	
Carbon credits	This can be a cost or revenue item depending on if the organization is a net-sequester or net-emitter.	Purchase/sale of carbon credits depending on if the organization is a net-sequester or net-emitter.
Financing Costs		
Stock holding costs	These costs include cost of capital, excess handling, obsolescence, deterioration, stock administration and insurance	These costs include cost relating to warranty returns such as excess handling, deterioration, stock administration and insurance
Debtors costs	None	These costs include cost of capital and the risk of bad debts

Table 5.1   (continued)

Areas of cost reduction or revenue generation via efficient carbon cost management	Pre-sale environmental impact	Post-sale environmental impact*
	Financing Costs	
Carbon tax	This tax could be an additional cost or revenue item (tax credit) depending on if the organization is a net-sequester or net-emitter	

Note: *These post-sale environmental costs can be incorporated into product costs using probability estimates.

For example if a company is subject to a government imposed rationing scheme, a number of options are available for it to manage its emissions liability: (1) do nothing and buy carbon credits from the government or from a carbon market to make up the shortfall; (2) reduce its carbon liability by undertaking *internal* projects that use new technologies to lower the carbon emissions of its resources and activities; (3) invest in *external* projects (e.g. wind farms, reforestation, etc.) that sequester carbon in order to offset its carbon liability and sell excess carbon credits generated (if any) in emission trading markets; or (4) a combination of both internal and external investments. Decisions to make such internal and external investments in carbon management projects, termed *carbonvestments*, fall under the general area of investment appraisal and management accounting (Smith and Nau 1995; Trigeorgis, 1996; Haka, 2007; Labatt and White, 2007).

SUMMARY

The concentrations of greenhouse gases in the atmosphere have risen dramatically, leading to an out of balance greenhouse effect that most scientists believe will continue to cause a very rapid warming of the world's climate. The possibility of costly disruption from rapid climate change, either globally or locally, calls for greater attention and precautionary measures to be put in place. Governments, business entities and consumers would be impacted by the extent to which such precautionary measures are incorporated in their decision making process.

Governments need to consider carbon regulation policy issues such as rationing or taxing of net CO_2 emitting entities and providing credit allowances or tax-breaks for net CO_2 absorbing entities. Business entities need to consider issues such as trading in carbon allowances or permits, investment in low CO_2 emission technologies, counting the costs of carbon regularity compliance and passing on the increased cost of carbon regulation to consumers through higher prices. Consumers need to consider if given a choice, they are willing to pay a higher price for CO_2 neutral products and services so as to play their part in reducing CO_2 emissions.

These decisions and their consequences will impact the accounting and auditing profession significantly. Unfortunately the current financial accounting and assurance frameworks appear to be ill-equipped to provide the reliable and relevant information required by companies to meet the challenge of global warming. This is mainly because accounting information systems based on the accounting equation are not designed to cope with non-monetary measures such as CO_2 sources and sinks. As such despite emissions trading being prevalent in most developed countries (within and outside the Kyoto Protocol) the accounting standard setters have yet to come up with an acceptable standard to account for such activity.

Cost and strategic management accounting issues also need to be considered in this new economy that global warming has forced upon us. New costing techniques need to be considered to evaluate the whole-of-life costs in terms of carbon emissions relating to products and services. Similarly new thinking will be required to provide strategic management accounting information for investment strategies and the resultant evaluation of performance evaluation.

Clearly the new carbonomics environment will produce winners and losers in both the product and allowances markets, and in organizations and countries. The accounting profession is also scrambling to be a winner in this new economic paradigm.

NOTES

1. By 2011, 192 states and one regional economic integration organization had become Kyoto signatories.
2. In 2007 Australia ratified the protocol but did not agree to any mandatory emissions target limits.
3. This has not eventuated to date, with the EU ETS being the only multi-country ETS operating under Kyoto.
4. As carbon is not the only greenhouse gas (GHG) that is measured, the term GHG emissions disclosure is also used. In this chapter the term 'CES accounting' captures all GHG emissions.
5. The IPCC along with Al Gore, the former USA Vice-President, won the 2007 Nobel Peace Prize for their work on reducing global warming.

6. Sergey Brin, the founder of Google, is reported as having bought carbon credits to offset the immense amount of CO_2 emitted by his private Boeing 767, but confesses he is not sure if it really achieves anything (Krauthammer, 2007).
7. Essentially the protocol covers three types, or scopes, of greenhouse gas emissions. Scope one refers to direct emissions from sources owned or controlled by a company – for example, emissions from combustion in boilers, furnaces and vehicles. Scope two refers to indirect emissions from consumption of purchased electricity, heat or steam. Scope three refers to other indirect emissions (such as airline travel) generated in the wider economy as a consequence of a company's activities but which are physically produced by others.
8. However, IFRIC 3 was unpopular in Europe and was subsequently withdrawn in June 2005. Financial reporting and valuation issues relating to ETS were reintroduced on the IASB agenda December 2007; however the IASB still appears to be a long way from developing a comprehensive accounting standard on carbon emission rights reporting.
9. If intangible assets arise due to a third party transaction such as a purchase of a carbon allowance, then it can meet the accounting profession's reliability test. However, carbon credits created internally by carbon sinks cannot be recognized until they are sold in open trading. An inconvenient truth is that the profession has great difficulty with internally generated intangible assets such as brand values and intellectual property, and it is still coming to terms with reporting issues arising due to carbon trading (Ratnatunga, 2007).
10. Questions as to whether such revenue is taxable or exempt from tax will be based on a specific country's tax policy.
11. The fair value would be based on market values if a trading scheme exists. Similar questions of 'fair value' pertain to share investments, that is, there are reporting differences if the shares are held as investments or as inventory in a fund management company.
12. Note that a liability is a present obligation arising from past events. The issue of a carbon permit relating to a possible future event is more a contingent liability, although the IASB has recommended abolishing this latter term.
13. http://www.fasb.org/project/emission_allowances.shtml (accessed 18 April 2007).
14. Pricing of allowances may be difficult to determine in the absence of a liquid market. The suggested approach of adopting mark-to-market accounting could have a significant impact on a company's profit and loss. The volatility in prices would need to be reflected in the income statement; as such profit and loss figures could be subject to disturbances with severe price spikes (that could easily happen in a thin market).
15. This pertains to intangible assets with the potential to generate future carbon credits, and not the value of the credits themselves; that is, in the case of tangible assets, the value of the machinery, not the value of the inventory produced by the machinery.
16. The IASB is however considering abolishing the term 'contingent liability'.
17. These cost categories are based on the nature of the expenditure items, such as the cost of raw materials, human input (labour) and overhead (rent, depreciation etc.)
18. Such as the energy used in mining and processing the materials.
19. See http://www.epa.gov/oppt/library/pubs/archive/acct-archive/index.htm

REFERENCES

Adams, C.A. (2004), 'The ethical, social and environmental reporting-performance portrayal gap', *Accounting, Auditing and Accountability Journal*, **17** (5), 731–57.

AICPA (2005), *Statement of Position 03-2: Attest Engagements on Greenhouse Gas Emissions Information*, New York: American Institute of Certified Public Accountants.

Cook, A. (2009), 'Emission rights: from costless activity to market operations', *Accounting, Organizations and Society*, **34** (3–4), 456–68.

Cooper, R. and Kaplan, R.S. (1988) 'Measure costs right: make the right decisions', *Harvard Business Review*, September–October, **66** (5), 96–103.

Dunn, J. (2007), 'Carbon trading leaves it to market forces', *The Weekend Australian Climate Change Special Report*, 24–25 March, 12.

Haka, S.F. (2007), 'A review of the literature on capital budgeting and investment appraisal: past, present, and future musings', in C.S. Chapman, A.G. Hopwood and M.D. Shields (eds), *Handbook of Management Accounting Research*, vol. 2, North Holland, Elsevier, pp. 697–728.

IAASB (2004), *ISAE 3000: Assurance Engagements Other Than Audits or Reviews of Historical Financial Information*, New York: International Auditing and Assurance Standards Board.

IAASB (2011), *ISAE 3410: Assurance Engagements on Greenhouse Gas Statements*, New York: International Auditing and Assurance Standards Board.

IPCC (2007), *Climate Change 2007: The Physical Science Basis*, Intergovernmental Panel on Climate Change.

King, A. and Simnett, R. (2010), *Green Accounting: Setting a Standard for Assurance Knowledge at an Australian School Of Business*, University of New South Wales.

Krauthammer, C. (2007), 'Limousine liberal hypocrisy', *TIME Magazine*, Commentary, 26 March, 16.

Labatt, S. and White, R.R. (2007), *Carbon Finance: The Financial Implications of Climate Change*, Hoboken: John Wiley and Sons.

Lohmann, L. (2009), 'Toward a different debate in environmental accounting: the cases of carbon and cost–benefit', *Accounting, Organizations and Society*, **34** (3–4), 499–534.

Mathews, M.R. (1997), 'Twenty-five years of social and environmental accounting research: is there a silver jubilee to celebrate?', *Accounting, Auditing and Accountability Journal*, **10** (4), 481–531.

Ratnatunga, J. (2007), 'An inconvenient truth about accounting', *Journal of Applied Management Accounting Research*, **5** (1), 1–20.

Ratnatunga, J. and Balachandran, K.R. (2009), 'Carbon business accounting: the impact of global warming on the cost and management accounting profession', *Journal of Accounting, Auditing and Finance*, **24** (2), 333–55.

Ratnatunga, J., Jones, S. and Balachandran, K.R. (2011), 'The valuation and reporting of organizational capability in carbon emissions management', *Accounting Horizons*, **25** (1), 127–47.

Sharma, R. and Ratnatunga, J. (1997), 'Traditional and activity based costing systems', *Accounting Education: An International Journal*, **6** (4), 337–45.

Simnett, R., Huggins, A. and Nugent, M. (2009), 'Developing an international assurance statement on greenhouse gas statements', *Accounting Horizons*, **23** (4), 347–64.

Smith, J.E. and Nau, R.F. (1995), 'Valuing risky projects: option pricing theory and decision analysis', *Management Science*, **41** (5), 795–816.

Tandukar, A. (2007), 'From neutral into drive', *BRW - Innovation*, 15–21 March, 74–5.

Trigeorgis, L. (1996), *Real Options: Managerial Flexibility and Strategy in Resource Allocation*, Cambridge, MA: MIT Press.

6. Sustainable marketing in principle and practice

Anne Sharp

INTRODUCTION

This chapter looks at what 'sustainable marketing' means for an organization, with particular focus on its implementation at the brand level. Drawing upon current scientific knowledge of consumer behaviour, the chapter examines what marketers can realistically expect in the way of consumer response to an organization's sustainable marketing efforts. The challenge of how best to communicate organizational sustainability efforts is discussed and the risks of not responding to consumer demand for more sustainable offerings are highlighted.

What Sustainable Marketing Really Means

A host of environmental and social issues, ranging from climate change through to fair working conditions, have brought sustainability increasingly to the forefront of organizational management attention. The issues are widely recognized as having their basis in human behaviour (Geller, 1989). The reality of consumers' unrelenting demand and purchasing power shapes the very fundamentals of consumer goods markets. Indeed consumer demand has such power that it drives producers to do things that destroy the long term prospects of their own industries. History repeatedly shows examples of industries following a boom and bust pattern in supply as producers struggle to meet consumer demand but overuse available resources to do so.

Sustainable marketing can be thought of as trying to explicitly acknowledge the conflict between short term and long term gains for both the organization and the consumer. In 1987 the UN World Commission on Environment and Development offered the now widely accepted definition of sustainability in its Brundtland Report, describing it as 'development that meets the needs of the present without compromising the ability of future generations to meet their own needs' (*Our Common Future*, 1987,

p. 55). In the context of marketing, it is about achieving long term organizational survival without causing harm to either the customer base an organization exchanges with or the resources that it uses in the exchange process.

A real challenge exists for industries and economies to move to this environmentally and socially sustainable path for the long term (Peattie, 2007; Crittenden et al., 2011). Marketing, as the core discipline of consumption, is uniquely positioned to help in this (Fuller, 1999; Crittenden et al., 2011). Marketing's focus must move from meeting immediate consumer demand to also considering the longer term environmental and societal well-being. Such a shift in focus requires organizations to consider questions such as the extent to which they should be responsive to customer demand if that means either consumer health or well being will suffer or resources will not last. Marketing also has a role in this transition through shaping consumer demand towards more sustainable consumption options and away from socially and environmentally detrimental ones. For example, many traditionally wild caught fish stocks, such as Mulloway, are now farmed. Marketing is needed to build awareness for the new sources of fish and also to help educate consumers to accept the visual look and taste of the new product.

Increasingly we are seeing organizations responding to this sustainability challenge. 'Sustainability' in an organization is now regarded as a competitive imperative (Mahler, 2007) and an important strategic goal (Closs et al., 2011). Organizations have introduced a plethora of programs and brands to the market with the aim of improved environmental and social outcomes and a longer term survival for the organization.

Accepting that we are a consumer driven society highlights the need for a clear understanding of what can be expected in the way of consumer response to such organizational efforts. While consumers frequently express sustainability as a general and global concern, little is still known as to how this translates into everyday purchasing behaviour. Marketing has an important role in engaging and educating consumers to help change the habits and culture of consumption, but this will be difficult. To increase the extent and speed of uptake of sustainability as an important buying criterion for a consumer, marketers need to understand how best to develop and communicate their sustainability efforts and also how to get their messages to cut through with consumers.

The Growth of Sustainable Marketing

Sustainable marketing has now entered the mainstream (Belz and Peattie, 2009), with forecasting and research companies consistently citing sustainability as a continuing key trend in consumer markets. For example, Mintel has held 'sustainability' as a top consumer trend in consumer goods for over five years, with both the environmental aspects of sustainability (such as reduced packaging) and the consumer aspects (improved health through sugar and fat reduction) making the top six in 2011 (Mintel, 2010). Every day the media run stories that purport strong consumer demand for more sustainable products. Today we see over 80 per cent of the world's 250 largest companies issuing sustainability reports (Handford, 2010) so that their efforts can be publicly seen.

One of the initial and most commonly documented ways an organization starts to improve the sustainability of its business practices is through improved cost effectiveness and process efficiencies. Supermarkets have made carbon footprint reductions and cost savings through streamlining stock-movement processes and energy contracts. Similarly manufacturers have adopted less and smaller packaging so that more products can be shipped within the same volume, saving transportation costs and reducing carbon emissions. Such process efficiencies, which result from 'greener' organizational practices, are a well-documented side of the sustainable business argument. But the marketing value of 'greening' a brand and the signalling of this to customers is less well understood; yet this is an important issue given the proliferation of 'green' brands in recent years in almost every consumer goods category. These green brands cover a range of sustainability claims starting with environmental concerns, such as material and energy consumption, but now covering issues such as sustainable sourcing of materials and organic production, or wider social concerns such as fair trade and non-animal testing.

Marketers have driven this growth in green brands based on the belief that this is an attribute that buyers will value and will show brand preference for. In this way it is seen as a means to attract new buyers to a brand (Vandermerwe and Oliff, 1990; Gordon, 2002). Additionally introducing a sustainability message on a brand creates news and a point of difference. This will help to gain the market's attention and thereby increase the likelihood of a brand being chosen over its competitor(s) (Sharp and Newstead, 2010); remember the novelty of the first Fairtrade endorsed candy bars or the first unbleached bathroom tissues. Given that the major challenge a brand faces is simply one for a customer's attention, this is a convincing argument. With an average of 30000 products in a supermarket (Sorensen, 2009), it is easy for a brand to simply not be noticed.

Yet despite these purported advantages of linking a brand to a sustainability message, most green brands remain small in terms of market share; unless of course they were big before they were 'greened' (Bonini and Oppenheim, 2008). Many companies experience lukewarm response to their efforts and only limited uptake of their offerings. One reason for this may be that historically green brands have had low quality associations (Alwitt and Berger, 1993; Peattie, 2001) and a perceived high price relative to their non-green counterparts (Peattie, 2001). They have also been perceived as 'niche' brands that only appeal to a specialist sub-set of a category's buyers (Vandermerwe and Oliff, 1990; Charter et al., 2002; Gordon, 2002; D'Souza, 2004; Pickett-Baker and Ozaki, 2008). Additionally studies have identified the amount of time or physical energy involved to find green brands, as well as a lack of information about them, as other key reasons for this deficit in expected performance (Stern, 1999). Following these arguments, a brand's growth could actually be inhibited rather than advanced through linking it to these limiting perceptions or encountering these barriers.

Alternatively the modest performance of green brands could be attributable to consumers simply not being as responsive to such sustainability claims as marketers would hope. It does appear that the increased public interest in sustainability issues is not often matched with changes in decisions people make as consumers (Cornelissen et al., 2008; Wright and Klÿn, 1998).

To have a proper understanding of the barriers and challenges to achieving cut through with sustainable marketing efforts, a good understanding of fundamental consumer behaviour is needed. Through knowing behavioural norms, realistic expectations for consumer response can be set. This requires knowledge of marketing science.

A MARKETING SCIENCE VIEW OF BUYER AND CONSUMER BEHAVIOUR

Much of marketing practice and literature is still underpinned by assumptions about buyer and consumer behaviour that do not bear out in reality. For example, it is widely held that a path to brand growth is through encouraging greater levels of loyalty amongst existing customers. Empirically this is shown not to be the case. Growth in market share comes from a brand attracting new buyers far more than it comes from getting existing buyers to give more of their category purchasing to that particular brand (Riebe et al., 2002).

Fortunately the last four decades of Marketing Science have seen substantial progress in moving away from non-empirically founded beliefs. Many regularities in consumer behaviour have been identified that have been found to hold across multiple markets, over time, and across countries (Sharp, 2010). These known regularities or patterns in consumer behaviour are relevant to marketers who are brand managers and to those charged with developing and communicating sustainability initiatives to the market. Through knowing what patterns are common in consumer behaviour, we can build a picture of how buyers choose between alternative options. This can serve as a framework for guiding marketing efforts – allowing for the realistic setting of performance targets and serving as a guide for where resources should be directed. Having an understanding of consumer decision making and how buyers choose between alternative options allows marketers to know how best to increase the probability of their brand being noticed and chosen. Sadly though, despite their relevance, many of Marketing Science's findings concerning consumer behaviour are still known only at modest levels amongst both industry and academia.

One important pattern relevant to the sustainability discussion is that consumer behaviour is highly routinized, especially in a shopping and consumer goods context (Rossiter and Winter, 1988; McDonald and Ehrenberg, 2002). When shopping for a category, consumers do not evaluate the whole category but instead choose from a subset of brands available. This reduced brand choice set saves shoppers from needing to constantly re-evaluate an entire category every time they need to visit the supermarket and helps them to navigate the myriad products found in a typical supermarket. Such habitual behaviour has also been noted in store choice and within price decisions (Ehrenberg and Uncles, 1995). These are all frequent behaviours with fairly low risk attached to them if a bad decision is made. Habitual behaviour allows the consumer to simplify repetitive choice decisions (Ehrenberg, 1972) and solve the immediate problem faster.

Another empirical pattern seen in consumer behaviour is that buyers have split loyalty across a repertoire of brands they buy from in a category. Total 100 percent brand loyalty is rare and tends to be found amongst lighter buyers of the category because, when you do not buy much, it is easier to exhibit loyalty to just one brand. Of course the extreme example of this is the single occasion buyer from the category where 100 percent brand loyalty is guaranteed. However most buyers make multiple purchases from a category over time and they tend to have a small repertoire of brands, each with a probability of being chosen on any one particular purchase occasion (Ehrenberg, 1972). These repertoires remain fairly stable for individuals but each individual will have their own repertoire of brands and probability of choice attached to them. The particular brand that will be chosen on any particular shopping occasion will be influenced by such things as 'out of stocks', price specials, or even recent exposure to an advertisement for the brand.

Knowing what patterns of buyer and consumer behaviour we expect to see around brand choice help sustainable marketers identify the challenges they face in making sustainability mainstream. It also helps to develop guidelines for how best to market an organization's sustainability efforts to consumers. Some of these are now highlighted and discussed.

SUSTAINABLE MARKETING FOR MAXIMUM RETURN

Understand the Breadth of Your Potential Market

Marketing Science knowledge has implications for the appeal that a green brand can be expected to have. Development of new or different product variants often occurs because marketers assume that the new offering will appeal to particular types of buyers. Niche brands are created out of this logic. Classic niche theory is that brands are niche when they are sold to a small group of highly loyal buyers. Although a profitable strategy in theory, unfortunately the niche phenomenon is extremely rare. Brands tend to be bought by fairly much the same sort of buyer, rather than a specialist sub set.

As an example, consider the cola category: diet colas should (in niche theory) sell to diet conscious people and diabetics. But in fact we find that most people who buy diet colas are normal cola buyers who occasionally feel like a less sugary, lower calorie, or different tasting option. Of course the diabetics and diet conscious buyers will buy the diet colas, but these few 'loyalists' make up only a small part of the variant's overall customer base. By far the bulk of sales will come from the relatively much larger base of normal cola buyers. And this is also seen for green brands.

In practice, while a brand with sustainability claims will probably attract some buyers who buy it frequently and are primarily motivated by the sustainable benefits purported, far more will just be 'normal' category buyers who have the brand as part of their repertoire and buy it occasionally. The customer base of any brand with a functional variant or feature (like fair-trade, organic etc.) will reveal this same pattern.

The positive implication of this knowledge is that having sustainability claims does not narrow your market appeal. However, by not realizing this broad appeal of your brand, you run the risk of missing out on mainstream category users. Cumulatively this is an extremely large and profitable group that may be missed by having communications restricted to only the environmentally or socially driven buyers.

Use Simple Messages and Calls-to-action

Despite the many studies that show most people value sustainability attributes such as 'buy local' and 'go green', empirically there is a low correlation between such environmental attitudes and green brand purchasing behaviour (Wright and Klÿn, 1998; Gupta and Ogden, 2009). There are several possible reasons for this, including the call to action being too hard and the message simply not being noticed.

The sustainability initiatives of consumer goods brands often call for changes in a consumer's everyday behaviours, be it choosing their particular brand over another usual choice in the store, or at a more general behavioural level in terms of how the product is used. Examining a mainstream category such as laundry powder sees consumers being asked in the last few years to change to washing in cold rather than hot water, and to reduce the volume of powders and liquids they use as concentrates have come on the market, developed for their lesser environmental impact.

Given the known high habituation of behaviour and consumer desire to minimize cognitive effort, any such calls to action need to be easy for the consumer to understand and act upon. They should also have a clear direct benefit the consumer can easily understand. They should not require additional infrastructure or behaviour steps for the benefit to be realized.

Since product choice is so quick, sustainability messages should only require minimal evaluation on the part of the consumer in order to be noticed and understood. The desired behaviour (for example, buy Fairtrade) or choice option (for example, recycle the container after use) should be spelt out with little evaluation of alternatives required. Difficult calls to action such as having to visit a web site or call a phone number in order to register, receive information, or qualify for a benefit, are likely to fail. Only a small sub-set of consumers will respond to such high involvement action calls.

This is not to say that consumers do not place a great deal of importance on sustainability. It is just that the average consumer does much of their consumption decision making quickly and automatically. While they may have good intentions to prioritize sustainability in their life, we know that what is bought is usually based on habit and convenience rather than on fully evaluated decisions.

An additional challenge is that consumers lack feedback for their behaviour at the shelf. Buying 'dolphin safe' tuna may sound appealing, but the consumer never gets to see the actual dolphin they have saved in any tangible way. They also do not get to see any harm they may do when choosing a non-dolphin safe brand. The immediate feedback loop is missing and so there is a disconnection between the moment of brand choice and the longer term impact of their consumption. Marketers must therefore try and give what immediate positive feedback they can to the consumer at the moment of choice and build on this this in their wider communications to reinforce the link.

Ensure Availability in the Mind and on the Shelf

Organizations are becoming increasingly aware that the success of their sustainability efforts lies not only in management's long term sustainable orientation, but also their marketing capacity to promote it (Barthel and Ivanaj, 2007).

Disappointingly most messages that marketers send about their brands simply fail to be noticed by consumers. Consumers are bombarded with messages every day from multiple sources and, as a result, many are either screened out or quickly forgotten. Therefore a key role of marketing communication is to ensure maximum availability in the mind, so that their brand or message (for example, make sure you buy 'free range') is more likely to be thought of at the point where the action is desired. Then the marketer also has to remind and reinforce the message, so the new behaviour is habituated. This means sustainability messages should be simple, consistent and repeated to the extent that they can act as triggers at the point of brand choice and reinforce new behaviours.

Likewise if a brand cannot be physically found it cannot be chosen. Ensuring maximum physical availability at the shelf is also a key challenge for marketers. Many smaller green brands face a challenge in getting valuable shelf frontage against their bigger and more established competitor brands. Consumer choice at the shelf is fast (Sorensen, 2009) and they have a host of other brands to choose from. They will not spend time trying to find a brand that is not immediately visible.

Sustainability signals are like any other product feature. They compete with all the other marketing stimuli for the consumer's attention at each purchase opportunity. And green brands compete against a range of other offers including specialist low cost, private label, premium, and country of origin brands.

This raises the important question of when a 'sustainable' product will be bought over a non-sustainable alternative. The answer is when it attracts attention, has good distribution and meets all the other performance features of competitor brands.

Do Not Forget the Basic Reason People Buy You

Sustainability attributes are not the key reason why a consumer buys from a product category. There is a wider need they are trying to satisfy, be it hunger (snack foods) or hygiene (hand wash). Sustainability issues are of secondary importance, playing an auxiliary role in brand choice (Fuller, 1999). While studies show us daily that most consumers want to be provided with more socially and environmentally beneficial goods and services, consumers are generally unwilling to compromise in terms of cost, performance and convenience at the point of choice (Carrigan, 2001; Vermeir and Verberke, 2006; Weatherell et al., 2003).

When consumers do not choose sustainable brand alternatives because they believe the sustainable attributes to have a lower quality (for example, recycled bathroom tissue, nature safe detergents), it is referred to as the 'green marketing myopia' (Ottman et al., 2006). Marketers must find the balance between emphasis on sustainable attributes to influence consumer preference and the message that their brand still meets the core benefit demanded of the category and can hold its own against competitors.

If marketers overemphasize sustainability attributes at the expense of core benefits, the product is likely to fail in the market or remain trapped as a small alternative niche choice (Carrigan and Attalla, 2001). Marketers need to ensure that the sustainability choices they make do not differentiate the product so far from the category norm as to be seen as an inferior alternative. For example, many fish stocks such as tuna are under enormous pressure from over fishing. Yet fish continues to be used in many cat food products. While taking tuna out of cat food might make sense in sustainability terms, educating and signalling this to consumers will be a challenge as customers may believe that pet food without tuna is of a lower quality, or that their cat might not like the alternative.

Use the Opportunity for News

Introducing a new sustainability element is news for a brand and gives the marketer an opportunity to say something about the brand that gets attention. For consumer goods, the chances for legitimate news are rare. However, while sustainability initiatives may be a talking point, typically it will not be one that remains unmatched by competitors for long. Most initiatives can be easily matched. Mature categories such as washing powder have undergone many rounds of new green advances such as two times, then three times and now 'ultra' concentrate (with a correspondingly shrinking box size), phosphate free, petrochemical free, chlorine free, biodegradable, no dyes or preservatives, dermatologically tested, grey water (garden) safe, organic stain remover added, with baking soda, with 75 per cent less sodium and plant-based. Nothing remains unmatched for long, but it may provide a marketer with a short term advantage.

Marketers should use their sustainability initiatives to form messages that can cut through competitive clutter and gain shelf space amongst distributors. At the very least, it may be the thing that gains attention over other brands at the shelf when a shopper finds their 'regular' brand is out of stock.

Growing and Protecting Sustainable Brands

Brands carrying sustainability claims still face all the normal marketing challenges. The biggest one of these is to maintain and grow mental and physical availability against all the competitor brands on offer.

In communicating sustainable aspects of a brand, an organization becomes protected from unwanted attention for not doing something that competitors are doing. To some extent all brands need to consider addressing sustainability concerns simply to ensure they are keeping up with the current industry standard. Sustainably sourced fish and trans fat free bakery products are examples of product categories where many competitive brands are working hard to show they are meeting (essentially the same) sustainability standard. Being proactive on sustainability can therefore help avoid customer-led criticism of your brand.

Finally, to gain mainstream adoption amongst organizations, sustainability must be presented as a business case that is competitive against existing business models. For this its impact has to be measurable and able to be interpreted within the framework of existing marketing metrics such as sales and profitability. This is where the next stage of the challenge lies.

REFERENCES

Alwitt, L.F. and Berger, I.E. (1993),'Understanding the link between environmental attitudes and consumer product usage: measuring the moderating role of attitude strength', *Advances in Consumer Research*, **20**, 189–94.

Barthel, P. and Ivanaj, V. (2007), 'Is sustainable development in multinational enterprises a marketing issue?', *The Multinational Business Review*, **15** (1), 67–87.

Belz, F.M. and Peattie, K. (2009), *Sustainability Marketing: A Global Perspective*, Cheltenham, UK: John Wiley & Sons.

Bonini, S. and Oppenheim, J. (2008), 'Cultivating the green consumer', *Stanford Social Innovation Review*, **6** (4): 56–61.

Carrigan, M. and Attalla, A. (2001), 'The myth of the ethical consumer – do ethics matter in purchase behaviour?', *Journal of Consumer Marketing*, **18** (7), 560–77.

Charter, M., Peattie, K., Ottman, J. and Polonsky, M.J. (2002), *Marketing and Sustainability*, Cardiff: Victoria University.

Closs, D.J., Speier, C. and Meacham, N. (2011), 'Sustainability to support end-to-end value chains: the role of supply chain management', *Journal of the Academy of Marketing Science*, **39** (1), 1–16.

Cornelissen, G., Pandelaere, M., Warlop, L. and Dewitte, S. (2008), 'Positive cueing: promoting sustainable consumer behavior by cueing common environmental behaviors as environmental', *International Journal of Research in Marketing*, **25** (1), 46–55.

Crittenden, V.L., Crittenden, W.F., Ferrell, L.K., Ferrell, O.C. and Pinney, C.C. (2011), 'Market-oriented sustainability: a conceptual framework and propositions', *Journal of the Academy of Marketing Science*, 1–15.

D'Souza, C. (2004), 'Ecolabel programmes: a stakeholder (consumer) perspective', *Corporate Communications*, **9** (3), 179–88.

Ehrenberg, A.S.C. (1972), *Repeat Buying: Theory and Applications*, New York: American Elsevier.

Ehrenberg, A.S.C. and Uncles, M.D. (1995), *Dirichlet-type Markets: Parts I and II*, London: South Bank Business School.

Fuller, D. (1999), *Sustainable Marketing: Managerial-Ecological Issues*, Thousand Oaks, California: SAGE.

Geller, E.S. (1989), 'Applied behavior analysis and social marketing: an integration for environmental preservation', *Journal of Social Issues*, **45** (1), 17–36.

Gordon, W. (2002), 'Brand green: mainstream or forever niche?', available at http://www.green-alliance.org.uk/grea_p.aspx?id=388 (accessed 12 June 2012).

Gupta, S. and Ogden, D. (2009), 'To buy or not to buy? A social dilemma perspective on green buying', *Journal of Consumer Marketing*, **26**, 376–91.

Handford, R. (2010), *Global Trends in Sustainability Performance Management*, available at http://footprinttalent.wordpress.com/2010/05/13/global-trends-in-sustainability-performance-management/ (accessed 1 June 2012).

Mahler, D. (2007), 'The sustainable supply chain', *Spotlight on Supply Management*, available at http://www.atkearneypas.com/knowledge/articles/2007/SCMR.spotlight.sustainability.pdf, (accessed 12 June 2012).

McDonald, C. and Ehrenberg, A.S.C. (2002), 'Personal buying is like "family" shopping', *Report 12 for Corporate Members*, Adelaide: Ehrenberg-Bass Institute for Marketing Science.

Mintel (2010), 'Mintel Report reveals consumer packaged goods trends for 2011', available at http://www.foodprocessing.com/industrynews/2010/114.html (accessed 30 May 2010).

Ottman, J.A., Stafford, E.R. et al. (2006), 'Avoiding green marketing myopia: ways to improve consumer appeal for environmentally preferable products', *Environment: Science and Policy for Sustainable Development*, **48** (5), 22–36.

Our Common Future: Report of the World Commission on Environment and Development (1987), available at http://www.un-documents.net/wced-ocf.htm (accessed 1 June 2012).

Peattie, K. (2001), 'Golden goose or wild goose? The hunt for the green consumer', *Business Strategy and the Environment*, **10** (4), 187–99.

Peattie, K. (2007), 'Sustainable marketing: marketing re-thought, re-mixed and re-tooled', in M. Saren, P. Maclaran, C. Goulding, R. Elliot, A. Shankar and M. Cattarall (eds), *Critical Marketing: Defining the Field*, London: Butterworth-Heinemann.

Pickett-Baker, J. and Ozaki, R. (2008), 'Pro-environmental products: marketing influence on consumer purchase decision', *Journal of Consumer Marketing*, **25** (5), 281–93.

Riebe, E., Sharp, B. and Stern, P. (2002), 'An empirical investigation of customer defection and acquisition rates for declining and growing pharmaceutical brands', in R.N. Shaw, S. Adam and H. McDonald (eds), *ANZMAC*, Melbourne.

Rossiter, J.R. and Winter, F.L. (1988), *Low Involvement Consumer Behaviour: An Operational Model Based on Purchase Pattern Matching with Repetitive or Stochastic Brand Choice*, Broadway, NSW: NSW Institute of Technology.

Sharp, A. and Newstead, K. (2010), *Green Brand Fatigue, ADMAP*, London: WARC.

Sharp, B. (2010), *How Brands Grow*, South Melbourne: Oxford University Press.

Sorensen, H. (2009), *Inside the Mind of the Shopper*, Upper Saddle River, New Jersey: Pearson Education Inc.

Stern, P.C. (1999), 'Information, incentives, and proenvironmental consumer behavior', *Journal of Consumer Policy*, **22** (4): 461–78.

Vandermerwe, S. and Oliff, M. (1990), 'Customers drive corporations green', *Long Range Planning*, **23** (6), 10–16.

Vermeir, I. and W. Verbeke (2006), 'Sustainable food consumption: exploring the "attitude-behaviour intention" gap', *Journal of Agriculture and Environmental Ethics*, **19** (2), 169–94.

Weatherell, C., J. Tregear, A. Allinson, et al. (2003), 'In search of the concerned consumer: UK public perceptions of food, farming and buying local', *Journal of Rural Studies*, **19** (2), 233–44.

Wright, M. and Klÿn, B. (1998), 'Environmental attitude – behaviour correlations in 21 countries', *Journal of Empirical Generalisations in Marketing Science*, **3**, 42–60.

7. Socially responsible human resource management: a conceptual framework

Jie Shen and John Benson

INTRODUCTION

The concept of sustainability is often seen by organizations as part of their corporate social responsibilities (CSR) rather than as an integral part of their corporate objectives (Nidumolu et al., 2009). Yet organizations that have paid attention to environmental integrity and social equity have improved their long-term economic prosperity (Russo and Fouts, 1997; Waddock and Graves, 1997). Whilst sustainability research has been linked to a variety of issues it has only been in the last decade that research has specifically focused on the relationship between sustainability and human resource management (HRM). Much of this work has been exploratory and conceptual in nature (Ehnert, 2009) and this chapter follows in this tradition. In particular we argue that the best way to explore the link between sustainability and HRM is through CSR. This will allow for HRM to be redefined in terms of socially responsible behaviour that a company adopts towards both its employees and the wider society.

The notion of CSR emerged in the 1950s (Bowen, 1953) and is now a global concern (Basu and Palazzo, 2008; Carroll, 1979, 1999; Lee, 2008; McWilliams et al., 2006). This interest has been due to an increased awareness of the power of multinational enterprises in the global economy and the potentially adverse effects of business activities on the environment, community and individuals (Fanning, 1990; Wilcox, 2006). Companies are urged to go beyond profits and shareholder returns and engage in CSR activities in relation to stakeholders that include customers, suppliers, governments, non-government organizations, unions, investment funds and the wider community (Becchetti et al., 2005; Matten and Moon, 2008; Waring and Lewer, 2004).

The World Business Council for Sustainable Development (WBCSD) has a wider perspective than most and defines CSR as a 'continuing

Figure 7.1   CSR, SR-HRM and sustainability

commitment by businesses to behave ethically and contribute to economic development while improving the quality of life of the workforce and their families as well as the local community and society at large' (Moir, 2001, p. 6). Unlike other definitions the WBCSD regards improving the quality of life of employees and their families as integral to CSR. However the prevailing CSR literature tends to focus on CSR as an organizational activity that meets the interests of external stakeholders, the so-called 'external CSR' (Rupp et al., 2006), whilst neglecting employees (Brammer et al., 2007; Rodrigo and Arenas, 2008; Rupp et al., 2006). While it has been pointed out that sustainability could encompass both human and natural environment issues 'there is a much greater emphasis on the physical rather than the social environment both in the research literature and in the actions and pronouncements of companies' (Pfeffer, 2010, p. 35). Thus in spite of the rapid development of the CSR literature over the past few decades, the focus has primarily been on the effects of CSR on shareholders and external stakeholders, such as customers and communities (Rodrigo and Arenas, 2008), so that little is known about the impact of CSR on employees, and on employees' role in, and reactions to, the formulation and delivery of CSR programs.

This is an important gap in the literature as employee support for, and participation in, CSR initiatives is crucial for their successful implementation and sustainability (Figure 7.1). The aim of this chapter is therefore to contribute to the development of the concept of socially responsible HRM (SR-HRM). The next section focuses on the definition of SR-HRM and discusses why SR-HRM practices can be conceived along two dimensions: whether HRM addresses the interest of employees, and whether it is adopted to implement external CSR programs. This is followed by an analysis of the relationship between the two categories of SR-HRM and employees' attitudes toward CSR and SR-HRM. The final substantive section explores the effects of SR-HRM on employee work attitudes and behaviour. Based on these discussions we develop a conceptual framework of SR-HRM which illustrates the relationships between employees' general attitude toward CSR, external CSR-oriented HRM, employee-oriented

SR-HRM and employee work attitudes and behaviour. The conceptual framework demonstrates how companies can sustain CSR initiatives and maintain positive employee attitudes and behaviour. We conclude with a consideration of the theoretical contributions and the practical implications of the conceptual framework.

SOCIALLY RESPONSIBLE HRM

One of the most widely accepted definitions of CSR is 'a firm's considerations of, and response to, issues beyond the narrow economic, technical, and legal requirements of the firm to accomplish social benefits along with the traditional economic gains which the firm seeks' (Davis, 1973, p. 312). Central to this definition is that CSR goes beyond business boundaries and legal minima. This definition is consistent with the ISO standard for CSR (standard 26000) which states that social responsibility 'is about organizational initiatives that start with, but go beyond meeting legal requirements and that contribute to social acceptance' (ISO, 2010, p. 13).

As suggested by the WBCSD, CSR has both internal and external components (see also Brammer et al., 2007). Internal CSR addresses the interests and needs of internal stakeholders, such as shareholders and employees. A range of organizational policies that fall within the HRM realm can be regarded as internal CSR that has implications for employees. According to Attribution Theory the perceived causes of these policies and practices will affect employees' emotional responses and work outcomes (Kelley, 1972). It also suggests that trust in another person is related to behaviours motivated by that other person's internal disposition rather than by external pressures (Kelley, 1972; Kelley and Michela, 1980). As a consequence it is likely that employees' trust in organizations will be enhanced when a fairness motive is perceived to underlie organizational policies and practices. On the other hand it is likely that employees' trust in organizations will not be enhanced if organizational policies and practices are adopted simply to comply with the law. We would therefore argue that HRM policies designed to meet the minimum legal conditions, such as minimum wages, maximum working hours, and the adoption of health and safety rules, whilst not reducing employee trust in organizations, will not enhance it. As such we define HRM that addresses the interests and needs of employees, and are also above and beyond legal minima, as 'employee-oriented SR-HRM'. On the other hand, HRM practices adopted to implement external CSR are defined as 'external CSR-oriented SR-HRM'.

Internal CSR: Employee-Oriented SR-HRM

Employee-oriented SR-HRM, as defined, includes a variety of HRM practices. As Pfeffer (2010) suggests, a number of policies such as providing life insurance, avoiding layoffs, enabling work-life balance, providing job control and maintaining equitable remuneration are important HRM practices for the health and wellbeing of employees. While these practices are internal, Johnston (2001) suggests that a company that does not treat its employees responsibly is unlikely to engage responsibly with its customers and its social and natural environments. The link between HRM and the external stakeholders is supported by Masterson (2001, p. 600) who found 'employees' perceptions of fairness were related to their organizational commitment, which in turn was positively related to customers' ratings of employees' effort and prosocial behaviours'.

Using SR-HRM as a criterion for assessing a company's CSR is not new. Waring and Lewer (2004) found that the definition of social performance utilized by socially responsible investment funds, such as the Domini Social Equity Fund, had employee relations dimensions that included diversity, management-union relations, employee involvement and retirement benefits (see also the ratings of labour standards by government and NGOs – Zappalá, 2004). The value of employee-oriented SR-HRM practices has been increasingly recognized through studies of training (Wilcox, 2006), flexible working time and employment (Guest, 2004), family-friendly policies (Bagraim and Sader, 2007), work-life balance (Bardoel et al., 2008), high commitment HRM (McElroy, 2001; Whitener, 2001) and high involvement HRM (Guthrie, 2001). For example Wilcox (2006) found training not only improved workers' employability and occupational safety but was important for career and succession planning. These HRM practices, it is contended, will improve worker wellbeing and the level of trust in management and so will have a major impact on employee commitment (McElroy, 2001; Whitener, 2001). The level of employee commitment is also positively associated with employees' perceptions of the benefit they receive from organizational membership (Shore and Wayne, 1993; Wayne et al., 1997).

External CSR-Oriented SR-HRM

In contrast to internal CSR, external CSR addresses the interests of the wider community and includes such issues as poverty reduction (Jenkins, 2005), climate change (Le Menestrel et al., 2002), environmental sustainability (Basu and Palazzo, 2008), disaster relief (Horwich, 1993) and corporate community involvement, including the provision of financial and in-kind assistance and contribution of time and expertise to the community (Zappalá, 2004). While external CSR is beyond the core business objectives, it requires strategies to be formulated and delivered by employees (Brammer et al., 2007; Collier and Esteban, 2007) and so companies need to develop appropriate HRM policies and practices. Without such external CSR-oriented SR-HRM policies, we contend that external CSR efforts are likely to be compromised and ineffectual.

Orlitzky and Swanson (2006) suggested that SR-HRM policies and practices include hiring employees for cognitive moral development and agreeableness, workforce diversity, developing skills in receptive stakeholder engagement and communication, and taking account of social contribution in performance appraisal and reward practices. The essence of this model is the recruitment, retention and development of socially responsible employees, although we recognize the inherent difficulties in adopting such an approach. Employing CSR-specific staff and taking account of social performance in promotion and reward belongs to this category of HRM practices. It has also been suggested that employees may be willing to sacrifice part of their salaries to support their company's CSR acts (Zappalá, 2004), although there is little firm evidence for this proposition. It may well be the case, however, that forms of wage adjustments or sacrifice could be part of the mix of external CSR-oriented SR-HRM policies.

EMPLOYEES' ATTITUDES TOWARD SR-HRM

It has been found that HRM that addresses the interests of employees, both within and beyond legal minima, such as family-friendly HRM, work-life balance, high involvement HRM and diversity management is positively related to perceived organizational support and justice (Mayes et al., in press). This in turn suggests that employees will react favourably to employee-oriented SR-HRM and develop positive work attitudes and behaviour.

Will employees have the same attitude toward external CSR-oriented SR-HRM? A number of writers have claimed that employees in general support organizational CSR initiatives and are a source of pressure on companies to engage in CSR (Aguilera et al., 2007; Brammer et al., 2007; Peterson, 2004). This claim is consistent with Social Identity Theory which suggests that individuals are happier when they associate themselves with organizations that have positive external reputations because it is the association with those organizations that enhances their self-esteem (Ashforth and Mael, 1989; Dutton et al., 1994). But it has also been claimed that notwithstanding their identification with companies with good reputations employees will not necessarily be positive toward CSR (Rodrigo and Arenas, 2008). This is because employees expect that if their companies are socially responsible toward external stakeholders they will behave similarly toward their employees (Zappalá, 2004). There is however evidence that some leading companies engage in CSR to protect corporate reputations and to attract customers and do little to protect vulnerable workers or provide good pay and conditions (Klein, 2001; Royle, 2005). As argued by Royle (2005, p. 51) while 'some corporations are keen to take on the rhetoric of CSR; they may be less keen to act in a socially responsible manner (particularly to their employees).'

We extend these arguments and suggest that the adoption of external CSR-oriented SR-HRM may threaten the interests of employees. For example hiring for cognitive moral development and agreeableness, and recruiting CSR-specific staff may affect the employment opportunities for other employees. The cost of CSR-specific training may reduce the firm's investment in other employee career development programmes. Taking account of social contribution in appraisals, promotion and reward may overshadow the significance of employee work performance. Community involvement and organizational philanthropic acts, such as disaster relief and financial contribution to poverty reduction and to the community, may impact on employees' income and/or their perceptions of fair wages. Clearly if this resulted in lower wages or wages growing at a lower rate than in other companies in similar industries, then some employees might adopt a less positive view of CSR. Moreover providing more employment, training, and development opportunities to local employees of MNEs may affect similar opportunities for other employees. It is also possible that companies may attempt to offset the costs caused by their external social goals by compromising employees' welfare, development and working conditions. However consistent with the Social Identity Theory we also argue that if the interests of employees are not perceived to be threatened by the adoption of external CSR-oriented SR-HRM then employees are likely to have a positive attitude toward this form of SR-HRM.

ANTECEDENTS TO EMPLOYEES' SUPPORT FOR EXTERNAL CSR-ORIENTED SR-HRM

Whether and how employees' support for external CSR-oriented SR-HRM develops depend on how its potential negative effects are offset by perceived organizational support and justice. Maslow (1943) argued that an individual's need for self-actualization only emerges when all his or her lower level needs are satisfied. Although this theory has been criticized as simplistic, recent studies have supported the existence of a needs hierarchy (see Latham and Pinder, 2005) and other studies have shown that its practical applications are well accepted (Ajila, 1997; Kamalanabhan et al., 1999). Based on the needs hierarchy theory it can be contended that the need to help others or having a strong concern for the wider society will usually be acted upon by individuals only after they have satisfied some basic physical and psychological needs. Thus the perceived adequacy of wages, working conditions, opportunities for personal development, organizational support for employee personal and family matters, and participation in decision-making are likely to be important pre-conditions for employees' support for external CSR-oriented SR-HRM and hence external CSR.

Yet even when an employee is satisfied with his or her employment conditions it cannot be assumed that the individual's pursuit of higher order needs will switch to external CSR. A key determinant will be altruism which, in an organizational setting, refers to the willingness of an employee to help co-workers or their company (Organ, 1988). This altruism behaviour is usually referred to as organizational citizenship behaviour which has been found to be positively associated with the employees' perceived level of organizational support and social justice (Masterson et al., 2000; Rhoades et al., 2001; Tekleab et al., 2005).

Employees' perceptions of organizational support and social justice are largely embedded in HRM policies and practices (Huselid, 1995; Meyer et al., 2002; Rhoades et al., 2001), such as training programs, flexible working time and employment, family-friendly policies, work-life balance practices, high commitment HRM and high involvement HRM. These types of HRM policies and practices largely overlap with employee-oriented SR-HRM. Hence a company's employee-oriented SR-HRM policies and practices are likely to be antecedents of employees' support for external CSR-oriented SR-HRM.

EFFECT OF EMPLOYEES' GENERAL ATTITUDES TOWARD CSR

Rodrigo and Arenas (2008) have classified employees' attitudes toward CSR as committed, indifferent or dissident. Committed employees 'have a positive perception of the new social role of the organization, which leads them to identify with it'; indifferent employees 'would not say they are for or against it'; dissident employees 'are not interested in the social significance of what they do' and their sense of social justice is 'focused toward themselves or their immediate group' (Rodrigo and Arenas, 2008, pp. 276–7). Such perceptions develop because employees' attitude towards CSR is influenced by family upbringing, traditional beliefs and customs and common practices in the industry (Abdul and Ibrahim, 2002) as well as by personal characteristics such as education and their environment in their formative years (Rodrigo and Arenas, 2008).

Even if employees have positive attitudes toward CSR in general, they may still react negatively to company specific CSR acts as well as to external CSR-oriented SR-HRM that delivers those acts. We suggest that this is because employees' attitudes toward external CSR-oriented SR-HRM are largely determined by whether and how these practices are in line with the day-to-day interests of employees (see also Golden, 2007 for a discussion on teleworkers and the impact on co-worker satisfaction). Nevertheless employees' attitudes toward general CSR will to some extent affect their attitudes toward external CSR-oriented SR-HRM. Hence employees' attitudes toward general CSR will impact on the relationship between employee-oriented SR-HRM and employee support for external CSR-oriented SR-HRM.

EFFECT OF SR-HRM ON EMPLOYEE WORK ATTITUDES AND BEHAVIOUR

Social exchange theory and the norm of reciprocity (Blau, 1964; Gouldner, 1960; Homans, 1961) would suggest that employee commitment to the organization and extra role performance derive from perceptions of the employer's commitment to and support of them (Rhoades and Eisenberger, 2002). If this is the case it could be argued that employees may interpret employee-oriented SR-HRM practices as an indicator of organizational support for and commitment to them. Hence they reciprocate such perceptions by making more effort in their work and exhibiting more organizational citizenship behaviour.

Employees are key stakeholders within the organization (Mitchell et al., 1997) and it is generally these employees who deliver CSR programs (Zappalá, 2004) and, at the same time, are affected by those programs (Brammer et al., 2007; Rupp et al., 2006; Zappalá, 2004). Employee perceptions of their company's CSR impact on their work attitudes and behaviours and eventually on their performance and the performance of their company (Rupp et al., 2006). A review of the literature found only two empirical studies that have explored the effect of CSR on employees' attitude and behaviour (Brammer et al., 2007; Riordan et al., 1997). Brammer et al. (2007) utilized a general and quite limited measure of CSR, namely that 'the company is a socially responsible member of the community', and concluded that perceived organizational social performance is positively related to employee organizational commitment. Riordan et al. (1997) found that perceived corporate image is directly related to employee job satisfaction and intention to leave. However this study used corporate leadership as an antecedent to perceived corporate image. Given this paucity of research little is known about the effect of external CSR acts and organizational policies and practices that are designed to implement CSR, particularly external CSR-oriented SR-HRM, on employee work attitudes and behaviour.

External CSR-oriented SR-HRM can affect employee work attitudes and behaviour in two contradictory ways. On the one hand, external CSR-oriented SR-HRM may incur significant organizational costs (McWilliams and Siegel, 2001; Paul and Siegel, 2006) that may redirect resources away from employees. Even though employees may support CSR in principle, if their interests are not adequately addressed then external CSR-oriented SR-HRM will likely impact negatively on employee work attitudes and behaviour. On the other hand if the interests of employees are adequately addressed, then we argue, in line with Social Identity Theory, employees will support external CSR-oriented SR-HRM. In this case external CSR-oriented SR-HRM will be positively related to employee work attitude and behaviour. We therefore contend that external CSR-oriented SR-HRM directly relates to employee work attitudes and behaviour, but how it impacts on employee work attitudes and behaviour largely depends on employees' perception of employee-oriented SR-HRM. In the light of the discussions above, we propose the following conceptual framework which links employee-oriented SR-HRM, external CSR-oriented SR-HRM, employee general attitude toward CSR and employee support for external CSR-oriented SR-HRM (Figure 7.2).

DISCUSSION

Despite the rapid expansion of the CSR literature over the last few decades, it remains limited in its application to employees and HRM for several reasons. First CSR is largely considered as organizational acts addressing the interests of external stakeholders. As a result CSR is typically regarded as a macro-level activity with macro-level consequences, and has thus received scant attention within the micro organizational behaviour literature (Rupp et al., 2006). So far little is known about the role of HRM in the formulation and implementation of CSR strategies and initiatives and the effect of external CSR on employees. Second it has been argued that employees in general support company CSR acts and are a source of pressure on companies to

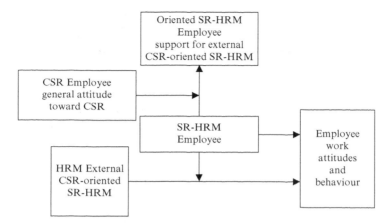

Figure 7.2   A conceptual framework of SR-HRM

engage in CSR. This argument is consistent with Social Identity Theory. Nevertheless we contend that research has largely ignored the potential threat to employees posed by external CSR and as such we know little about how employees feel about external CSR acts. Third while there are a small number of studies exploring the effect of CSR on employees, these studies have inadequate measures of CSR and fail to distinguish between external and internal CSR (Brammer et al., 2007; Riordan et al., 1997).

In this chapter we argue for a different approach than that provided by the prevailing CSR literature. In particular we contend that employees' general attitude toward CSR may be different from their attitude to their company's specific CSR acts, although we recognize that the former may affect the latter. Although employees tend to identify with organizations with good reputations, they may have a negative attitude toward company specific CSR acts and organizational policies and practices designed to implement CSR. We further argue that employees may react negatively to external CSR-oriented SR-HRM as it may threaten their interests and that such a reaction will be determined by how they perceive organizational support and social justice which are largely imbedded in employee-oriented SR-HRM. Hence we also contend that the perceived employee-oriented SR-HRM is associated with employees' support for organizational external CSR acts. Moreover we suggest that this relationship will be moderated by employees' general attitude toward CSR. External CSR-oriented SR-HRM we argue is directly related to employee work attitudes and behaviour, but again we suggest that this relationship will be moderated by the perceived level of employee-oriented SR-HRM.

The introduction of the concept of SR-HRM provides a way to incorporate the threats posed by external CSR to employees and to develop a more holistic approach to our understanding of CSR and sustainability. The concept of external CSR-oriented SR-HRM highlights the role of HRM in the successful formulation and implementation of external CSR programs. The focus on HRM allows CSR research to resolve the apparent contradiction between employees' general support for external CSR and their potential negative reactions to organizational specific CSR acts. Our proposed conceptual framework thus builds a bridge between external CSR activities and employees. Examining the antecedents to employees' support for external CSR-oriented SR-HRM will allow for a clearer understanding not only of the threats posed by external CSR to employees but also of organizational policies to address those threats. This approach thus allows predictions to be made about how successful a company's external CSR initiatives are likely to be. Moreover exploration of the possible moderating variables on the relationship between external CSR-oriented SR-HRM and employee work attitudes and behaviour will assist companies to develop appropriate HRM policies and practices to generate a positive effect of CSR on employees, and consequently on organizational performance.

THEORETICAL AND MANAGEMENT IMPLICATIONS

Our conceptual framework addresses three important shortcomings in the literature. First, employees and HRM have been largely neglected in the CSR and sustainability literature. Our conceptual framework suggests that employee-oriented SR-HRM is part of CSR and that external CSR-oriented SR-HRM delivers external CSR programs, and so provides a bridge between HRM and CSR. Second, the potential negative impact of external CSR on employees has been significantly underestimated in the literature. This neglect has serious consequences for the implementation of CSR initiatives. Through the introduction of the concept of SR-HRM our framework provides a way to ameliorate the threat to employee interests and to develop a more holistic approach to the study of CSR. Third, the CSR literature generally refers to external CSR activities and as a result, CSR is normally regarded as having 'mainly macro-level consequences' (Rupp et al., 2006, p. 537). The relationship between CSR, particularly external CSR, and employee attitudes and behaviour has not been researched. Our conceptual framework provides a way to understand the inherent contradictions of CSR and to find solutions to the potential lack of support for external CSR-oriented SR-HRM and for external CSR employees.

The framework presented in this chapter has significant implications for managers and HRM practitioners. Companies often find themselves in a dilemma when deciding whether or not to adopt CSR. On the one hand companies are informed that the successful implementation of CSR can have a range of organizational benefits, such as improving corporate reputation (Brammer and Pavelin, 2006; Fombrun, 2005), attracting talent (Albinger and Freeman, 2000; Turban and Greening, 1996), increasing customer loyalty (Bhattacharya and Sen, 2004), maintaining good relationships with governments, business associations and NGOs, and having access to socially responsible funds that take account of environmental, social and labour standards in investment decisions (Zappalá, 2004). On the other hand inadequate engagement in CSR is likely to incur negative consequences. Companies are increasingly realizing that CSR can help them to obtain legitimacy and social license and can be an important source of competitive advantage (Branco and Rodrigues, 2006), but some companies are under pressure from global competition and the strong demand from shareholders for short-term profits, preventing them from engaging in CSR that requires additional resources but does not necessarily yield greater returns (Ambec and Lanoie, 2008; McWilliams and Siegel, 2001; Paul and Siegel, 2006).

While there is pressure on companies to develop and effectively implement appropriate CSR initiatives, many are not yet equipped with the knowledge and understanding of how to effectively engage in CSR and how to minimize the potentially negative impact of external CSR initiatives on their employees. Over time this will seriously affect their competitiveness and sustainability in the global marketplace as well as negatively impact on their employees and other stakeholders. Hence many companies have found themselves in need of assistance (Collier and Esteban, 2007). A growing literature has been devoted to exploring how to effectively improve organizational social performance, and suggestions have been focused on understanding the complexity and suitability of CSR programs (Basu and Palazzo, 2008; Matten and Moon, 2008), although the role of HRM in the formulation and implementation of external CSR programmes has been almost entirely neglected.

As employees 'carry the main burden of responsibility for implementing ethical corporate behaviour in the daily working life of the company, the achievement of those outcomes will largely depend on employee willingness to collaborate' (Collier and Esteban, 2007, p. 20). This raises the question as to how a company can gain employees' full support for CSR acts and ensure that employees are motivated and committed to achieving the company's social objectives. We would contend that our conceptual framework demonstrates how this can be achieved and the advantages to be gained by companies adopting SR-HRM policies and practices. In short our argument is that while external CSR-oriented SR-HRM delivers external CSR, it is employee-oriented SR-HRM that underpins employee support for external CSR-oriented SR-HRM and thus organizational external CSR acts. Through addressing the interests and needs of employees the proposed conceptual framework demonstrates how to minimize the potential negative impact of external CSR on employees and so allow both these forms of SR-HRM to contribute to more positive employee work attitudes and behaviours, thus resulting in improved organizational performance and long-term sustainability.

CONCLUSIONS

We have argued in this chapter that employees' general attitude toward CSR may be different from their attitudes toward organizational specific external CSR acts, although we acknowledge that the former, to some extent, affects the latter. This means that companies need to consider a more holistic approach to achieving their social objectives. We provide such an approach by expanding upon the theoretical underpinnings of past CSR research, developing the concept of CSR-oriented SR-HRM, and by drawing upon motivational theory and the concept of organizational citizenship behaviour to establish the determinants of employee support for external CSR-oriented SR-HRM. The resultant framework enables a better understanding of how to increase employee support for external CSR-oriented SR-HRM, and through such support to implement external CSR programs more effectively. This approach, we suggest, will ensure the sustainability of corporate CSR initiatives as it demonstrates the essential SR-HRM policies necessary for the successful implementation of CSR initiatives and their longer term impact on employees and corporate performance.

REFERENCES

Abdul, M. and Ibrahim, S. (2002), 'Executive and management attitudes towards corporate social responsibility in Malaysia', *Corporate Governance*, **2** (4), 10–16.
Aguilera, R., Rupp, D., Williams, C. and Ganapathi, J. (2007), 'Putting the S back in corporate social responsibility: a multilevel theory of social change in organizations', *Academy of Management Review*, **32** (3), 836–63.

Ajila, C. (1997), 'Maslow's hierarchy of needs theory: applicability to the Nigerian industrial setting', *IFE Psychologia: An International Journal*, **5** (1), 162–74.

Albinger, H. and Freeman, S. (2000), 'Corporate social performance and attractiveness as an employer to different job seeking populations', *Journal of Business Ethics*, **28** (3), 243–53.

Ambec, S. and Lanoie, P. (2008), 'Does it pay to be green? A systematic overview', *Academy of Management Perspectives*, **22** (4), 45–62.

Ashforth, B. and Mael, F. (1989), 'Social identity theory and the organization', *Academy of Management Review*, **14** (1), 20–39.

Bagraim, J. and Sader, R. (2007), 'Family-friendly human resource practices and organisational commitment', *Management Dynamics*, **16** (4), 2–10.

Bardoel, E., De Cieri, H. and Mayson, S. (2008), 'Bridging the research-practice gap: developing a measurement framework for work-life initiatives', *Journal of Management and Organization*, **14** (3), 239–58.

Basu, K. and Palazzo, G. (2008), 'Corporate social responsibility: a process model of sensemaking', *Academy of Management Review*, **33** (1), 122–36.

Becchetti, L., di Giacomo, S. and Pinnachio, D. (2005), 'Corporate social responsibility and corporate performance: evidence from a panel of US listed companies', Centre for Economic and International Studies, Research Paper No. 26–78.

Bhattacharya, C. and Sen, S. (2004), 'When, why, and how consumers respond to social initiatives?', *California Management Review*, **47** (1), 9–24.

Blau, P. (1964), *Exchange and Power in Social Life,* New York: Wiley.

Bowen, H. (1953), *Social Responsibilities of the Businessman,* New York: Harper and Row.

Brammer, S. and Pavelin, S. (2006), 'Corporate reputation and social performance: the importance of fit', *Journal of Management Studies*, **43** (3), 435–55.

Brammer, S., Millington, A. and Rayton, B. (2007), 'The contribution of corporate social responsibility to organizational commitment', *International Journal of Human Resource Management*, **18** (10), 1701–19.

Branco, M. and Rodrigues, L. (2006), 'Corporate social responsibility and resource-based perceptive', *Journal of Business Ethics*, **69** (2), 111–32.

Carroll, A. (1979), 'A three dimensional conceptual mode of corporate performance', *Academy of Management Review*, **4** (4), 497–505.

Carroll, A. (1999), 'Corporate social responsibility: evolution of a definitional construct', *Business and Society*, **38** (3), 268–95.

Collier, J. and Esteban, R. (2007), 'Corporate social responsibility and employee commitment', *Business Ethics: A European Review*, **16** (1), 19–33.

Davis, K. (1973), 'The case for and against business assumption of social responsibilities', *Academy of Management Journal*, **16**, 312–23.

Dutton, J., Dukerich, J. and Harquail C. (1994), 'Organizational images and member identification', *Administrative Science Quarterly*, **39** (2), 239–63.

Ehnert, I. (2009), *Sustainable Human Resource Management: A Conceptual and Exploratory Analysis from a Paradox Perspective*, Heidelberg: Physica, Springer-Verlag.

Fanning, D. (1990), 'Coping in industries that the public hates', *New York Times*, 19 August, p. 25.

Fombrun, C. (2005), 'A world of reputation, research, analysis and thinking – building corporate reputation through CSR initiatives: evolving standards', *Corporate Reputation Review*, **8** (1), 7–12.

Golden, T. (2007), 'Co-workers who telework and the impact of those in the office: understanding the implications of virtual work for co-worker satisfaction and turnover intention', *Human Relations*, **60** (11), 1641–67.

Gouldner, A. (1960), 'The norm of reciprocity: a preliminary statement', *American Sociological Review*, **25** (2), 161–78.

Guest, D. (2004), 'Flexible employment contracts, the psychological contract and employee outcomes: an analysis and review of the evidence', *International Journal of Management Reviews*, **5/6** (1), 1–19.

Guthrie, J. (2001), 'High involvement work practices, turnover and productivity: evidence from New Zealand', *Academy of Management Journal*, **44** (1), 180–90.

Homans, G. (1961), *Social Behavior*, New York: Harcourt, Brace, and World.

Horwich, G. (1993), 'The role of the for-profit private sector in disaster mitigation and response', *International Journal of Mass Emergences and Disasters*, **11** (2), 189–205.

Huselid, M. (1995), 'The impact of human resource management practices on turnover, productivity and corporate financial performance', *Academy of Management Journal*, **38** (3), 635–72.

ISO (2010), *Draft ISO 26000 Standard for Social Responsibility*, The International Organization for Standardization, available at http://www.iso.org/iso/home.html (accessed 11 May 2010).

Jenkins, R. (2005), 'Globalization, corporate social responsibility and poverty', *International Affairs*, **81** (3), 525–40.

Johnston, P. (2001), 'Corporate responsibility in employment standards in a global knowledge economy', in S. Zadek, N. Hojensgard and P. Raynard (eds), *Perspectives on the New Economy of Corporate Citizenship*, Copenhagen: The Copenhagen Centre, pp. 43–7.

Kamalanabhan, T., Uma, J. and Vasanthi, M. (1999), 'A delphi study of motivational profile of scientists in research and development organizations', *Psychological Reports*, **85** (3), 743–9.

Kelley, H. (1972), 'Attribution in social interaction', in E. Jones, D. Kanouse, H. Kelley, R. Nisbett, S. Valins and B. Weiner (eds), *Attribution: Perceiving the Causes of Behavior*, Morristown, NJ: General Learning Press, pp. 1–26.

Kelley, H. and Michela, J. (1980), 'Attribution theory and research', *Annual Review of Psychology*, **31**, 457–501.

Klein, N. (2001), *No Logo*, London: HarperCollins.

Latham, G. and Pinder, C. (2005), 'Work motivation theory and research at the dawn of the twenty-first century', *The Annual Review of Psychology*, **56**, 485–516.

Le Menestrel M., van den Hove, S. and de Bettignies, H. (2002), 'Processes and consequences in business ethics dilemmas: the oil industry and climate change', *Journal of Business Ethics*, **43** (3), 253–61.

Lee, M. (2008), 'A review of the theories of corporate social responsibility: its evolutionary path and the road ahead', *International Journal of Management Review*, **10** (1), 53–73.

Maslow, A. (1943), 'A theory of human motivation', *Psychological Review*, **50** (4), 370–96.

Masterson, S. (2001), 'A trickle-down model of organizational justice: relating employees' and customers' perceptions of and reactions to fairness', *Journal of Applied Psychology*, **86** (4), 594–604.

Masterson, S., Lewis, K., Goldman, B. and Taylor, M. (2000), 'Integrating justice and social exchange: the differing effects of fair procedures and treatment on work relationships', *Academy of Management Journal*, **43** (4), 738–48.

Matten, D. and Moon, J. (2008), '"Implicit" and "explicit" CSR: a conceptual framework for comparative understanding of corporate social responsibility', *Academy of Management Review*, **33** (2), 404–24.

Mayes, B., Gillespie, T., Johnson, T., Shen, J. and Lin, Y. (in press), 'Effect of human resource practices on perceived organizational support in the People's Republic of China', *International Journal of Human Resource Management*.

McElroy, J. (2001), 'Managing workplace commitment by putting people first', *Human Resource Management Review*, **11** (3), 327–36.

McWilliams, A. and Siegel, D. (2001), 'Corporate social responsibility: a theory of firm perspective', *Academy of Management Review*, **25** (1), 117–27.

McWilliams, A., Siegel, D. and Wright, P. (2006), 'Corporate social responsibility: strategic implications', *Journal of Management Studies*, **43** (1), 1–18.

Meyer, J., Stanley, D., Herscovitch, L. and Topolnytsky, L. (2002), 'Affective, continuance, and normative commitment to the organization, a meta-analysis of antecedents, correlates and consequences', *Journal of Vocational Behaviour*, **61**, 20–52.

Mitchell, R., Agle, B. and Wood, D. (1997), 'Toward a theory of stakeholder identification and salience: defining the principle of who and what really counts', *Academy of Management Review*, **22** (4), 853–86.

Moir, L. (2001), 'What do we mean by corporate social responsibility?', *Corporate Governance*, **1** (2), 16–22.

Nidumolu, R., Prahalad, C. and Rangaswami, M. (2009), 'Why sustainability is now the key driver of innovation', *Harvard Business Review*, **87** (9), 57–64.

Organ, D. (1988), *Organizational Citizenship Behaviour: The Good Soldier Syndrome*, Lexington, Massachusetts/Toronto: D.C. Heath and Company.

Orlitzky, M. and Swanson, D. (2006), 'Socially responsible human resource management', in J. Deckop (ed.), *Human Resource Management Ethics*, Charlotte, North Carolina: Information Age Publishing.

Paul, C. and Siegel, D. (2006), 'Corporate social responsibility and economic performance', *Journal of Productivity Analysis*, **26** (3), 207–11.

Peterson, D. (2004), 'The relationship between perceptions of corporate citizenship and organizational commitment', *Business and Society*, **43**, 296–319.

Pfeffer, J. (2010), 'Building sustainable organizations: the human factor', *Academy of Management Perspectives*, **24** (1), 34–45.

Rhoades, L. and Eisenberger, R. (2002), 'Perceived organizational support: a review of the literature', *Journal of Applied Psychology*, **87** (4), 698–714.

Rhoades, L., Eisenberger, R. and Armeli, S. (2001), 'Affective commitment to the organization: the contribution of perceived organizational support', *Journal of Applied Psychology*, **86** (5), 825–36.

Riordan, C.M., R.D. Gatewood and J. Bill (1997), 'Corporate image: employee reactions and implications for managing corporate social performance', *Journal of Business Ethics*, **16** (4), 401–12.

Rodrigo, P. and Arenas, D. (2008), 'Do employees care about CSR programmes? A typology of employees according to their attitudes', *Journal of Business Ethics*, **83** (2), 265–83.

Royle, T. (2005), 'Realism or idealism? Corporate social responsibility and the employee stakeholder in the global fast-food industry', *Business Ethics: A European Review*, **14** (1), 42–55.

Rupp, D., Ganapathi, J., Aguilera, R. and Williams, C. (2006), 'Employee reactions to corporate social responsibility: an organizational justice framework', *Journal of Organizational Behaviour*, **27** (4), 537–43.

Russo, M. and Fouts, P. (1997), 'A resource-based perspective on corporate environmental performance and profitability', *Academy of Management Journal*, **40** (3), 534–59.

Shore, L. and Wayne, S. (1993), 'Commitment and employee behaviour: comparison of affective commitment and continuance commitment with perceived organizational support', *Journal of Applied Psychology*, **78** (5), 774–80.

Tekleab, A., Takeuchi, R. and Taylor, M. (2005), 'Extending the chain of relationships among organizational justice, social exchange, and employee reactions: the role of contract violations', *Academy of Management Journal*, **48** (1), 146–57.

Turban, D. and Greening, D. (1996), 'Corporate social performance and organizational attractiveness to prospective employees', *Academy of Management Journal*, **40** (3), 658–72.

Waddock, S. and Graves, S. (1997), 'The corporate social performance-financial performance link', *Strategic Management Journal*, **18** (4), 303–19.

Waring, P. and Lewer, J. (2004), 'The impact of socially responsible investment on human resource management: a conceptual framework', *Journal of Business Ethics*, **52** (1), 99–108.

Wayne, S., Shore, M. and Liden, R. (1997), 'Perceived organizational support and leader-member exchange: a social exchange perspective', *Academy of Management Journal*, **40** (1), 82–111.

Whitener, E. (2001), 'Do "high-commitment" human resource practices affect employee commitment? A cross-level analysis using hierarchical linear modelling', *Journal of Management*, **27** (5), 515–35.

Wilcox, T. (2006), 'Human resource development as an element of corporate social responsibility', *Asia Pacific Journal of Human Resources*, **44** (2), 184–96.

Zappalá, G. (2004), 'Corporate citizenship and human resource management: a new tool or a missed opportunity?' *Asia Pacific Journal of Human Resources*, **42** (2), 185–201.

8. Examining the influence of common core virtues in leader-member exchange (LMX): connecting virtue-based leadership traits to sustainable performance in a moderated mediation model

Erich C. Fein and Aharon Tziner

INTRODUCTION

In recent years the number of sustainability related publications in top management journals has increased rapidly, with over 100 articles appearing in the major journals of the Academy of Management on sustainability or sustainability related concepts since 2005. In the majority of these articles, sustainability takes on a social as well as environmental dimension. In accord with the growing recognition that social sustainability is an important complement to environmental and economic sustainability, we focus on social sustainability as related to the quality of relationships within firms. In this chapter we argue that one core mechanism of the sustainability of social systems within firms is based in the reciprocal influence processes within Leader-Member Exchange (LMX). We build on an established core of research that explains how LMX relationships help to produce higher individual performance, which in turn helps drive the economic sustainability of organizations (Gerstner and Day, 1997; Kamder and Van Dyne, 2007; Liden et al., 1997; Sparrowe et al., 2006). However the unique contribution of this chapter is to highlight the under-studied role of individual virtues as moderators in driving sustainable performance and to do so in the context of a moderated mediation model. Within this model we build on an established core of LMX research, but we also nominate a set of primary enacted virtues as unique moderating factors. The consideration of such virtues as psychological strengths has been growing with the rise of positive psychology research (Dahlsgaard et al.,

2005) and investigations into ethical leadership (Ilies et al., 2005), but the connections of these virtues to LMX theory remains underdeveloped. To address this gap we focus on the potential interaction between LMX and virtues as a contribution to the social sustainability of the firm. By doing so we discuss both social and economic sustainability – two of the three elements of the 'triple bottom line' at the interface of business and society (Elkington, 1994).

LEADER-MEMBER EXCHANGE

LMX is an approach to understanding leadership processes where elements of persons and situations are simultaneously considered. This connects LMX theory to the work adjustment literature (Dawis and Lofquist, 1981; Lofquist and Dawis, 1972; Tziner and Elizur, 1987). A primary assumption within LMX theory is that managers do not exhibit the same leadership style to all subordinates, but rather develop different types of social exchange relationships with different employees. These may range from high quality exchanges that extend beyond the employment contract, to low quality relationships based on formal job requirements (Sparrowe et al., 2006). Accordingly employees who enjoy high quality LMX with their superiors typically receive more growth opportunities (Liden et al., 1997; Wayne et al., 2002), emotional support and cooperative interactions than those in low quality LMX relationships (Kamdar and VanDyne, 2007; Liden and Maslyn, 1998). Furthermore because LMX is premised on the notions of social exchange (Blau, 1964) and reciprocity (Adams, 1965), subordinates offered high quality LMX are expected to feel compelled to reciprocate the positive treatment they receive from their supervisor. Here we note that the notion of mutual sustainability is inherent to the exchange within high quality LMX relationships. This is supported by core tenets within LMX theory, which emphasize the development and maintenance of an ongoing exchange relationship between leaders and members whereby both parties mutually sustain one another (Sparrowe et al., 2006; Sparrowe and Liden, 1997; Wang et al., 2005). The positive affect, respect, loyalty and perceived obligation characteristic of high quality LMX should motivate better job performance and organizational citizenship behaviours such as working overtime and offering extra help to coworkers and supervisors (Kamdar and Van Dyne, 2007). However individual differences can moderate the effectiveness of LMX, and preferences for specific leadership behaviours may be affected by the values inherent in a particular cultural and national environment (Fein et al., 2010).

LMX theory has had a long history and has produced an abundance

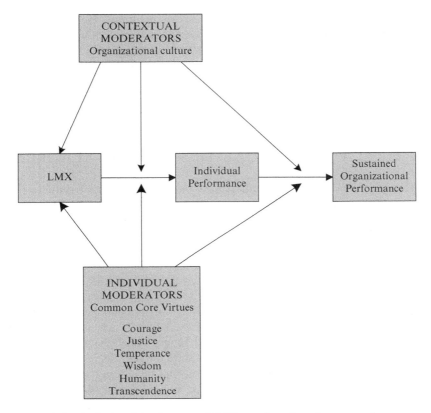

Figure 8.1   Relationships between LMX, moderating virtues, and sustainable performance

of empirical support, but there is still a lack of clarity in regard to many antecedents, consequences and moderating conditions surrounding the leader-member relationship (Van Breukelen et al., 2006). Several moderators of the LMX performance relationship have been proposed, including perceived organizational support (Erdogan and Enders, 2007), employee traits such as extraversion (Bauer et al., 2006), communication (Kacmar et al., 2003) and other follower characteristics (Zhu et al., 2009). We would add elements of individuals' value structures to this list of potential moderators.

In this chapter we address a specific weakness in LMX research: namely that values-based moderators and correlates of LMX have been under-specified at both the individual and organizational levels. Figure 8.1 represents our proposed relationships between LMX, individual and contextual moderators, and performance outcomes in organizations. Here we suggest there are direct effects from several contextual and individual factors on LMX, including paths from the core virtues as a key contribution of this chapter. In addition, and as another point of unique contribution, we depict these contextual and individual factors as both first and second stage moderators of the relationship between LMX, individual performance, and organizational performance in a moderated mediation model.

THE RELATIONAL QUALITIES OF GOOD LEADERS

There is evidence that good leadership by its nature can contribute to the sustainability of organizations. For example, leadership competencies, which are clusters of skills and knowledge essential to good leadership behaviours, are based somewhat in primary social skills (Bernardin, 2007). Because such competencies are applied in the dynamic context of relationships across time, accomplished leaders may have a competitive advantage in producing relationships that are sustainable. Furthermore accomplished leaders may be particularly skilled at treating people with individually focused positive regard, which can result in more effective long-term influence. Certain theories of leadership, such as transformational leadership theory (Antonakis and House, 2002; Avolio and Bass, 1991) and servant leadership (Blanchard and Hodges, 2003) are explicit in emphasizing the means that leaders can use in developing and caring for individuals within their scope of influence. Indeed the classic behavioural dimensions of consideration and the initiation of structure are based in powerful assumptions regarding the welfare of individuals in organizations (Judge et al., 2004). Thus underpinning our model in Figure 8.1, we assert the following proposition:

Proposition 1:   Leadership is connected to sustainable performance through positive relationships.

The concept of consideration was one of two behavioural meta concepts to emerge from the Ohio State leadership studies in the 1950s (Judge et al., 2004). Later theories such as Leader-Member Exchange have produced more detailed descriptions of how leaders may interact with their environments, and also how they engage in transactional as well as consideration based behaviours (Van Breukelen et al., 2006). Several scholars suggest that these later contingency approaches improve the applicability of leadership models to the workplace (Dienesch and Liden, 1986; Liden et al., 1997), although more recent scholarship argues that the simplicity of consideration based interventions result in better utility, especially for developing managers with limited experience (Yukl et al., 2002). For instance, Tziner and Vardi (1983) reported that performance effectiveness was high among tank crews when people orientation (that is, a consideration based style) of commanders was combined with low cohesiveness, and people oriented and task oriented styles were exhibited with highly cohesive crews. In addition there is also evidence that the strength of consideration based behaviours varies across cultures (House et al., 2004; Javidian and House, 2001; Offerman and Hellman, 1997). A basic premise in our approach is that effective leaders will generally attempt to develop positive exchange relationships with the individuals they supervise. This is consistent with a prescriptive dimension of LMX that suggests leaders at least try to develop high quality exchange relationships with most of their subordinates (Graen and Uhl-Bien, 1995). In this regard although LMX theory has been criticized for paying little attention to possible moderators of the relationship between LMX, job performance and organizational citizenship, there are strong elements of consideration within LMX (Schriesheim et al., 2000).

In addition to the concept of consideration there are other perspectives that relate the nature of a leader's relational qualities with follower outcomes. One recent example is the work of Ilies et al. (2005) on the concept of authentic leadership, which is largely related to the connections between qualities in the leader-subordinate relationship and desired outcomes. Specifically this perspective examines well-being, where behaviours such as authentic behaviours and authentic relational orientation are drawn from authenticity theory (Ilies et al., 2005). Such behavioural factors are hypothesized to connect with positive organizational outcomes and individual well-being (Schyns et al., 2007). A more recent example relates to virtuous outcomes within leadership behaviours (Neubert et al., 2009). Finally various theories of leadership discuss the issue of credibility as a linchpin in the effectiveness of leadership influence processes, most notably from a communications-based perspective (Gilley and Dixon, 2008). Here the emphasis is generally on the reliability and trust in the leader over time. However within each of these various leadership concepts, the links to existing leadership theories and practice need further explication. Also the concepts tend to be uni-dimensional, in the sense of considering either individual differences or contextual elements in isolation, which may prove to offer limited utility. We feel that including the effects of the core virtues within a comprehensive multi-level model as displayed in Figure 8.1 would enhance the utility of contextual moderators and other individual differences as moderators.

INCORPORATING ORGANIZATIONAL CONTEXT

The relationship between organizational culture and leadership has received limited attention in the empirical leadership literature (Xenikou and Simosi, 2006). Some studies have shown that specific leadership behaviours are associated with distinct organizational cultural characteristics (Lok and Crawford, 1999; Tsui et al., 2006). Moreover organizational culture might be a contextual factor leading to the emergence of a specific leadership style (Pillai, 1995). Schein (2004) even claims that organizational culture controls the manager more than the manager controls the culture, via the automatic sense making processes. Therefore although LMX is based on the dyadic employee-manager interaction, it also is likely to be affected by cultural dimensions, which is displayed in Figure 8.1.

According to Schein the most salient defining feature of culture is a pattern of shared basic assumptions (2004), which include artifacts, or visible structures within organizations, espoused values and beliefs, and the underlying assumptions and beliefs that shape thinking and action within the organization. Organizational culture has also been defined as observed behavioural regularities and norms, which are connected to cognitive habits and mental models. Culture in this sense is viewed in the literature as a multifaceted abstraction with several dimensions that have varying degrees and direction of effect on both employees' behaviour (Sheridan, 1992) and organizational performance (Denison, 1984).

In respect to our model proposed in Figure 8.1, the performance management system of an organization can be considered a cultural artifact. Within this system, leadership development programs and the general balance between developmental versus control efforts within performance management systems can also be thought of as cultural artifacts. At the second level of culture, espoused beliefs that could be related to these artifacts could be value statements such as 'we take care of our people' and 'this organization invests in training.' There are deeper dimensions of belief around which shared basic assumptions form, including beliefs related to the nature of human beings in general, the nature of activity within organizations, and the nature of human relationships (Schein, 2004). Important questions related to these themes might revolve around the basic trustworthiness of employees and how to develop correct ways of interaction between managers and subordinates. Finally, as illustrated in Figure 8.1, we note that leaders can embed and transmit culture through various types of leadership activities including LMX. Some of these are particularly salient to LMX concerns, such as the types of behaviours that leaders attend to and measure, which people leaders select for promotion and higher degrees of investment such as more focused teaching and coaching, and, at a secondary level, how leaders design performance management systems. Therefore we include organizational culture as a contextual moderator in Figure 8.1 and distinguish two moderating effects, one for the relationship between LMX and individual performance and a second moderating force between individual performance and sustainable organizational performance.

UNDERSTANDING VALUES AND VIRTUE

The study of values is important in organizations because knowing about individual and group level value structures can help managers understand and predict attitudes, motivational processes and important organizational outcomes (Meglino and Ravlin, 1998). Many types of connections between values and work related behaviours have been documented (Dawis, 1991; Rokeach, 1973) and individual level value constructs have played important roles in need based theories of motivation such as Self-Determination Theory (Deci and Ryan, 2002). Values may be defined as personal beliefs in the relative desirability of different modes of conduct and end states of achievement (Rokeach, 1973). In addition to understanding values as beliefs, values can be considered as transformations of psychological need (Super, 1995) where values may be aligned to categories of needs, and as such may be considered 'second-order needs' (Loftquist and Dawis, 1972). We feel that values are best defined as belief structures that are also connected to particular categories of needs (Tziner and Elizur, 1987). As such, values represent common elements in need dimensions and they serve as reference dimensions for the description of needs. Through their connection to needs, values can produce states of psychological tension, which lead to cognition, affect, and behaviour. Also particular values operate together as elements of individuals' value systems, which are collections of beliefs that together address the desirability of multiple modes of conduct and end states (Rokeach, 1973). Such value systems can be particularly effective at predicting important work-related behaviours (Maio and Olson, 1998; Schwartz and Bilsky, 1990), and there is sound evidence that values promote positive work relationships (Dawis, 1991; Meglino and Ravlin, 1998). This leads to a second proposition to illustrate the logic within Figure 8.1:

Proposition 2: Pro-social values contribute to positive relationships.

We note that values are related to traits and interests because each of these constructs is derived from needs (Super, 1995). Therefore psychological needs serve as antecedents for traits (general patterns of behaviour, affect, and cognition), interests (specific objects and associated behaviours) and values. Because values serve as a representation and transformation of needs, they are enduring, but because they address multiple modes of conduct or end states of existence, they are broader and more basic than interests. Finally, based on this network of relationships – namely, connections between psychological needs, and antecedent traits, values, and interests – values can be thought of as standards that determine behaviour across a wide range of situations.

While values are similar to virtues there are some important differences. Values are transformations of needs and represent preferences for particular types of conduct or end states. Virtues are similar, in that they represent types of conduct or typical patterns of behaviour. However the virtues refer to character strengths, implying that an individual typically manifests a category of positive or pro social behaviours across multiple situations and time. In this sense the virtues are akin to personality traits, which refer to relatively fixed patterns of behaviour across situations. Rather than simply expressing preferences for ways of behaving, individuals who possess particular virtues have shown a consistent pattern of acting on their values for certain types of behaviours and goals. In fact this recognition of the habit of taking appropriate action is a distinctive component of the virtues and of the virtue ethics tradition.

Based on our objective in understanding the connections between values and the LMX-performance relationship, we have chosen to focus on several distinctions drawn by Solomon (1999) in distinguishing between individual values and the enactment of these values. According to Solomon (1999) the concept of virtue is essentially the consistent enactment of values. Thus a virtuous leader is proactive and consistently reliable in respect to positive behaviour. In making sense of how virtues are manifest we turn to two key elements that must be considered under traditional notions of virtue ethics (Solomon, 1999). First, the notion of a collection or synthesis of virtues must be considered because virtues cannot exist in isolation. As individuals have systems of values, these values are also enacted within a synthesis of virtues so that many virtues work together and in balance to form a coherent whole. Thus in a virtuous person there exists a full range of individual virtues (Solomon, 1999).

Second, there are many types of specific behaviours that might manifest an individual's virtue, and the frequency and range of such behaviours is determined by interactions between the individual and the environment. For example, contentment and courage can both be considered virtues, yet the first is manifest during opportunity and the latter during situations of danger. The notion of positive moral behaviour must also be considered, for if values are to result in virtue they must be connected to positive outcomes for individuals and their social groups. From the Aristotelian tradition, modern concepts of virtue ethics have inherited the notion of the organization as a community rather than a collection of autonomous, self-sufficient individuals. Thus for the virtues to be considered good, they must collectively contribute to organizational viability. Taking the first notion of coherence and a synthesis of enacted values, as well as this idea of collective benefit into account, we can articulate a framework for individual virtue in the context of the LMX-performance relationship. Referring back to Figure 8.1, we place the core virtues as individual moderators of the relationship between LMX and individual performance and as a moderating force between individual performance and sustainable organizational performance. This logic, which underlies the connection between values and virtues leads to our third proposition:

Proposition 3:   Consistently enacted values may be conceptualized as virtues.

HISTORIC CORE VIRTUES

There is strong evidence that a relatively small set of virtues, which include the classic or cardinal virtues, have been central components of human wellness throughout cultures and history. Therefore rather than proposing an exhaustive list of virtues within our model, we follow the work of Dahlsgaard et al. (2005), who found six core virtues which are generally common across the philosophical and religious traditions of Western, South Asian and Confucian civilizations. This is why we label these as 'common core virtues' in Figure 8.1. These virtues include the four cardinal virtues of Plato and Aristotle, which are courage, justice, temperance and wisdom, but also embrace the virtues of humanity and transcendence. Of these, *courage* relates to decisive goal striving under opposition, *justice* refers to civil strengths that promote community, *temperance* refers to character strengths that allow one to self-regulate against excess and *wisdom* relates to cognitive strengths in learning and the use of important knowledge (Dahlsgaard et al., 2005). In addition, the virtue of *humanity* is discussed as a strength that enables the care of others, and *transcendence* is considered as a set of strengths that help one forge connections beyond the self to provide meaning (Dahlsgaard et al., 2005). We refer back to the earlier section of this chapter on the relational quality of good leaders, specifically the notion of consideration based behaviours, to illustrate that at least one of these virtues – that of humanity – has long been connected with effective leadership processes. We next illustrate the role of other virtues in our model by reference to two specific virtues that have appeared as important factors within the sustainability literature – the virtues of temperance and transcendence.

In respect to temperance, the notion of control of excess appears mostly in ecological sustainability contexts external to firms (Egri and Herman, 2000; Waldman and Siegel, 2008). However Waldman also defends the notion that action based in moral values can be a strong driver of socially sustainable behaviour. He argues that moral conviction can be a powerful force in producing sustainability and suggests that those leaders with a disposition towards responsibility are able to consistently temper their own behaviours, and their decisions on behalf of organizations, through personal means. Here we note that the notion of temperance understood as a cardinal virtue means precisely this idea – that one should be able to self-regulate one's own passions. The concept of temperance along with the other cardinal virtues has underpinned what has been considered morally good behaviour for centuries across several major cultural traditions of the world, and we feel it has much to offer research and practice on sustainability.

As another example, Egri and Herman (2000) discuss the value of transcendence in relation to leaders' pro sustainability orientations in the North American environmental sector, and they provide evidence that transcendent values are related to positive environmentally sustainable leadership. While the focus of sustainability may be external and environmental, it may also be internal to the firm and social. In our model we propose an internal, employee-centric model of sustainability that is still consistent with the underlying concerns for sustainability expressed by many ecological models. Although Egri and Herman discuss the value of self-transcendence in relation to external environmental sustainability, we discuss the virtue of transcendence in relation to the sustainability of social systems within firms. It makes sense that the same values, beliefs, and assumptions that have been shown to underpin change efforts to promote environmental sustainability would also drive leadership processes that help sustain the social relationships within firms. Therefore by implication the virtue of transcendence should play an important role in socially sustainable behaviours within firms.

In addition to the virtues of humanity, temperance and transcendence, there are the three remaining cardinal virtues of justice, wisdom and courage. The potential connections of these virtues to leadership and sustainability have also been addressed in the management literature. In respect to justice, which can be considered the virtue that best promotes civil strength and stability, the risk management literature in particular relates to the positive or altruistic motivation by some leaders to punish corporate wrongdoing that threatens the sustainability of firms. Here the notion is proposed that good leadership requires leaders and government officials to exert pressure on companies to bear the costs of managing risks that threaten sustainability and potentially to provide sanctions to motivate compliance in effective sustainability management. For example, in the case of wrongdoing by WorldCom/MCI the justice motivated responses of a former US Attorney General show effective leadership because the responses at a national level influenced similar responses from state officials in Oklahoma (Anderson, 2005).

The virtue of wisdom has also been strongly displayed in areas of corporate leadership. One example is the effective promotion of Life Cycle Assessment (LCA) processes and Design for Environment (DfE) risk management programs (Anderson, 2005). This notion of corporate direction at companies such as Procter and Gamble, a world leader in LCA, shows a strong resonance with wisdom. There is evidence that corporate leaders in companies such as Procter and Gamble show their influence at multiple levels of their organizations in reducing pollution while implementing DfE programs (Anderson, 2005).

Finally individual leader-member relationships can be strongly affected by the exercise of the final cardinal virtue of courage. In particular, within the practice of performance management in leader-member dyads the virtue of courage is important to promote the application of effective performance management skills, such as in the case of delivering negative feedback to subordinates. For example, with the collaborative performance coaching processes, leaders must ask questions to diagnose performance problems and strive to provide advice to correct poor performance. Aguinis (2012) notes that providing negative feedback is critical to organizational performance, yet leaders are often afraid to do so because of potential negative employee reactions, consequences for the leader-member work relationship, and defensiveness concerning future feedback. We note that the exercise of providing negative feedback in spite of these potential dangers calls for the virtue of courage, which is related to the pursuit of action under perceived opposition.

TESTABLE COMPONENTS OF A MODERATED MEDIATION MODEL

In our model, the mediating role of individual performance is primarily affected by LMX, which is influenced by contextual and individual moderators. In this sense we keep with the tradition that leader-follower outcomes are a specific type of performance that has received extensive attention (Ilies et al., 2005; Schyns et al., 2007). Furthermore within the leadership literature there are many studies that examine connections between traits and leader behaviours (De Hoogh et al., 2005; Judge and Bono, 2000). While there is no shortage of work that examines connections between leadership and traits, there is less work that considers the relationships between values, value related traits such as the core virtues, and consequent leadership behaviours (Szabo et al., 2001). With the exception of several recent studies (for example, Kark and Van Dijk, 2007) there is a need in the leadership literature to address the influence of personal values on leadership styles of managers. Also when existing studies have examined connections between leadership behaviour and value structures, these connections have frequently been examined from the perspective of shared values (Offermann and Hellman, 1997). An even smaller number of studies have addressed connections between personal level values and leadership from a cross cultural perspective. We hope that this gap may be addressed by empirical research based on the relationships in Figure 8.1, because there is strong evidence that the six core virtues are applicable across cultures (Dahlsgaard et al., 2005).

To further articulate our contribution, we here unite the three propositions which underpin the logic behind Figure 8.1:

Proposition 1: *Leadership is connected to sustainable performance through positive relationships.*

Proposition 2: *Pro-social values contribute to positive relationships.*

Proposition 3: *Consistently enacted values may be conceptualized as virtues.*

Together these propositions lead to the central claim of our chapter, which is that the virtues contribute to the link between leadership and sustainable performance in organizations. We now articulate how virtues strengthen these links between leadership and sustainable performance through the use of a moderated mediation model.

In our model, which is illustrated in Figure 8.1, we specifically posit direct effects and multiple moderating effects between LMX, virtues and values, organizational culture, and performance. However, rather than propose initial empirical tests between all six of the virtues and the LMX-performance relationship, we suggest that empirical work begin with the four cardinal virtues of courage, justice, temperance, and wisdom. This is because there are existing scales with reasonable psychometric properties for investigating these four virtues (Riggio et al., 2010) and there are measures of other constructs such as justice and conscientiousness that could serve as useful components of validation studies. Here wisdom (termed 'prudence') is operationalized as balancing information across multiple decision criteria to do what is appropriate in a given situation (for example, 'Considers a problem from all angles and reaches the best decision for all parties involved'). Courage (termed 'fortitude') is operationalized as perseverance under adversity or fear to produce the best possible outcomes (for example, 'Would rather risk his/her job than do something that was unjust'). Temperance is operationalized as self-control with the moderation of emotions and psychological and physical appetites (for example, 'Is not overly concerned with his/her own accomplishments'). Finally justice is operationalized as seeking to give what is deserved and respecting the welfare of others (for example, 'Gives credit to others when credit is due') (Riggio et al., 2010).

We began hypothesis generation with our initial proposal that individual components of values and virtue are considered to have direct effects on LMX because virtuous leaders and followers will be considerate of the mutual obligations to the organization as well as to each other. This led to several hypotheses related to direct effects of leader and member virtues on LMX levels related to group and organizational performance:

H1a: *The virtue of **courage** will display a direct positive effect on LMX level.*

H1b: *The virtue of **justice** will display a direct positive effect on LMX level.*

H1c: *The virtue of **temperance** will display a direct positive effect on LMX level.*

H1d: *The virtue of **wisdom** will display a direct positive effect on LMX level.*

In our model we propose that virtue will have moderating effects between LMX and individual performance and between individual performance and organizational performance. These connections are justified by the ample evidence that shows LMX is related to individual and group level performance. This also illustrates the notions of first stage and second stage moderation for the enacted virtues, which are key propositions within this chapter. Following the logic of Edwards and Lambert (2007), a first stage moderation effect occurs when a variable changes the relationship between an antecedent and another variable that serves as a mediator in a model. This leads to the following hypotheses.

*H2a: The virtue of **courage** will serve as a first stage moderator between LMX and individual performance.*

*H2b: The virtue of **justice** will serve as a first stage moderator between LMX and individual performance.*

*H2c: The virtue of **temperance** will serve as a first stage moderator between LMX and individual performance.*

*H2d: The virtue of **wisdom** will serve as a first stage moderator between LMX and individual performance.*

In our model based on the empirical support of LMX theory, we also propose that virtue will have moderating effects between individual performance and group performance. This illustrates the notion of second stage moderation for the enacted virtues, which following the logic of Edwards and Lambert (2007) occurs when a variable changes the relationship between the mediating variable and the outcome variable in a model. This leads to the following hypotheses, which we note will require multilevel methods for investigation:

*H3a: The virtue of **courage** will serve as a second stage moderator between individual performance and group performance.*

*H3b: The virtue of **justice** will serve as a second stage moderator between individual performance and group performance.*

*H3c: The virtue of **temperance** will serve as a second stage moderator between individual performance and group performance.*

*H3d: The virtue of **wisdom** will serve as a second stage moderator between individual performance and group performance.*

In conclusion we believe that this model, and subsequent tests of this model, have the potential to fuel promising research into new areas. Such emergent findings may offer a better understanding not only of how the quality of social exchange between a leader and subordinates (LMX) channels its impact on the sustainability of organization performance, which is a process mediated by individual performance, but also how the core virtues, as under-studied individual factors, may moderate these relationships. Although many of these enacted virtues have not been invoked in the past while studying LMX-behavioural outcomes connections, they are certainly part of what DeGeorge (2011) calls the new mandate for business, which illustrates the developing expectation that business organizations must pay attention to the ethical quality of their actions, especially as related to sustainability outcomes. Furthermore we advocate these empirical tests within a moderated mediation model. In recent years the inclusion and testing of both moderation and mediation process together has become an important contribution to research in the social sciences (Edwards and Lambert, 2007). We note that it will be necessary to employ measures of the core virtues along with measures of established constructs such as organizational justice and organizational commitment to conduct validation research in this area. However with the ubiquitous presence of the core virtues across cultures, such a program may advance cross cultural studies of leadership in a positive psychology framework. To further such a research program we hope that the hypotheses proposed in this paper will provide fruitful starting points for empirical investigations.

REFERENCES

Adams, J.S. (1965), 'Inequity in social exchange', in L. Berkowitz (ed.), *Advances in Experimental Social Psychology*, New York: Academic Press, **2**, pp. 267–99.

Aguinis, H. (2012), *Performance Management*, 3rd edn, Upper Saddle River, NJ: Pearson Prentice Hall.

Anderson, D.R. (2005), *Corporate Survival: The Critical Importance of Sustainability Risk Management*, New York: iUniverse.

Antonakis, J. and House, R.J. (2002), 'The full-range leadership theory: the way forward', in Bruce J. Avolio and Francis J. Yammarino (eds), *Transformational and Charismatic Leadership: The Road Ahead*, New York: JAI Press, pp. 3–34.

Avolio, B.J. and Bass, B.M. (1991), *A Manual for Full-Range Leadership Development*, Binghamton, NY: Center for Leadership Studies.

Bauer, T.N., Erdogan, B., Liden, R. and Wayne, S. (2006), 'A longitudinal study of the moderating role of extraversion: LMX, performance, and turnover during new executive development', *Journal of Applied Psychology*, **91**, 298–310.

Bernardin, H.J. (2007), *Human Resource Management*, 4th edn, New York: McGraw Hill.

Blanchard, K. and Hodges, P. (2003), *The Servant Leader*, Nashville, TN: J. Countryman.

Blau, P. (1964), *Exchange and Power in Social Life*, New York: John Wiley & Sons.

Dahlsgaard, K., Peterson, C. and Seligman, M.E.P. (2005), 'Shared virtue: the convergence of valued human strengths across culture and history', *Review of General Psychology*, **9** (3), 203–13.

Dawis, R. and Lofquist, L. (1981), *Job Satisfaction and Work Adjustment: Implications for Vocational Education*, Columbus, US: The Ohio State University.

Dawis, R.V. (1991), 'Vocational interests, values, and preferences', in M.D. Dunnette and L.M. Hough (eds), *Handbook of Industrial and Organizational Psychology, Vol. 2*, 2nd edn, Palo Alto, CA: Consulting Psychologists Press.

Deci, E.L. and Ryan, R.M. (2002), 'Self-determination research: reflections and future directions', in Edward L. Deci and Richard M. Ryan (eds), *Handbook of Self-Determination Research*, Rochester, NY: University of Rochester Press.

DeGeorge, R. (2011), *Business Ethics*, 7th edn, Upper Saddle River, NJ: Pearson Education.

DeHoogh, A.H.B., Den Hartog, D. and Koopman, P.L. (2005), 'Linking the big five-factors of personality to charismatic and transactional leadership: perceived dynamic work environment as a moderator', *Journal of Organizational Behavior*, **26** (7), 839–65.

Denison, D.R. (1984), 'Bringing corporate culture to the bottom line', *Organizational Dynamics*, **13**, 5–22.

Dienesch, R.M. and Liden, R.C. (1986), 'Leader-member exchange model of leadership: a critique and further development', *Academy of Management Review*, **11** (3), 618–34.

Edwards, J.R. and Lambert, S. (2007), 'Methods for integrating moderation and mediation: a general analytical framework using moderated path analysis', *Psychological Methods*, **12** (1), 1–22.

Egri, C.P. and Herman, S. (2000), 'Leadership in the North American environmental sector: values, leadership styles, and context of environmental leaders and their organizations', *Academy of Management Journal*, **43** (4), 571–604.

Elkington, J. (1994), 'Toward the sustainable corporation: win-win-win business strategies for sustainable development', *California Management Review*, **36** (2), 90–100.

Erdogan, B. and Enders, J. (2007), 'Support from the top: supervisors' perceived organizational support as a moderator of leader-member exchange to satisfaction and performance relationships', *Journal of Applied Psychology*, **92** (2), 321–30.

Fein, E.C., Tziner, A. and Vasiliu, C. (2010), 'Age cohort effects, gender, and Romanian leadership preferences', *Journal of Management Development*, **29**, 364–76.

Gerstner, C.R. and Day, D. (1997), 'Meta-analytic review of leader-member exchange theory: correlates and construct issues', *Journal of Applied Psychology*, **82**, 827–44.

Gilley, A. and Dixon, P. (2008), 'Characteristics of leadership effectiveness: implementing change and driving innovation in organizations', *Human Resource Development Quarterly*, **19** (2), 153–69.

Graen, G.B. and Uhl-Bien, M. (1995), 'Relationship-based approach to leadership: development of leader-member exchange (LMX) theory of leadership over 25 years: applying a multi-level multi-domain perspective', *The Leadership Quarterly*, **6** (2), 219–47.

House, R.J., Hanges, P.J., Javidan, M. and Dorfman, P.W. (2004), *Leadership, Culture, and Organizations: The GLOBE Study of 62 Societies*, Thousand Oaks, CA: Sage.

Ilies, R., Morgeson, F. and Nahrgang, J. (2005), 'Authentic leadership and eudaemonic well-being: understanding leader-follower outcomes', *Leadership Quarterly*, **16** (3), 373–94.

Javidan, M. and House, R.P. (2001), 'Cultural acumen for the global manager: lessons from project GLOBE', *Organizational Dynamics*, **29** (4).

Judge, T.A. and Bono, J.E. (2000), 'Five-factor model of personality and transformational leadership', *Journal of Applied Psychology*, **85** (5), 751–65.

Judge, T.A., Piccolo, R.F. and Ilies, R. (2004), 'The forgotten ones? The validity of consideration and initiating structure in leadership research', *Journal of Applied Psychology*, **89** (1), 36–51.

Kacmar, K.M., Witt, L., Zivunska, S. and Gully, S. (2003), 'The interactive effect of leader-member exchange and communication frequency on performance ratings', *Journal of Applied Psychology*, **88**, 764–72.

Kamdar, D. and Van Dyne, L. (2007), 'The joint effects of personality and workplace social exchange relationships in predicting task performance and citizenship performance', *Journal of Applied Psychology*, **92** (5), 1286–98.

Kark, R. and Van Dijk, D. (2007), 'Motivation to lead, motivation to follow: the role of self-regulatory focus in leadership processes', *Academy of Management Review*, **32** (2), 500–528.

Liden, R.C. and Maslyn, J.M. (1998), 'Multidimensionality of leader-member exchange: an empirical assessment through scale development', *Journal of Management*, **24** (1), 43–72.

Liden, R.C., Sparrowe, R.T. and Wayne, S. (1997), 'Leader-member exchange theory: the past and potential for the future', in G.R. Ferris (ed.), *Research in Personnel and Human Resources Management*, **15**, 47–119.

Lofquist, L.H. and Dawis, R. (1972), 'Applications of the theory of work adjustment to rehabilitation and counseling', in *Minnesota Studies in Vocational Rehabilitation*, University of Minnesota.

Lok, P. and Crawford, J. (1999), 'The relationship between commitment and organizational culture, subculture, leadership style and job satisfaction in organizational change and development', *Leadership and Organization Development Journal*, **20**, 365–73.

Maio, G.R. and Olson, J. (1998), 'Values as truisms: evidence and implications', *Journal of Personality and Social Psychology*, **74** (2), 294–311.

Meglino, B.M. and Ravlin, E.C. (1998), 'Individual values in organizations: concepts, controversies, and research', *Journal of Management*, **24** (3).

Neubert, M., Carlson, D. et al. (2009), 'The virtuous influence of ethical leadership behavior: evidence from the field', *Journal of Business Ethics*, **90** (2), 157–70.

Offermann, L.R. and Hellmann, P. (1997), 'Culture's consequences for leadership behavior: national values in action', *Journal of Cross-Cultural Psychology*, **28** (3), 342–51.

Pillai, R. (1995), 'Context and charisma: the role of organic structure, collectivism, and crisis in the emergence of charismatic leadership', *Academy of Management Proceedings*, 332–6.

Riggio, R.E., Zhu, W., Reina, C. and Maroosis, J.A. (2010), 'Virtue-based measurement of ethical leadership: the leadership virtues questionnaire', *Consulting Psychology Journal: Practice and Research*, **62** (4), 235–50.

Rokeach, M. (1973), *The Nature of Human Values*, New York: Free Press.

Schein, E.H. (2004), *Organizational Culture and Leadership*, 3rd edn, San Francisco: Jossey-Bass.

Schreisheim, C.A., Castro, S. and Yammarino, F.J. (2000), 'Investigating contingencies: an examination of the impact of span of supervision and upward controllingness on leader-member exchange using traditional and multivariate within and between entities analysis', *Journal of Applied Psychology*, **85**, 659–77.

Schwartz, S.H. and Bilsky, W. (1990), 'Toward a theory of the universal content and structure of values: extensions and cross-cultural replications', *Journal of Personality and Social Psychology*, **58** (5), 878–91.

Schyns, G., Felfe, J. and Blank, H. (2007), 'Is charisma hyper-romanticism? Empirical evidence from new data and a meta-analysis', *Applied Psychology: An International Review*, **56** (4), 505–25.

Sheridan, J.E. (1992), 'Organizational culture and employee retention', *Academy of Management Journal*, **35**, 1036–1056.

Solomon, R. (1999), *A Better Way To Think About Business*, London: Oxford University Press.

Sparrowe, R.T. and Liden, R.C. (1997), 'Process and structure in leader-member exchange', *Academy of Management Review*, **22**, 522–52.

Sparrowe, R.T., Soetjipto, B. and Kraimer, M. (2006), 'Do leaders' influence tactics relate to members' helping behavior? It depends on the quality of the relationship', *Academy of Management Journal*, **49** (6), 1194–1208.

Super, D.E. (1995), 'Values: their nature, assessment, and practical use', in D.E. Super and B. Sverko (eds), *Life Roles, Values, and Careers: International Findings of the Work Importance Study*, San Francisco: Jossey-Bass.

Szabo, E., Reber, G., Weibler, J., Brodbeck, F. and Wunderer, R. (2001), 'Values and behavior orientation in leadership studies: reflections based on findings in three German-speaking countries', *Leadership Quarterly*, **12** (2), 219–44.

Tsui, A.S., Zhang, Z., Wang, H., Xin, K. and Wu, J. (2006), 'Unpacking the relationship between CEO leadership behavior and organizational culture', *Leadership Quarterly*, **17** (2), 113–37.

Tziner, A. and Elizur, D. (1987), 'Work values as "reinforcer groups": is the underlying structure method free?', *Quality and Quantity*, **21**, 377–92.

Tziner, A. and Vardi, Y. (1983), 'Ability as a moderator between cohesiveness and tank crews' performance', *Journal of Occupational Behavior*, **4** (2), 137–43.

van Breukelen, W., Schyns, B. et al. (2006), 'Leader-member exchange theory and research: accomplishments and future challenges', *Leadership*, **2** (3), 295–316.

Waldman, D.A. and Siegel, D. (2008), 'Defining the socially responsible leader', *Leadership Quarterly*, **19** (1), 117–31.

Wang, H., Law, K., Hackett, R., Wang, D. and Chen, Z. (2005), 'Leader-member exchange as a mediator of the relationship between transformational leadership and followers' performance and organizational citizenship behavior', *Academy of Management Journal*, **48**, 420–32.

Wayne, S.J., Shore, L., Bommer, W. and Tetrick, L. (2002), 'The role of fair treatment and rewards perceptions of organizational support and leader-member exchange', *Journal of Applied Psychology*, **87**, 590–98.

Xenikou, A. and Simosi, M. (2006), 'Organizational culture and transformational leadership as predictors of business unit performance', *Journal of Managerial Psychology*, **21**, 566–79.

Yukl, G., Gordon, A. and Tabor, T. (2002), 'A hierarchical taxonomy of leadership behavior: integrating a half century of behavior research', *Journal of Leadership & Organizational Studies*, **9** (1), 15–32.

Zhu, W., Avolio, B.J. and Walumba, F. (2009), 'Moderating role of follower characteristics with transformational leadership and follower work engagement', *Group & Organization Management*, **34** (5), 590–619.

9. Strategic risk assessment for pursuing sustainable business in the construction industry: diagnostic models

Nicholas Chileshe, Lou Wilson, Jian Zuo, George Zillante and Stephen Pullen

INTRODUCTION

This chapter provides a broad overview of the sustainable business in practice, highlighting the necessary strategic risk assessment models desirable for pursuing sustainable business in the construction industry. Synergies are highlighted between the disciplines of project management through the underlying concepts of risk management, strategic management and organization behaviour (OB) in exploring the diagnostic models for pursuing sustainable business.

The chapter reviews the literature and describes the strategic risk assessment framework in the form of a diagnostic model: a three dimensional framework which can be used for diagnosing the effectiveness of construction organizations intending to pursue sustainable business practices and other social systems. The framework can then be used to select an appropriate intervention. The concepts of agency and structure using the underlying saturation theory are utilized to provide the elements of a model to assess risk in the construction industry. In identifying the challenges associated with pursuing sustainable business, this chapter discusses the strategic risk assessment from two perspectives, namely the outer and inner environment. The factors that need to be considered within the outer environment are political; economic and social, while organizations seek to pursue sustainable businesses are considered to reside within the inner environments and could inherently be affected or influenced by a number of factors such as structure; cultural and political.

THE NECESSITY OF STRATEGIC RISK ASSESSMENT

At the 2011 seminar organized by Zero Waste SA, Adelaide Thinkers in Residence and 5000+ series, Paul Hawken, the renowned environmentalist, entrepreneur, journalist and author, stated 'everything we do every day "as individuals" is about sustainability' (Hawken, 2011). Hawken further observed that in making a business case for sustainable practices, organizations had to embrace the economic, ecological and sustainability issues. The basic premise or tenet was that sustainability was about systems thinking. Most importantly, the view was that businesses hold the future of the planet in their hands. Hawken (2011) pointed out that fundamental notions about commerce and its role in shaping our future are transforming, and far-sighted companies are seizing the opportunity to not only survive but to prosper. It is against that background that the basis of this chapter is formed. In realizing the views of Hawken, this chapter suggests that strategic risk assessment models are not only desirable but necessary for pursuing sustainable business in the construction industry.

Calandro and Lane (2006) state that the accelerating growth in global risk levels has led to an intense current demand for risk management solutions. While the need for pursuing a sustainable business practice might be taken within the local context, there are a number of firms or organizations which seek to diversify and have international business operations. As pointed out by Christopher et al. (2011), this diversification or global sourcing, while it can bring many benefits to organizations, can also expose them to a number of risks. It could thus be argued that, in pursuing an 'international sustainable business', managers have to assess global sourcing risks across the entire supply chain and what actions they might take to mitigate those risks (Christopher et al., 2011).

The need for conducting strategic assessment, which is part of risk management, is further amplified by Fernie and Thorpe (2007) who argue that strategy is heavily rooted in understanding the marketplace (and its structure and contours) and refining and executing a strategy to exploit current and future opportunities to better the organization (Fernie and Thorpe, 2007, p. 323). According to Gupta (2011), risk management (RM) is an integral part of the decision making process, and effective risk management can proactively help in overcoming the possibilities of business failures. The linkages between 'risk management' and 'strategy' are further highlighted by Sheehan (2010) who states that managers need to monitor the appropriateness of their firm's strategy in light of environmental changes. Accordingly, Sheehan (2010) suggests paying close attention to those risks that pose the greatest threat to its strategy as the starting point. The proposed diagnostic model in the chapter is intended to offer

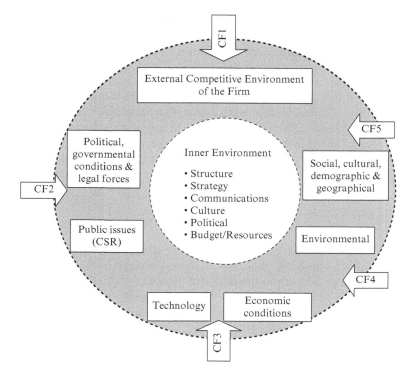

Figure 9.1   Contextualization of internal and external environments for sustainable practices

that opportunity of identification of the risk associated with sustainable business for the strategic decision makers.

CONTEXTUALIZING THE BUSINESS ENVIRONMENT

Organizations pursuing sustainable practices often operate within internal and external environments. In order to explore the links between the business competitive environment in which organizations operate and the internal environment, there is a need to illustrate this inter-connectedness. Figure 9.1 presents the contextualization of internal and external environments for sustainable practices.

The CF_1 through CF_5 in Figure 9.1 denote 'Competitive Forces'. These environments are manifested through a number of factors which influence the overall performance. Li and Ye (1999) used two frames of reference to describe the environment. Firstly, they divided the environment into different segments such as customers, competitors and governmental agencies, to help identify relevant factors in the environment. The second description of the environment was along a variety of critical characteristics. The elements contained within the critical characteristics are twofold: environmental dynamism and environment munificence. On the other hand, as demonstrated by Chileshe (2004), the environment segments help to identify relevant factors in the environment, whereas environmental dynamism is the critical dimension of an organization environment. Environmental dynamism involves the degree and instability of change in the firm's environment.

DEFINITIONS AND BACKGROUND

Before discussing the necessary strategic risk assessment models desirable for pursuing sustainable business in the construction industry and the factors inherent within the internal and external context of the business, it is necessary to define the following terminology: 'risk', 'strategic risk assessment', 'diagnostic models', 'sustainable business' and 'external and internal business environment'.

Risks

Construction is a very competitive and risky business (Chan et al., 2006). Sheehan (2010) defines risks as 'internal' and 'external' events that will increase the firm's costs or decrease its revenue, and hence negatively impact its financial performance. Risk is also generally considered as a threat to project objectives (Stretton, 2012). The Project Management Institute (PMI) (2000) defined project risk as 'an uncertain event or condition that, if it occurs, has a positive or a negative effect on a project objective'. In the construction context, risk is the likelihood of the occurrence of a definite event/factor or combination of events/factors which occur during the whole process of construction, to the detriment of the project (Wang et al., 2004).

Strategic Risk Assessment (SRA)

According to the Institute of Risk Management (IRM) (2002), 'risk management is a central part of any organization's strategic management. It is the process whereby organizations methodically address the risk attached to their activities with the goal of achieving sustainable benefit within each activity and across the portfolio of all activities,' whilst Edwards and Bowen (1998) define risk management as an important tool to cope with construction risks. While these definitions place the emphasis on risk management, the Department of Infrastructure and Planning (2010) defines strategic risk management from the strategic perspective as a means of coordinating, oversighting and modelling the interrelationship of important risk factors across an organization's functions.

Diagnostic Models

According to Harrison and Shirom (1999), 'the term or terminology diagnosis refers to investigations that draw on concepts, models, and methods from the behavioural sciences in order to examine an organization's current state and help clients find ways to solve problems or enhance organization effectiveness'. Within the context of this chapter, it could thus be argued that the diagnostic models are based on the concepts drawn from risk management aimed at identifying the risks associated with the sustainable business and strategic management concepts. This chapter is premised on the sharp-image diagnosis model as advocated by Harrison and Shirom (1999). Accordingly this (sharp-image diagnosis) model which is structured around two entry stages, namely the application of theoretical frames and development of a diagnostic model, is composed of the following four critical steps:

1. The gathering of data to obtain comprehensive overview of operations;
2. Usage of theoretical frames to organize core problems and challenges;
3. The development of a diagnostic model to identify the root cause of ineffective outcomes; and
4. Feedback model and relevant data to clients.

Another diagnostic model found in the literature (Harrison and Shirom, 1999), is the Weisbord's six-box model which centres on diagnostic analysis of the following six organizational factors: the organization's strategy, structures, rewards, internal relationships, helpful mechanisms, and leadership. These are also depicted as part of the inner environment (see Figure 9.1).

Sustainable Business

While there are many definitions of 'sustainability' and 'sustainable business', Vasconcellos e Sá et al. (2011) highlight the challenges and changes, both in terms of new risks and new opportunities, arising from the impact of globalization. Whereas Stonebraker et al. (2009) provide the differentiation of corporate sustainability and operational robustness in terms of profitability and costs and go on to define and develop internal, external, and uncontrollable fragility factors, Vasconcellos e Sá et al. (2011) argue that there is a need for consideration as to how a firm should define its business in light of the impact of globalization. Accordingly, in providing the business mission of any organization, and subsequently the terminology, 'sustainable business' needs to take into account the following three things: geographical area, distribution channels, and time location. Notwithstanding the definitions provided, a study by Smith and Sharicz (2011), which was aimed at assessing the extent to which organizations in practice had shifted towards sustainability, found a number of key elements missing in their quest for developing sustainability. These were identified as follows:

- Governance
- Leadership
- Business plan
- Measure and report
- Organization learning
- Culture
- Information systems

This chapter aims at identifying the similarities between these missing key elements and the concepts of risk management planning as a vehicle for organizations pursuing sustainable business. Other definitions of sustainable business as suggested in the literature can be found in Jeurissen (2000) and Larson et al. (2000). For example Jeurissen (2000) defines sustainable business as: '[a business that] lives up to the triple bottom line of economic prosperity, environmental quality and social justice [which] are interrelated, interdependent, and partly in conflict' (Jeurissen 2000, p. 229). Indeed sustainable business is 'environmentally and socially aware business strategies and operating practices that both guide firms to a cleaner and healthier world and offer an avenue to improved profitability' (Larson et al., 2000, p. 1). In other words the focus of firms will be on creating value, not only financially, but also ecologically and socially (Cramer, 2002). In this chapter, sustainable business is used interchangeably with corporate sustainability.

External Business Environment

The external business environment is considered through external variables as competitive forces (Porter, 1990) and this in turn links to the field of Industrial Organization. The competitive forces affecting the firm's environment as identified by Porter (1990) are as follows:

- CF_1 = The organization's competitive position
- CF_2 = The bargaining power of the customers
- CF_3 = The possibility (or threat) of new or potential competition
- CF_4 = The ability to reduce construction uncertainties
- CF_5 = The ability to redefine market uncertainties

Porter's (1980) framework for the analysis of competition in specific industries shows that an industry has a high level of competition rivalry when it is easy to enter, both buyers and suppliers have bargaining power, and finally there is a threat of substitute products/services. While Porter's analysis of competitive forces does not specifically address risk management processes, it can provide a framework for establishing the role that strategic risk assessment can play in pursuing sustainable business and enhancing an organization's competitive strategy.

The implications that thus emerge are that any organization seeking to pursue sustainable practices would have to take stock of its competitive position as this affects its ability to redefine market uncertainties. Using the construction industry as an example, there is always a need to explore the relationships between the possibility (and threats) of new potential competition (CF_3) and the ability to redefine market uncertainties (CF_5). Adoption of a strategic risk assessment framework in the form of diagnostic models such as identification of risks can contribute to effectively controlling these uncertainties.

This chapter draws extensively from the construction industry as a premier illustration, given that it (construction industry) is relatively easy to enter due to low capital requirements and the nature of sub-contracting. According to Dikmen et al. (2010), this makes the bankruptcy phenomenon more of a threat compared to other industries. Construction-related organizations are therefore encouraged to adopt and implement risk assessment mechanisms prior to pursuing sustainable practices, to guard against possible competition. Other primary influencers or factors affecting the external environment as shown in Figure 9.1 relate to the social, cultural, political, legal, regulatory, financial, technological and economical. According to Larson and Gray (2011), these external influences could occur at international, national, state, regional or local levels.

Political stability
Political stability is one of the key factors that needs to be considered when implementing a project in a foreign country (Larson and Gray, 2011). For

example, lack of political stability such as frequent change in governments can lead to investors questioning the need of pursuing sustainable business practices in any particular country.

Internal Business Environment

According to Boyle and Desai (1991 cited in Arditi et al., 2010), the internal environment includes events under management control. As illustrated in Figure 9.1, organizations' pursuit of sustainability is considered to reside within the inner environment and could inherently be affected or influenced by structural, cultural and political factors. Smallman (1996) further identifies structure, strategy and culture among the three factors which effectively define an organization's approach to managing risk. Some of these are discussed as follows.

Structure
Kuei et al. (1995) define structure as an antecedent which is a degree of constraint on employee behaviour by rules, regulations and formal procedures. For any organization developing diagnostic models for pursuing sustainable business for the first time, the focus needs to be on developing a strategy for defining the overall objectives that will guide all the participants. The connections between organizational structure and strategy for pursuing sustainable business are amplified by Lynch (2003) who postulates that strategy and structure are more closely interrelated. According to Lynch (2003), the two existing differing perspectives on strategy and structure, namely 'the prescriptive approach' and 'the emergent approach', provide conflicting definitions or purposes of organizational structures. While the prescriptive approach defines the purpose of organizational structure as to allocate the work and administrative mechanisms that are necessary to control and integrate the strategies of an organization (Lynch, 2003, p. 565), the emergent perspective takes a different view. The rationale provided is that organizations may restrict or enhance the strategies that are proposed.

Strategy
Smallman (1996) describes strategy as the nature and combination of techniques used in risk management. As observed by Chileshe (2004), top managers spend more time and energy on implementing strategies than choosing them. Strategies that are well chosen fail because of poor implementation. Getting the organization structures right for a particular strategy is thus clearly critical to practical success in pursuing sustainable business. It is also worth noting that a number of factors may influence the

structure of an organization. Needle (1989) identifies some of these factors or influencers: technology, size, changes in the environment, culture and interest groups. While it is beyond the scope of this chapter to discuss them all, the issue of culture is reflected within the Internal Environment as illustrated in Figure 9.1 and discussed in the subsequent section, while the factor of 'interest groups' is included within the Risk Management process as part of 'establishing the context'.

Culture
Organizational culture dictates the way a business operates and how employees respond and are treated. Organizational culture contains such elements as a guiding philosophy, core values, purpose and operational beliefs. These elements have to be integrated within a mission statement which interprets the cultural theory into tangible targets bounded by closed objectives. Pearse (2010) states that organizational culture change can be approached from two broad view points, namely levels of culture and types of culture. It is beyond the scope of this chapter to discuss these in detail; however, in relation to the internal and external environments for pursuing sustainable practices (see Figure 9.1), the two levels of organizational culture identified by Schien (1984 cited in Pearse, 2010) range from visible artefacts to invisible values or basic assumptions. According to Schien (1984 cited in Pearse, 2010), as this organization culture develops, two sets of problems emerge, namely external adaptation and internal integration. The process of risk management offers the potential to determine which risks may affect the project, and to document their characteristics.

Having provided the definitions associated with the 'strategic risk assessment', 'diagnostic models', 'sustainable business', 'external business environment' and 'internal business environment', it is important that the theoretical issues underpinning this chapter and discussion of the diagnostic model for strategic risk assessment are set forth. The following section presents a critique and discussion of the theoretical issues. The saturation theory and the argument for human agency and structures within the context of the construction industry form the basis of the discussion.

THEORETICAL ISSUES: AGENCY AND STRUCTURE

The concepts of agency and structure provide elements of a diagnostic model to assess strategic risk in the construction industry. Structure refers to rules for acting, thinking, and feeling that are general throughout a society, or an organization, and the available material and non-material resources that are needed for action to take place (Giddens, 1984, 1991). Structures act as constraints over the actions of members of a society or an organization. Human agency refers to the capacity for human beings to make choices and to take action to implement those choices (Barker, 2005).

Anthony Giddens, the former director of the London School of Economics and the classic theorist of stucturation theory, has argued that the relationship between structure and agency is an interdependent duality (Giddens, 1984). This duality can be illustrated in relation to the development of a project. People as thinking and speaking agents with the capacity to make choices and implement them, are the agents by which a project is conceived, established, implemented and evaluated. At the same time these agents are constrained by the choices that they and others external to the project have made. For example developing project plans requires a process involving choices, which once entered into constrains the choices that are made by agents later in the project. Construction projects must also follow building codes and adhere to planning regulations that have been developed and codified by other agents external to the project. Building codes and regulations are developed by human agents in relation to accepted behaviour in terms of risk, safety and public amenity. Thus to understand the causes of outcomes in project management it is necessary to consider that causality is dualistic, and is affected by both human action and the constraints of structures in a dynamic process of change and reconstitution.

Giddens's conception of the relationship between agency and structure presents certain ontological and epistemological problems if it is to be utilized as an analytical model in risk assessment, as a recent study by Mutch and Mole (2010) suggests. Ontologically, structure and agency in Giddens's conception are subjective and intertwined, which makes it difficult to analyse both at the same time. Moreover structure is purely subjective until action takes place because it is held in the minds of agents until it affects their actions by constraining or enabling the choices they make in relation to the rules or the resources available to implement their choices. Hence structure and agency can only be analysed in the present sense since the decisions of agents depend on how they interpret structures and apply resources. This presents methodological challenges in deploying this approach to assess risk. For example it would seem to preclude making generalizations from survey data to predict action by agents in relation to structures, and hence to assess risk to projects based on those predictions. This matter was addressed in a study by Sarason et al. (2006) who argued for longitudinal studies using repeated interviews with individuals, so that it would be possible to offer individual case studies of action over time.

This model lends itself to understanding why actions happen but is limited in its capacity to predict outcomes.

In contrast to Giddens, Archer (1995, 2003) holds structure to be objective. That is, structures possess emergent properties because their existence depends upon material resources, both physical and human (Archer, 2007, 1995). The latter might include structures that change over time such as the competitive environment (see Figure 9.1) of the firm, or financial liquidity. Agents in Archer's (2003) model have histories of action in relation to structure. Understanding these histories might suggest how agents respond to change over time. This proposed diagnostic risk management and sustainable business model also opens the possibility of examining both the successes of agents in relation to projects, and their failures, or in other words their understanding of the objective reality of their interaction with their environment, what has worked and what has not, thus providing an understanding of agents as fallible and reflexive. Agents according to Archer are not fully constrained by their environment but have the capacity to reflect and act on past actions. In this sense Archer refers to the tension between agents being conditioned to do things in one way by structural norms but being able to visualize doing them another way to effect change.

Archer (2003, 2007) is offering an analytic model of structure and agency rather than the conceptual model offered by Giddens (1984, 1991). Archer nonetheless recognizes the interdependence of structure and agency, that is to say, without people there can be no structures. However she argues that agency and structure operate on different timescales, which produce dynamic outcomes. At any point in time previously existing structures both constrain and enable agents. These interactions have outcomes, which might reproduce or change the initial structure. The new structure then provides a context of human action for future agents. While recognizing that structure and agency are interdependent, Archer argues that it is possible to separate them for the purpose of analysis. That is, by separating out structural factors which establish the context in which the actions for human agents take place, or how human activities shape structures, it is possible to investigate how those factors shape future interactions of agents with structures and how those interactions change the initial structural context.

Archer's model offers a means to investigate the causal dynamics of how construction projects are established, proceed and have outcomes, by unpacking the relationship between human action and the structures that constrain and enable action, and which are also transformed by the actions of human agents. In doing so it is possible to give empirical accounts of how projects might evolve over time with clear implications for risk assessment.

A CRITICAL REVIEW OF THE EXISTING DIAGNOSTIC MODELS FOR STRATEGIC RISK ASSESSMENT

A number of diagnostic models for strategic risk assessment currently exist in the literature. These have ranged from incorporation of integrated risk management systems for public-private partnerships (PPP) (Fischer et al., 2010); measurement models such as balanced scorecard (Calandro and Lane, 2006; Zou et al., 2008); risk-adjusting performance (Calandro et al., 2008); risk-based approach to strategy (Sheehan, 2010); risk management of knowledge loss (Jafari et al., 2011); enterprise-wide risk management (Gupta, 2011); classification of risks associated with global sourcing (Christopher et al., 2011); supply chain fragility (Stonebraker et al., 2009).

A study by Calandro and Lane (2006) which aimed at introducing the concept of an Enterprise Risk Scorecard used the basis of Kaplan and Norton's scorecard approach as the basis for applying an effective risk measurement, management and communication tool. Despite the importance of the study it was limited as two separate scorecards, one for risk and the other for performance, were not integrated. Calandro and Lane (2006) postulate that integration of risk and performance scorecards could provide strategy-focused organizations with a more comprehensive diagnostic control system. Within the construction industry, projects undertaken can be for either public or private sector clients. On the other hand, large infrastructure projects which involve many stakeholders might utilize a different mechanism for allocation of risk where this is negotiated between the public sector and private sector (Zou et al., 2008). Some frameworks such as Kaplan and Norton's Balanced Scorecard (1996, 2001, 2004, 2008) focused on improving the firm's capability needs to be acknowledged. However as observed by Sheehan (2010), these frameworks have limitations as risk is not addressed.

Fischer et al. (2010) developed an Integrated Risk Management System (IRMS) aimed at enhancing the capabilities and accuracy of the decision making processes. A study by Christopher et al. (2011) which aimed at understanding how managers assess global sourcing risks across the entire supply chain and what actions they take to mitigate those risks proposed a new categorization for global sourcing risks and offered a characterization of global sourcing risk mitigation strategies applicable to different industries. Practical approaches for integrated performance management and risk management have been proposed by Calandro et al. (2008).

Accordingly, this risk-adjustment approach is aimed at evaluating performance in the context of the relative volatility in which business operations are undertaken. Some new areas which have received attention and are associated with growing concern to business executives, are those of robustness and operational sustainability. Sheehan (2010) proposed a risk-based approach to strategy execution. The main steps included within this approach were as follows:

- Strategy mapping tool;
- Identification and assessing of key organizational risks;
- Designing of management control systems; and
- Monitoring risk on an ongoing basis.

A CRITICAL REVIEW OF COMMON RISKS ASSOCIATED WITH SUSTAINABLE DEVELOPMENT AND SUSTAINABLE BUSINESS

Having provided the critical review of the existing diagnostic models for strategic risk assessment, this section presents a summary of a selection of studies on common risks associated with 'sustainable development' and 'sustainable businesses'. The Institute of Risk Management (IRM) (2002) classified the business activities and decisions as following into strategic, financial, knowledge management, and compliance. Given that the focus of this chapter is on strategic risk assessment, it is worth singling out the definition of 'strategic decisions' as provided by IRM (2002). The guide defines them as those concerning the long-term strategic objectives of the organization. Accordingly, they can be affected by such areas as capital availability, sovereign and political risks, and legal and regulatory changes in the physical environment (Figure 9.1). Within the context of supply chain management, which is normally aligned with sustainable business, Christopher et al. (2011) proposed the classification of risks covering four categories: supply, process and control, environmental, and sustainability risks. Examples associated with the environmental and sustainability risks were as follows: fluctuations on interest rates, quota restrictions, unanticipated resource requirements, high levels of CO_2 carbon footprint emissions during the global sourcing activity.

Sustainable Business Specific Risks

There are a number of risks associated with sustainable business, which can be broadly classified into the following two categories, namely 'go' risks (risks to pursue corporate sustainability), and 'not to go' risks (risks associated with not to pursue corporate sustainability).

'Not to go' risks

Apparently there are a number of risks if firms ignore the growing demand for sustainability features of products they provide (for example building and its components in the construction industry). An argument for not to go sustainable business was related to the cost savings as there is no extra expenditure on sustainable practice, for example research and development of new technologies or methods leading to lower level of environmental loading. However, the introduction of life cycle costing helps to justify the upfront cost while responsibility to the broader community has gained a wider acceptance in the business society. Azapagic (2003, p. 307) concluded that the risks of unsustainable business were:

Technical   For example, financial and environmental inefficiency (material, energy) due to continuous use of conventional and inefficient technologies.

Legislative   For example, higher level of greenhouse gas emission tax (carbon tax in Australia context) leading to increase of business costs.

Environmental   For example, penalties, even long-term liability, due to poor environmental performance.

Social   For example, damage to the business brand and negative public image, which may cause the business to be unattractive to quality staff.

Indeed Hopwood et al. (2010) asserted that environmentally unsustainable business practice will ultimately lead to financial loss to the company. Azapagic (2003) suggested that corporate sustainability provides a useful tool to manage business risks.

'Go' risks

Significant risks exist even though firms choose to pursue corporate sustainability. The main risks identified by prior studies are:

Social   Social acceptance has been a critical issue for the success of the adoption of technological innovation, for example, renewable energies integrated with buildings (Yuan et al., 2011). Social and psychological related factors present significant changes to environmental sustainable design and construction (Hoffman and Henn, 2008). Efforts are required to enhance the awareness and willingness to accept the sustainable features with associated cost.

Human resource related   Capabilities and competence for innovation is paramount for addressing the business focus on sustainability (van Kleef and Roome, 2007). Therefore the lack of human resources with innovation oriented competence and capability presents a significant risk for sustainable business. As a consequence Lambrechts et al. (2012) have called for integrating competence on sustainable development into the undergraduate programmes on management. It is logical to strengthen the sustainable business related knowledge and skill set into professional education (for example, in the form of continuous professional development).

Communication related risks   The realization of sustainable built environment involves all actors (e.g. contractor, architect, engineer, property valuer, facility manager, etc.) in the supply chain (Saari and Aalto, 2006). Interactions amongst various professions and organizations are required. It is also necessary to engage the end users to provide feedback for the purpose of improving the future designs (Cole et al., 2010). As a result effective communication and cooperation is essential (Häkkinen and Belloni, 2011).

OVERVIEW OF THE DIAGNOSTIC RISK MANAGEMENT AND SUSTAINABLE BUSINESS

Figure 9.2 presents and summarizes the main steps and components of the 'Diagnostic Risk Management and Sustainable Business'. The three components are as follows:

- Communication and consultation;
- General framework for the sustainable risk management process, composed of six sub steps;
- Monitoring and review.

While the need to integrate 'sustainability' and 'risk management' has been explored before, there is a paucity of studies that have focussed on developing strategic risk assessment models for pursuing sustainable business in the construction industry.

The linkages between sustainable business and risk assessment are further demonstrated by Calandro et al. (2008). They suggest that a key objective of risk management is to evaluate performance in the context of the relative volatility in which business operations are undertaken.

Establishing the Context

The first step of the second component within the 'diagnostic model' starts with establishing the context. In addition to identifying key stakeholder demands, this step also provides the opportunity to prioritize them within a framework of constrained resources (Asif et al., 2011). Within the context of risk management processes, this involves establishing the context, which in essence includes sub activities such as the external context; internal context; the risk management context; developing risk evaluation criteria; and definition of the structure for the risk analysis. This is similar to activities undertaken in existing diagnostic models such as the 'Weisbord six-box' and 'sharp-image diagnosis' which offers some scope for usage with the key activities associated with risk management.

For example the first step of sharp-image diagnosis developed by Harrison and Shirom (1999) involves the gathering of data to obtain the comprehensive overview of the operations, the focus of which is to identify specific problems or challenges for subsequent analysis. This is similar to the range of activities associated with the 'establishment of the context', which mainly deals with the audit of the internal and external environment.

Figure 9.2 can also be interpreted from the external and internal environment context as shown in Figure 9.1. As noted by Searcy (2009), this stage would be similar to the activities undertaken during the situational diagnostic. Searcy (2009) recommends the systematic survey of the following three key areas:

- Interpreting sustainability in the corporate context;
- Surveying the internal environment; and
- Surveying the external environment.

There are some other considerations that need to be taken into account within this stage, such as identification of dominant factors. For example Stonebraker et al. (2009) identifies the following four factors: increasing complexity of products, processes, and technologies; increasing structural complexity of supply chains; increasing diversity and global nature of business systems; and the environmental costs and impacts of extended supply chains.

Identifying the Risk

Having established the context, the second step within the risk management process is that of 'identifying the risk' which is a sub set of the risk

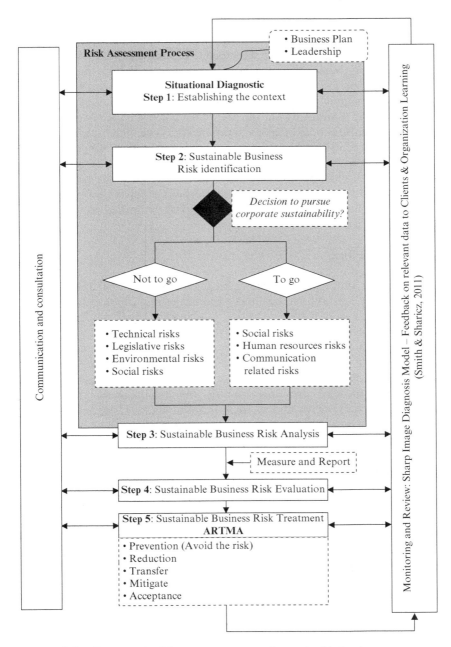

Figure 9.2   Diagnostic risk management and sustainable business

assessment process. As observed by Chileshe (2011), for sustainability initiatives to be effective, the first step of identifying the potential influences of the factors affecting the social, economic and environmental issues requires consideration. Christopher et al.'s (2011) study of how managers assess global risk, found that most organizations did not have a structured supply chain risk management and mitigation system. This study is highly relevant within the international context for organizations seeking to venture outside the local domiciles. As an illustration from the procurement of PPP infrastructure projects, Zou et al. (2008) established that properly assessing and managing the risks (such as financial, government/political and public acceptance/rejection) from a project life cycle perspective led to the success of projects. However for the purpose of this chapter, the identification of the common risk is limited to sustainable development and sustainable business.

Analysing the Risk

This stage is aimed at establishing an understanding of the risk associated with the 'sustainable business'. Fischer et al. (2010) also point out the main purpose of this stage as that of using the significance of the risk as a basis for making informed decisions about required strategies and resources. As observed by Lynch (2003) most worthwhile strategies are likely to carry some degree of risk which requires some form of analysis. For example for the financial risk, Lynch (2003) recommends a number of analyses such as cash flow analysis, break-even analysis, company borrowing requirements and financial ratio analysis. Using construction organizations or business as an example, some tools such as probability/impact matrixes, strength/weakness/opportunity/threat analysis (SWOT), and top ten risk tracking techniques have also been suggested (Kululanga and Kuotcha, 2010).

Evaluating Risks

The fourth step of the diagnostic risk management and sustainable business process, constituting the third stage of the 'risk assessment' process, involves the evaluation of the risk. According to the Department of Infrastructure and Planning (2010), the purpose of risk evaluation is to make decisions, based on outcomes of the risk analysis, about which risks need treatment, whether an activity should be undertaken, and treatment priorities. Chileshe (2011) in acknowledging that risk management can act as a catalyst for the evaluation of sustainability issues within the discipline of Construction and Project Management suggested that the area of risk management could focus on the identification and evaluation of the factors that might affect the implementation of sustainability initiatives.

Treating Risks

The fifth step of the diagnostic risk management and sustainable business process involves the treatment or mitigation of the risk. Fischer et al. (2010) describe this process as the practice that can either reduce the likelihood of occurrence of risk, or impact of the consequences if it does occur. While a number of mitigation strategies practices exist such as prevention, reduction, transfer and acceptance, Fischer et al. (2010) observe that the most commonly used risk mitigation practice is that of transference of risk to another party which is in a better position to manage and control the risk.

Monitoring and Review

The last stage of the diagnostic risk management and sustainable business process involves monitoring and review. Within the context of project management, this is normally associated with reporting and reviewing structure to ensure that risks associated with sustainable business are effectively identified and assessed and that appropriate controls and responses are in place (IRM, 2002). As pointed out by Harrison and Shirom (1999), one of the requirements or conditions that should be met by a good diagnostic model is that of provision of feedback. Accordingly this diagnostic feedback should help the clients and other members of the client organization to understand the nature and sources of organizational ineffectiveness and to focus on more promising levers for introducing change (Harrison and Shirom, 1999, p. 93). This stage of 'monitoring and review' also offers the potential of addressing the missing key element of 'organization learning' in defining sustainability as suggested by Smith and Sharicz (2011).

CONCLUSIONS

The strategic risk assessment diagnostic model presented in this chapter provides a mechanism of integrating the principles and processes of risk management in the planning of corporate activities. The model identifies, evaluates (through the qualitative and quantitative assessment methods), treats and monitors risks associated with sustainable business with particular reference to the construction industry. Using the theoretical underpinnings of 'agency and structures' theory, and fulfilling the underlying conditions or requirements for the sharp-image diagnosis, the proposed conceptual diagnostic model offers strategic decision makers the guidelines that require consideration during the assessment of risks associated with the sustainable business.

REFERENCES

Archer, M. (1995), *Realist Social Theory: The Morphogenetic Approach*, New York: Cambridge University Press.
Archer, M. (2003), *Structure, Agency, and the Internal Conversation*, New York: Cambridge University Press.
Archer, M. (2007), *Making Our Way Through the World*, Cambridge: Cambridge University Press.
Arditi, D., Koksal, A. and Kale, S. (2000), 'Business failure in the construction industry', *Engineering, Construction and Architectural Management*, **7** (2), 120–32.
Asif, M., Searcy, C., Zutshi, A. and Ahmad, N. (2011), 'An integrated management system approach to corporate sustainability', *European Business Review*, **23** (4), 353–67.
Azapagic, A. (2003), 'Systems approach to corporate sustainability: a general management framework', *Process Safety and Environmental Protection*, **81** (5), 303–16.
Barker, C. (2005), *Cultural Studies: Theory and Practice*, London: Sage.
Calandro, J., Jr. and Lane, S. (2006), 'An introduction to the Enterprise Risk Scorecard', *Measuring Business Excellence*, **10** (3), 31–40.
Calandro, J., Jr., Lane, S. and Dasari, R. (2008), 'A practical approach for risk-adjusting performance', *Measuring Business Excellence*, **12** (4), 4–12.
Chan, A.P.C., Chan, D.W.M., Fan, L.C.N., Lam, P.T.I. and Yeung, J.F.Y. (2006) 'Partnering for construction excellence: a reality or myth?', *Building and Environment*, **41** (12), 1924–33.
Chileshe, N. (2004) 'The application of TQM within small and medium sized construction related organizations', PhD thesis, Sheffield Hallam University, UK.
Chileshe, N. (2011), 'Delivering sustainability through construction and project management: principles, tools and practices', in Roetman, P.E.J and Daniels, C.B. (eds), *Creating Sustainable Communities in a Changing World*, Adelaide: Crawford House Publishing.
Christopher, M., Mena, C., Khan, O. and Yurt, O. (2011), 'Approaches to managing global sourcing risk', *Supply Chain Management: An International Journal*, **16** (2), 67–81.
Cole, R.J., Brown, Z. and McKay, S. (2010), 'Building human agency: a timely manifesto', *Building Research & Information*, **38** (3), 339–50.
Cramer, J. (2002), 'From financial to sustainable profit', *Corporate Social Responsibility and Environmental Management*, **9** (2), 99–106.
Dalmau, T. and Dick, B. (1991), *A Diagnostic Model for Selecting Interventions for Community and Organization Change*, 2nd edition, Chapel Hill: Interchange.

Department of Infrastructure and Planning (2010), September, Report available at http://dlgp.qld.gov.au/resources/policy/integrated-risk-management-framework-strategy.pdf

Dikmen, I., Birgonul, M.T., Ozorhon, B. and Sapci, N.E. (2010), 'Using analytic network process to assess business failure risk of construction firms', *Engineering, Construction and Architectural Management*, **17** (4), 369–86.

Edwards, P.J. and Bowen, P.A. (1998), 'Risk and risk management in construction: review and future directions for research', *Engineering, Construction and Architectural Management*, **5** (4), 339–49.

Fernie, S. and Thorpe, A. (2007), 'Exploring change in construction: supply chain management', *Engineering, Construction and Architectural Management*, **14** (4), 319–33.

Fischer, K., Leidel, K., Riemann, A. and Alfen, H.W. (2010), 'An integrated risk management system (IRMS) for PPP projects', *Journal of Financial Management of Property and Construction*, **15** (3), 260–82.

Giddens, A. (1984), *The Constitution of Society: Outline of the Theory of Structuration*, Berkeley, CA: University of California Press.

Giddens, A. (1991), *Modernity and Self-identity*, Cambridge: Polity.

Gupta, P.K. (2011), 'Risk management in Indian companies: EWRM concerns and issues', *The Journal of Risk Finance*, **12** (2), 121–39.

Häkkinen, T. and Belloni, K. (2011), 'Barriers and drivers for sustainable building', *Building Research & Information*, **39** (3), 239–55.

Harrison, M.I. and Shirom, A. (1999), *Organizational Diagnosis and Assessment: Bridging Theory and Practice*, Thousand Oaks, CA: Sage.

Hawken, P. (2011), 'Business survival: a sustainable and profitable model', presentation to Zero Waste SA, Adelaide Thinkers in Residence and 5000+ series seminar, 20 October, Palace Cinema, Adelaide.

Hoffman, A.J. and Henn, R. (2008), 'Overcoming the social and psychological barriers to green building', *Organization & Environment*, **21** (4), 390–419.

Hopwood, A., Unerman, J. and Fries, J. (2010), *Accounting for Sustainability: Practical Insights*, London: Earthscan.

Institute of Risk Management (IRM) (2002), *A Risk Management Standard*, London, UK: AIRMIC/ALARM/IRM.

Jafari, M., Rezaeenour, J., Mazdeh, M.M. and Hooshmandi, A. (2011), 'Development and evaluation of a knowledge risk management model for project-based organizations', *Management Decision*, **49** (3), 309–29.

Jeurissen, R. (2000), 'John Elkington, Cannibals With Forks: The Triple Bottom Line of 21st Century Business, book review', *Journal of Business Ethics*, **23**, 229–31.

Kaplan, R.S. and Norton, D.P. (1996), *The Balanced Scorecard*, Boston, MA: Harvard Business Publishing Press.

Kaplan, R.S. and Norton, D.P. (2001), *The Strategy Focussed Organization*, Boston, MA: Harvard Business Publishing Press.

Kaplan, R.S. and Norton, D.P. (2004), *Strategy Maps*, Boston, MA: Harvard Business Publishing Press.

Kaplan, R.S. and Norton, D.P. (2008), *The Execution Premium*, Boston, MA: Harvard Business Publishing Press.

Kuei, C.H., Madu, C.N., Lin, X.C. and Lu, M.H. (1995), 'An empirical investigation of the association between quality management practices and organizational climate', *International Journal of Quality Science*, **2** (2), 121–37.

Kululanga, G. and Kuotcha, W. (2010), 'Measuring project risk management process for construction contractors with statement indicators linked to numerical scores', *Engineering, Construction and Architectural Management*, **17** (4), 336–51.

Lambrechts, W., Mulà, I., Ceulemans, K., Molderez, I. and Gaeremynck, V. (2012), 'The integration of competences for sustainable development in higher education: an analysis of bachelor programs in management', *Journal of Cleaner Production*, in press, available at dx.doi.org/10.1016/j.jclepro.2011.12.034 (accessed 25 May 2012).

Larson, A.L., Teisberg, E.O. and Johnson, R.R. (2000), 'Sustainable business: opportunity and value creation', *Interfaces*, **30** (3), 1–12.

Larson, E.W. and Gray, C.F. (2011) *Project Management: The Managerial Process*, 5th edition, McGraw-Hill Irwin.

Li, M. and Ye, R. (1999), 'Information technology and firm performance: linking with environmental, strategic and managerial contexts', *Information and Management*, **35**, 43–51.

Lynch, R. (2003), *Corporate Strategy*, 3rd edition, Prentice Hall.

Mutch, K. and Mole, M. (2010), 'Entrepreneurship as the structuration of individual and opportunity: a response using a critical realist perspective', *Journal of Business Venturing*, **25**, 230–37.

Needle, D. (1998), *Business in Context*, Van Nostrand Reinhold (International).

Pearse, N.J. (2010), 'Towards a social capital theory of resistance to change', *Journal of Advances in Management Research*, **7** (2), 163–75.

Porter, M.E. (1980), *Competitive Strategy*, New York: Free Press.

Porter, M.E. (1990), 'The competitive advantage of nations', *Harvard Business Review*, March–April.

Project Management Institute (2000), *A Guide to the Project Management Body of Knowledge (PMBOK Guide)*, Newtown Square, PA: Project Management Institute, Inc.

Project Management Institute (2008), *A Guide to the Project Management Body of Knowledge*, Newtown Square, PA: Project Management Institute, Inc.

Saari, A. and Aalto, L. (2006), 'Indoor environment quality contracts in building projects', *Building Research & Information*, **34** (1), 66–74.

Sarason, Y., Dean, T. and Dillard, J. (2006), 'Entrepreneurship as the nexus of individual and opportunity: a structuration view', *Journal of Business Venturing*, **21**, 286–305.

Searcy, C. (2009), 'Setting a course in corporate sustainability performance measurement', *Measuring Business Excellence*, **13** (3), 49–57.

Sheehan, N.T. (2010), 'A risk-based approach to strategy execution', *Journal of Business Strategy*, **31** (5), 25–37.

Smallman, C. (1996), 'Risk and organizational behaviour: a research model', *Disaster Prevention and Management*, **5** (2), 12–26.

Smith, P.A.C. and Sharicz, C. (2011), 'The shift needed for sustainability', *The Learning Organization*, **18** (1), 73–86.

Stonebraker, P.W., Goldhar, J. and Nassos, G. (2009), 'Weak links in the supply chain: measuring fragility and sustainability', *Journal of Manufacturing Technology Management*, **20** (2), 161–77.

Stretton, A. (2012), 'Project management in the 2000s', *Project Manager Journal*, December/January, 28–30.

The State of Queensland (Queensland Treasury) (2011), *A Guide to Risk Management*, Queensland Government.

van Kleef, J.A.G. and Roome, N.J. (2007), 'Developing capabilities and competence for sustainable business management as innovation: a research agenda', *Journal of Cleaner Production*, **15** (1), 38–51.

Vasconcellos e Sá, J.A., Olão, F. and Pereira, M. (2011), 'From Levitt to the global age: one more time, how do we define our business?', *Management Decision*, **49** (1), 99–115.

Wang, S.Q., Dulaimi, M.F. and Aguria, M.Y. (2004), 'Risk management framework for construction projects in developing countries', *Construction Management & Economics*, **22**, 237–52.

Yuan, X., Zuo, J. and Ma, C. (2011), 'Social acceptance of solar energy technologies in China – end users' perspective', *Energy Policy*, **39** (3), 1031–6.

Zou, P.X.W., Wang, S. and Fan, D. (2008), 'A life-cycle risk management framework for PPP infrastructure projects', *Journal of Financial Management of Property and Construction*, **13** (2), 123–42.

PART III

Sustainable Business in Practice

10. Sustainable entrepreneurship in family businesses

Shruti R. Sardeshmukh

INTRODUCTION: SUSTAINABLE ENTREPRENEURSHIP IN FAMILY BUSINESSES

Increasing awareness of the fragility of our environment and of the limited nature of our natural resources has highlighted the importance of ecological sustainable development. Ecologically sustainable development is defined as 'development that improves the total quality of life, both now and in the future, in a way that maintains the ecological processes on which life depends' (Australian Government, 1999). Ecologically sustainable development can take place through innovation and pursuit of sustainable entrepreneurial opportunities (Porter and Kramer, 2011). This conceptual chapter argues that the stewardship oriented governance characteristics of family businesses, honed through their long term focus and continuity, also create an excellent platform for the family businesses to identify and pursue ecologically sustainable entrepreneurship opportunities.

Recognizing the importance of ecological sustainability, many initiatives have been undertaken at the international, national and individual level. International bodies have formed agreements to undertake initiatives that will help protect the natural resources. The Stockholm convention and Kiev protocol in the early 2000s created legally binding agreements among European Union (EU) nations to promote sustainability. Similarly many local, state and national government bodies have responded by enacting legislation such as an Environment Protection and Biodiversity Conservation Act (Australian Government, 2011). These actions are not limited to institutional actors. Private citizens and individuals are known to undertake voluntary actions such as participating in and championing recycling and organic living, as well as reducing reliance on non-renewable resources such as petroleum.

On the other hand the business community has had a mixed reaction to environmental regulations. Initially many industries resisted environmental

regulation legislation, particularly if there were any negative profit implications, but many have eventually embraced the environmental reforms
(Sandhu, 2010; Porter and Kramer, 2011). While even today, business
organizations are in the news for violating the environmental legislation,
in general there is a greater acceptance that business organizations have a
responsibility to the environment and many organizations have adopted
Proactive Environmental Strategies (PES) that go well beyond complying
with the regulations (Sharma and Sharma, 2011; Sandhu, 2010). We also
know that by undertaking a proactive environmental strategy (Sharma
and Sharma, 2011), organizations can help mitigate and even reverse
some of the damage to the natural environment. While there is a plethora
of research on environmental sustainability and corporate actions, it has
primarily focused on large public organizations. The role of the most
common organizational form, the family business, remains understudied
in the sustainability context. In this chapter I propose to explore the role
of governance characteristics in family business (stewardship) and develop
propositions related to the role of stewardship in identifying and pursuing
ecologically sustainable opportunities.

We know that family businesses are the 'dominant organizational
form' all over the world (Sharma and Sharma, 2011, p. 309). They contribute 57 per cent of the employment numbers and a similar proportion
of gross domestic product in the US (Astrachan and Shanker, 2003), and
constitute about 60 per cent of all businesses in the world (Déniz and
Suárez, 2005). Similar to the world statistics more than two thirds of
all Australian businesses are family owned (KPMG, 2011). On average
Australian family businesses employ 37 people, with an average annual
turnover of $12 million and an estimated total wealth of around $4.2
trillion (FBA, 2011). Given the economic gravitas of family businesses, a
good understanding of ecologically sustainable family business behaviour
patterns can make a substantial difference in the sustainability outcomes
in Australia and beyond. This chapter conceptually develops propositions
arguing that the characteristics of stewardship associated with successful
family business governance, can provide impetus to pursue opportunities
for ecologically sustainable entrepreneurship to mitigate market imperfections and market failures that may lead to environmental degradation.
In the next section I briefly discuss family businesses, and the governance characteristics commonly associated with family businesses, and
the importance of stewardship characteristics in the context of ecological
sustainability.

FAMILY BUSINESSES

Family businesses are businesses that are also 'family institutions' (Chrisman et al., 2003, p. 442). While family businesses have been defined in various ways, this chapter adheres to the definition by Chua et al. (1999, p. 25); they define a family business as:

> The family business is a business governed and/or managed with the intention to shape and pursue the vision of the business held by a dominant coalition controlled by members of the same family or a small number of families in a manner that is potentially sustainable across generations of the family or families.

Since in the rest of the chapter the term sustainability refers to ecological sustainability, a clarification is in order; in this definition of family business, the term sustainable is used to imply intergenerational continuity in the family business. This definition of family business articulates the importance of long term perspective and intergenerational continuity for family business. It also highlights the point that family business strategies, including environmental strategies, are shaped by a coalition of family members, who are influenced by the forces from the family sphere. In fact this overlap of family and business offers family businesses their unique familiness (Pearson et al., 2008; Rutherford et al., 2008; Zellweger et al., 2010), which can be a source of competitive advantage. These deep connections between family and business also give the family businesses a unique reason for stewardship behaviours (Miller et al., 2008). In fact Chua et al. (2005) eloquently state, 'family firms exist because of the reciprocal economic and noneconomic value created through the combination of family and business systems.'

Family business research has had multidisciplinary origins. Recent research related to governance issues in family businesses is influenced by agency theory (Schulze and Gedajlovic, 2010; Schulze et al., 2003; Schulze et al., 2001) and stewardship theory (Davis et al., 1997; Donaldson and Davis, 1991; Hernandez, 2012). Agency theory posits that the divergence in the goals of the principal (owner) and the agent (manager) create agency costs. While family businesses show overlap of ownership and control, in spite of the convergence of ownership and control, family businesses are argued to suffer from agency costs (Schulze and Gedajlovic, 2010; Schulze et al., 2003; Schulze et al., 2001).

Originating in psychology and sociology, stewardship theory offers a contrast to the agency theory governance model. Stewardship is defined as 'the extent to which an individual willingly subjugates his or her personal interests to act in protection of others' long-term welfare' (Hernandez,

2012, p. 174). Stewardship theory (Davis et al., 1997) posits that managers and leaders of organizations are motivated not just by individual self-interest, but strive to act in their organization's best interest and attain the objectives of the organization. Stewardship theory makes the assumption that the interests of the managers extend well beyond just individualistic and economic goals. Organizational identification and pride in the achievement of the organization can be a source of intrinsic rewards for the stewards of the business. Family businesses are seen as an appropriate field for application of stewardship theory (Corbetta and Salvato, 2004; Eddleston and Kellermanns, 2007) as the key psychological mechanisms of stewardship, 'long term orientation' and 'affective sense of connection' (Hernandez, 2012, p. 175) are observed in the family business context. For example the family business owner/managers are interested in intergenerational continuity of the business, and experience a sense of pride and identity with the family business. Family business owner/managers also hold the belief that they are merely stewards of the business, protecting and nurturing it for the next generation.

Related to the notion of stewardship, family businesses are also characterized by the motivation to preserve socio-emotional wealth associated with having and controlling their family business (Berrone et al., 2010; Gómez-Mejía et al., 2007; Stockmans et al., 2010). These socio-emotional concerns extend well beyond the rational-economic reasons of monetary returns from the family business. In fact family business owners report pride (Zellweger and Nason, 2008) about their family business and make investments in family reputation (Dyer and Whetten, 2006; Sorenson et al., 2009). Overall family businesses tend to merge the family identity with the organizational identity (Gómez-Mejía et al., 2007; Zellweger et al., 2011).

Another set of important and related features of family businesses governance systems are parsimony, particularism and personalism (Carney, 2005). Carney (2005) argues that with families' personal wealth being involved, family businesses are more prudent with their money, demonstrating *parsimony*. Family members and senior managers also have a great deal of control over the strategy of the family business, allowing the family to direct and implement its values and visions for the business. With the *personalization* of authority and close socio-emotional ties with the business, family businesses often operate on criteria not solely limited to rational-economic criteria. In fact, they often use *particularistic* criteria to make decisions. These particularistic criteria are not always positive (for example, nepotism) but pave the way for family firms to make decisions which reflect their personal values and exploit entrepreneurial opportunities that emerge from who they are (Sarasvathy, 2001, p. 258).

FAMILY BUSINESS STEWARDSHIP AND ECOLOGICAL SUSTAINABILITY

While family business stewardship in its limited form relates to the preservation and continuity of the family business for the next generation, the characteristics associated with stewardship are relevant to ecological sustainability. Stewardship in family business focuses on both economic and non-economic value. In fact socio-emotional value associated with family business stewardship goes well beyond the traditional economic values. We also know that the sphere of stewardship extends beyond the immediate family to employees as well as customers (Miller et al., 2008). With the merger of family identity and the firm identity, strong incentives to invest in reputation of the family business are created. I argue that the acknowledgement and appreciation of the non-economic value, and long term perspective, and the overlapping family and business identity predispose the family businesses to undertake stewardship initiatives in the community. While these initiatives may take the form of a wider range of corporate social responsibility initiatives (Dyer and Whetten, 2006), I focus on recognition and pursuit of ecologically sustainable entrepreneurial opportunities. In the next section I briefly discuss the nature of entrepreneurial opportunities and origins of sustainable opportunities.

Entrepreneurial Opportunities

Entrepreneurial opportunities are defined as 'situations in which new goods, services, raw materials, markets and organizing methods can be introduced through the formation of new means, ends, or means-ends relationships' (Eckhardt and Shane, 2003, p. 336). We know that entrepreneurship involves the nexus of individual and opportunity (Shane and Venkataraman, 2000) and the entrepreneurship literature has demonstrated that opportunities are triggered by a 'complex pattern of changing conditions – changes in technology, economic, political, social and demographic conditions' (Baron, 2006, p. 107). Yet these opportunities cannot come into existence unless they are recognized or created by an entrepreneur (Kirzner, 1997). While the opportunities are triggered by the business environment for everyone, not all are poised to pursue these opportunities. Because of who they are, what they know, and whom they know (Sarasvathy, 2001, p. 258), entrepreneurs have differential access to information and resources, enabling some but not all to exploit these opportunities.

Sustainable entrepreneurial opportunities thus emerge from the business environmental context. They may be triggered by changes in technology, creation of new information, or changes in the markets' needs and wants (Baron, 2006), yet the opportunities cannot exist unless they are recognized or created by an entrepreneur (Kirzner, 1997). Consistent with Baron's work, Gregoire et al. (2009, p. 3) define the *process of recognizing opportunities* 'as effort to make sense of signals of change (e.g., new information about new conditions) to form beliefs regarding whether or not enacting a course of action to address this change could lead to net benefits.' Their definition suggests that the process of opportunity recognition has two sub-phases: (a) a phase when the opportunity exists, and an individual recognizes it as such, regardless of ability to pursue it; and (b) a phase when the opportunity is evaluated in relationship to one's self, determining whether or not one has the abilities and motivation to pursue it (Gregoire et al., 2009). This indicates that just identifying the environmental context and a market opportunity is not enough, it is also important that the individual recognizes the opportunity as appropriate for herself or himself.

Family businesses provide an excellent context for conversion of a third person opportunity into a first person opportunity. The perception about whether one has the ability and motivation to pursue the opportunity is rooted in the notion of Entrepreneurial Self Efficacy (ESE) (Chen et al., 1998; Zhao et al., 2005). Grounded in the social cognitive theory, self efficacy is an individual's belief that he or she can successfully perform certain behaviours. In this context self efficacy relates to the belief about one's ability to successfully pursue opportunities and to perform entrepreneurial tasks. Working within a family business contributes to the family member/ entrepreneur's ESE as the experience of working in your own business instils a sense of success and develops skills and competencies (Vallejo, 2009) as well as idiosyncratic knowledge (Bjuggren and Sund, 2005). Not surprisingly family business owners and successors often have high ESE, allowing them to identify new opportunities as first person opportunities and pursue the opportunities as they are identified.

Further, given the personalism principle of governance used by family businesses, family business entrepreneurs and successors have a strong influence on the strategy of the firm, influencing the direction as well as the entrepreneurial initiatives undertaken by the family business. Therefore family business entrepreneurs and successors are not only likely to identify third and first person opportunity, they are also likely to have the ability and authority to undertake those initiatives for the family business.

Opportunities for Sustainable Entrepreneurship

There is an increasingly acute understanding that our environmental resources are unique, and often not renewable. Therefore many sustainable entrepreneurial opportunities have emerged for entrepreneurs. Dean and McMullen (2007, p. 51) define sustainable entrepreneurial activities as 'alleviation of environmentally relevant market failures through the exploitation of potentially profitable opportunities.' These sustainable opportunities emerge out of market imperfections (Cohen and Winn, 2007) and market failures (Dean and McMullen, 2007). These imperfections offer excellent Kirznerian opportunities (Kirzner, 1973, 1997), which allow the entrepreneur to generate profits by mitigating inefficiencies and restoring the market equilibrium. While these opportunities are available to all, this chapter makes the case that the unique characteristics of family businesses enable them to better identify and pursue these opportunities to mitigate environmental market failure.

Cohen and Winn (2007) identify four types of market imperfections that contribute to the detrimental impact on the environment: inefficient firms, externalities, flawed pricing mechanisms, and information. Similarly, Dean and McMullen (2007) discuss five different types of market failures: public goods, externalities, monopoly power, inappropriate government intervention, and imperfect information; and they argue that entrepreneurial action can help resolve these market imperfections. In this chapter I focus on the four market imperfections identified by Cohen and Winn (2007) and articulate how the stewardship patterns associated with successful family businesses can help them identify the sustainable entrepreneurial opportunities to mitigate these market imperfections. Recall that family business entrepreneurs and successors often have high ESE, which allows them to not only identify these opportunities in the environment but to pursue them as first person opportunities.

INEFFICIENT FIRMS

Market imperfections take place when firms in the market are inefficient. Such inefficiencies can create Kriznerian oportunities for entrepreneurs who engage in efficiency enhancing actions to mitigate these inefficiencies, cut costs and improve profitability. Family businesses, with their focus on parsimony, are well poised to identify these efficiency oriented opportunities (Figure 10.1). Further, with the personalistic and particularistic governances, they are more likely to pursue these efficiency oriented opportunities. For example we all know that modern product packaging creates an enormous amount of waste. Family businesses that specialize in packaging products made from recycled materials can improve these inefficiencies. Often these opportunities are in small niches, making it less worthwhile for the large corporate players to exploit them. However

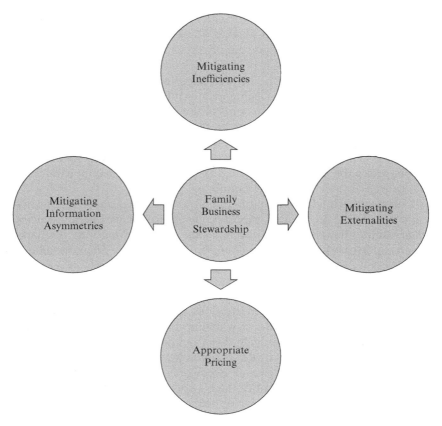

*Figure 10.1   Family business stewardship mitigating market inefficiencies
for sustainable entrepreneurship*

family businesses, with personalistic decision making and focus on parsimony can quickly identify and exploit these opportunities.

*Proposition 1:   Stewardship in family businesses will be manifested in
entrepreneurship through identification and pursuit of opportunities that
mitigate inefficiencies and improve profitability.*

EXTERNALITIES

As York and Venkataraman (2010, p. 453) articulate, 'Many environmental problems are inherently problems of resource distribution and

allocation.' Externalities come into the picture when costs or benefits to all of the stakeholders are not accurately reflected in the price of the commodity. The environmental economics literature is abundant with examples of negative externalities imposed by firms polluting the environment (Cohen and Winn, 2007). Such behaviour is a consequence of lack of a longer term perspective. Less tied to the quarterly profitability reports, family businesses have a longer term orientation (Zahra et al., 2004), a key psychological component of stewardship (Hernandez, 2012). Family business senior executives also enjoy longer tenures (Cruz et al., 2010) and have the patient capital that creates a long-term multigenerational outook (Sirmon and Hitt, 2003). Family businesses are also more interested in building trust based long term relationships with employees and customers over time (Miller et al., 2008). Moreover, family businesses more likely to have strong local roots, are also more likely to be involved in the community where they operate, be aware of community stakeholders and sensitive to immediate environmental issues (Gallo, 2004). This affective involvement is also a key component of their stewardship (Hernandez, 2012). In fact, Carrigan and Buckly (2008) found that family businesses were considered the 'glue' holding together both urban and rural communities, indicating that they were very aware and active of the issues of the communities in which they operate.

Family business governance is also marked by personalism, echoing the substantial personal role of individual members of the family senior management team. Further, family identity is closely tied to the organizational identity, creating a direct linkage between corporate reputation and family's standing in the society (Berrone et al., 2010). Therefore the organizational good and bad deeds reflect accordingly on the family and the reputational damage due to environmental misbehaviour is likely to impact the family business and the family senior management personally. I argue that family businesses will be interested in proactive environmental strategies in protecting the environmental interests of the community in which they operate.

Proposition 2: Stewardship in family businesses will be manifested in entrepreneurship through identification and pursuit of opportunities that mitigate negative externalities to the community in which they operate.

FLAWED PRICING

One way to mitigate the negative externalities is to incorporate the full costs to the stakeholders in different investment and pricing decisions.

As Berrone et al. (2010, p. 84) state, 'if people cared enough about pollution, firms would have a market based incentive to reduce toxic emissions and therefore little contamination would exist.' However, often the prices in the marketplace do not reflect the negative environmental impact. Family businesses with a strong stewardship perspective are more likely to incorporate the cost of negative externalities into their business model. The personal values and interests of the family business entrepreneurs and successors are more likely to influence the business strategy, and as the stewards of family businesses and more, if they value the fair price approaches, they are more likely to implement them. For example many family businesses in Australia pride themselves on local fair wage production. Further many family businesses may use the fair pricing as a product differentiation and reputation strategy to signal good quality and good values to the customer. While there may be economic benefits to the differentiation strategy, part of the rationale can be traced back to the identity, socio-emotional value and stewardship of the family businesses. The press release by the DFID about Taylor's ethically sourced beverages highlights the role of stewardship of that family business (DFID, 2012).

Proposition 3: Stewardship in family businesses will be manifested in entrepreneurship through identification and pursuit of opportunities that differentiate their products through appropriate pricing mechanisms such as selling fair price products.

INFORMATION ASYMMETRIES

Classical economics theory makes the assumption that information is available to all actors in the market. However, given bounded rationality, we know that economic actors have limited ability to make strategic decisions (Williamson, 1985). Reflecting this, some actors may have a different set of information, creating information asymmetry as a cause for market failure (Akerlof, 1970). However we also know that entrepreneurs leverage their knowledge and experience to identify opportunities. In fact prior knowledge (Shane, 2000) and information, and learning asymmetries between individuals (Corbett, 2005; Shane, 2000) can lead individuals down different information corridors (Ronstadt, 1988; Venkataraman, 1997).

In the context of sustainability and entrepreneurship, Cohen and Winn (2007) offer an example where consumers' lack of knowledge about energy consumption in the house can create an imperfection where consumers make uninformed purchase decisions that are costly for themselves as well as for the environment. This presents an excellent sustainable entrepreneurial opportunity to bridge the information gap. Family businesses have a sense of stewardship towards their customer relationships (Miller et al., 2008) and customers have a greater degree of trust (Orth and Green, 2009) towards family business. These attributes allow the family businesses to disseminate information about sustainability products while maintaining a trust-based relationship with the consumer base. For example, family nurseries may disseminate information about how to use organic methods in the consumers' gardens, while also generating business on the organic gardening tools and equipment.

Proposition 4: Stewardship in family businesses will be manifested in entrepreneurship through identification and pursuit of opportunities that reduce the information asymmetry for their customers with respect to sustainability products and services.

DISCUSSION AND CONCLUSION

Family businesses, a commonly found form of organization all over the world, can make a substantial contribution to the agenda of ecological sustainability. Successful family businesses also display characteristics of stewardship governance. We also know that such stewardship is associated with successful family businesses. Responding to the call for research by Sharma and Sharma (2011), I developed a nuanced argument outlining the role characteristics of family business stewardship in identifying and pursuing sustainable entrepreneurship opportunities. These initiatives may take different forms as family businesses are poised to pursue opportunities that mitigate different market imperfections.

In doing so I pulled together three strands of literature: opportunity recognition, stewardship in family business and sustainable entrepreneurship. The sustainable entrepreneurship literature is based on the concepts associated with economics and market imperfection. Opportunity recognition literature is rooted in cognitive psychology, while the stewardship theory literature is developed from management and used in family business research literature. This chapter identifies the strength of stewardship that family business possesses and how that strength can be utilized to identify and pursue opportunities for sustainability. By understanding how the stewardship governance in family business can contribute to identification and pursuit of sustainable opportunities has several implications for family business, entrepreneurship and ecological sustainability literature.

Opportunity recognition in family businesses is important for long term continuity and growth of the family business. Family businesses are often associated with stagnation (Miller et al., 2008), risk aversion and lack of growth (Ward, 1997), yet pursuing new opportunities is an essential aspect of the process of strategic renewal (Sardeshmukh and Corbett, 2011) and growth agenda (Ward, 1997) for continuation of the family business. Family businesses that pursue entrepreneurial opportunity are more likely to show better performance and growth (Kellermanns and Eddleston, 2006; Memili et al., 2010). We also know that family businesses driven by attitudes of stewardship, are strongly focused on continuity, long-term preservation and nurturing their business (Miller et al., 2008), and their behaviours extend beyond the pecuniary concerns to include community and connections with the external environment (Miller et al., 2008). These attributes poise them perfectly to undertake sustainable entrepreneurship activities to further develop the family business. By integrating these with the sustainable entrepreneurship literature, we show how different forms of market imperfections can be mitigated by some of the stewardship approaches associated with family business.

Given that family business forms are pervasive, understanding the role inherent family business attributes such as stewardship can play for pursuit of sustainable opportunities can help us better reach the majority of businesses in the world. This chapter indicates that sustainability initiatives can not only fit well with the essential familiness of family business, but can also help them grow. Further if the large majority of businesses can be encouraged into making sustainability a priority, highlighting the fit with their familiness, it can help make great strides in the context of environmental sustainability. Similar to York and Venkataraman (2010), I argue that sustainable entrepreneurship is not antithetical to making profits. In fact, entrepreneurial business can generate profits while doing the right thing for sustainability. However pursuing opportunities for sustainability requires a broader stewardship view of profitability to mitigate environmental market failures.

This chapter is a conceptual study and the propositions can be empirically tested to improve our understanding of family businesses' contribution to the sustainability issues. A multi-method study investigating opportunity recognition and sustainable entrepreneurship in family business can empirically shed light on this important phenomenon. Further, this of course does not imply that all family businesses will have environmental consciousness and will be successful in pursuing the sustainable entrepreneurship opportunities. Nor does this chapter imply that other businesses and entrepreneurs cannot exploit these opportunities. While we acknowledge that not all family businesses exhibit stewardship behaviours, research shows that successful and intergenerationally sustainable family businesses do indeed show stewardship characteristics.

In conclusion family businesses that approach their family, business, and community with a stewardship perspective, are well poised to identify and pursue sustainable entrepreneurship opportunities which can lead to strategic renewal and growth of their family businesses while maintaining and building upon their 'familiness'. Highlighting these benefits to a large majority of business forms throughout Australia and the world can help us reach important sustainability milestones.

REFERENCES

Akerlof, G.A. (1970), 'The market for "lemons": quality uncertainty and the market mechanism', *The Quarterly Journal of Economics*, 488–500.

Astrachan, J.H. and M.C. Shanker (2003), 'Family businesses' contribution to the U.S. economy: a closer look', *Family Business Review*, **16**, 211–19.

Australian Government (1999), *Guidelines for Section 516A reporting: Environment Protection and Biodiversity Conservation Act 1999*, Canberra: Government of Australia.

Australian Government (2011), available at http://www.environment.gov.au/about/legislation.html (accessed 12 April 2011).

Baron, R.A. (2006), 'Opportunity recognition as pattern recognition: how entrepreneurs "connect the dots" to identify new business opportunities', *The Academy of Management Perspectives*, **20** (1), 104–19.

Berrone, P., Cruz, C., Gomez-Mejia, L.R. and Larraza-Kintana, M. (2010), 'Socioemotional wealth and corporate responses to institutional pressures: do family-controlled firms pollute less?', *Administrative Science Quarterly*, **55** (1), 82–113.

Bjuggren, P. and Sund, L. (2005), 'Organization of transfers of small and medium-sized enterprises within the family: tax law considerations', *Family Business Review*, **18** (4), 305–19.

Carney, M. (2005), 'Corporate governance and competitive advantage in family-controlled firms', *Entrepreneurship Theory and Practice*, **29** (3), 249–65.

Carrigan, M. and Buckley, J. (2008), '"What's so special about family business?" An exploratory study of UK and Irish consumer experiences of family businesses', *International Journal of Consumer Studies*, **32** (6), 656–66.

Chen, C.C., Greene, P.G. and Crick, A. (1998), 'Does entrepreneurial self-efficacy distinguish entrepreneurs from managers?', *Journal of Business Venturing*, **13** (4), 295–316.

Chrisman, J.J., Chua, J.H. and Sharma, P. (2005), 'Trends and directions in the development of a strategic management theory of the family firm', *Entrepreneurship Theory and Practice*, **29** (5), 555–76.

Chrisman, J.J., Chua, J.H. and Steier, L.P. (2003), 'An introduction to theories of family business', *Journal of Business Venturing*, **18** (4), 441–8.

Chua, J.H., Chrisman, J.J. and Sharma, P. (1999), 'Defining the family business by behavior', *Entrepreneurship Theory and Practice*, **23** (4), 19–39.

Cohen, B. and Winn, M.I. (2007), 'Market imperfections, opportunity and sustainable entrepreneurship', *Journal of Business Venturing*, **22** (1), 29–49.

Corbett, A.C. (2005), 'Experiential learning within the process of opportunity identification and exploitation', *Entrepreneurship Theory and Practice*, **29** (4), 473–91.

Corbetta, G. and Salvato, C. (2004), 'Self-serving or self-actualizing? Models of man and agency costs in different types of family firms: a commentary on "comparing the agency costs of family and non-family firms: conceptual issues and exploratory evidence"', *Entrepreneurship Theory and Practice*, **28** (4), 355–62.

Cruz, C.C., Gomez-Mejia, L.R. and Becerra, M. (2010), 'Perceptions of benevolence and the design of agency contracts: CEO-TMT relationships in family firms', *The Academy of Management Journal*, **53** (1), 69–89.

Davis, J.H., Schoorman, F.D. and Donaldson, L. (1997), 'Toward a stewardship theory of management', *Academy of Management Review*, **22** (1), 20–47.

Dean, T. and McMullen, J. (2007), 'Toward a theory of sustainable entrepreneurship: reducing environmental degradation through entrepreneurial action', *Journal of Business Venturing*, **22** (1), 50–76.

Déniz, M.C.D. and Suárez, M.K.C. (2005), 'Corporate social responsibility and family business in Spain', *Journal of Business Ethics*, **56** (1), 27–41.

Department for International Development (DFID) (2012), 'International development minister praises Harrogate's ethical tea and coffee' (Press Release 17-2-2012).

Donaldson, L. and Davis, J.H. (1991), 'Stewardship theory or agency theory: CEO governance and shareholder returns', *Australian Journal of Management*, **16** (1), 49–64.

Dyer, W.G. Jr. and Whetten, D.A. (2006), 'Family firms and social responsibility: preliminary evidence from the S&P 500', *Entrepreneurship Theory and Practice*, **30** (6), 785–802.

Eckhardt, J.T. and Shane, S. (2003), 'Opportunities and entrepreneurship', *Journal of Management*, **29**, 333–49.

Eddleston, K. and Kellermanns, F. (2007), 'Destructive and productive family relationships: a stewardship theory perspective', *Journal of Business Venturing*, **22** (4), 545–65.

Family Business Australia (FBA) (2011), *Australian Family Business Sector Statistics*, Melbourne: Family Business Australia.

Gallo, M. (2004), 'The family business and its social responsibilities', *Family Business Review*, **17** (2), 135–49.

Gómez-Mejía, L.R., Haynes, K.T., Núñez-Nickel, M., Jacobson, K.J.L. and Moyano-Fuentes, J. (2007), 'Socioemotional wealth and business risks in family-controlled firms: evidence from Spanish olive oil mills', *Administrative Science Quarterly*, **52** (1), 106–37.

Gregoire, D.A., Shepherd, D.A. and Lambert, L.S. (2009), 'Measuring opportunity-recognition beliefs: illustrating and validating an experimental approach', *Organizational Research Methods*, **13** (1), 114–45.

Hernandez, M. (2012), 'Toward an understanding of the psychology of stewardship', *Academy of Management Review*, **37** (2), 172–93.

Kellermanns, F.W. and Eddleston, K.A. (2006), 'Corporate entrepreneurship in family firms: a family perspective', *Entrepreneurship Theory and Practice*, **30** (6), 809–30.

Kirzner, I. (1973), *Competition and Entrepreneurship*, Chicago, IL: University of Chicago Press.

Kirzner, I. (1997), 'Entrepreneurial discovery and the competitive market process: an Austrian approach', *Journal of Economic Literature*, **35** (1), 60–85.

KPMG (2011), *Stewards: Moving Forward, Moving Onward. KPMG and Family Business Australia's Family Business Survey 2011*, Sydney: KPMG Australia.

Memili, E., Eddleston, K.A., Kellermanns, F.W., Zellweger, T.M. and Barnett, T. (2010), 'The critical path to family firm success through entrepreneurial risk-taking and image', *Journal of Family Business Strategy*, **1**, 200–209.

Miller, D., Le Breton-Miller, I. and Scholnick, B. (2008), 'Stewardship vs. stagnation: an empirical comparison of small family and non-family businesses', *Journal of Management Studies*, **45** (1), 51–78.

Orth, U.R. and Green, M.T. (2009), 'Consumer loyalty to family versus non-family business: the roles of store image, trust and satisfaction', *Journal of Retailing and Consumer Services*, **16** (4), 248–59.

Pearson, A.W., Carr, J.C. and Shaw, J. (2008), 'Toward a theory of familiness: a social capital perspective', *Entrepreneurship: Theory and Practice*, **32** (6), 949–69.

Porter, M.E. and Kramer, M.R. (2011), 'The big idea: creating shared value. How to reinvent capitalism – and unleash a wave of innovation and growth', *Harvard Business Review* (Jan–Feb), 63–77.

Ronstadt, R. (1988), 'The corridor principle', *Journal of Business Venturing*, **3** (1), 31–40.

Rutherford, M.W., Kuratko, D.F. and Holt, D.T. (2008), 'Examining the link between "familiness" and performance: can the F-PEC untangle the family business theory jungle?', *Entrepreneurship Theory and Practice*, **32** (6), 1089–1109.

Sandhu, S. (2010), 'Shifting paradigms in corporate environmentalism: from poachers to gamekeepers', *Business and Society Review*, **115** (3), 285–310.

Sarasvathy, S. (2001), 'Causation and effectuation: toward a theoretical shift from economic inevitability to entrepreneurial contingency', *Academy of Management Review*, **26** (2), 243–63.

Sardeshmukh, S.R. and Corbett, A.C. (2011), 'The duality of internal and external development of successors: opportunity recognition in family firms', *Family Business Review*, **24** (2), 111–25.

Schulze, W.S and Gedajlovic, E.R. (2010), 'Whither family business?', *Journal of Management Studies*, **47** (2), 191–204.

Schulze, W.S., Lubatkin, M.H. and Dino, R.N. (2003), 'Exploring the agency consequences of ownership dispersion among the directors of private family firms', *Academy of Management Journal*, **46** (2), 179–94.

Schulze, W.S., Lubatkin, M.H., Dino, R.N. and Buchholtz, A.K. (2001), 'Agency relationships in family firms: theory and evidence', *Organization Science*, **12**, 99–116.

Shane, S. (2000), 'Prior knowledge, and the discovery of entrepreneurial opportunities', *Organization Science*, **11** (4), 448–69.

Shane, S. and Venkataraman, S. (2000), 'Entrepreneurship as a field of research', *Academy of Management Review*, **25**, 217–26.

Sharma, P. and Sharma, S. (2011), 'Drivers of proactive environmental strategy in family firms', *Business Ethics Quarterly*, **21** (2), 309–34.

Sirmon, D.G and Hitt, M.A. (2003), 'Managing resources: linking unique resources, management, and wealth creation in family firms', *Entrepreneurship Theory and Practice*, **27** (4), 339–58.

Sorenson, R.L., Goodpaster, K.E., Hedberg, P.R. and Yu, A. (2009), 'The family point of view, family social capital, and firm performance: an exploratory test', *Family Business Review*, **22** (3), 239–53.

Stockmans, A., Lybaert, N. and Voordeckers, W. (2010), 'Socioemotional wealth and earnings management in private family firms', *Family Business Review*, **23** (3), 280–94.

Vallejo, M. (2009), 'Analytical model of leadership in family firms under transformational theoretical approach: an exploratory study', *Family Business Review*, **22** (2), 136–50.

Venkataraman, S. (1997), 'The distinct domain of entrepreneurship research', *Advances in Entrepreneurship, Firm Emergence and Growth*, **3**, 119–38.

Ward, J.L. (1997), 'Growing the family business: special challenges and best practices', *Family Business Review*, **10** (4), 323–37.

Williamson, O.E. (1985), *The Economic Institutions of Capitalism: Firms, Markets, Relational Contracting*, New York: The Free Press.

York, J.G. and Venkataraman, S. (2010), 'The entrepreneur-environment nexus: uncertainty, innovation, and allocation', *Journal of Business Venturing*, **25** (5), 449–63.

Zahra, S.A., Hayton, J.C. and Salvato, C. (2004), 'Entrepreneurship in family vs. non-family firms: a resource-based analysis of the effect of organizational culture', *Entrepreneurship Theory and Practice*, **28** (4), 363–81.

Zellweger, T.M. and Nason, R.S. (2008), 'A stakeholder perspective on family firm performance', *Family Business Review*, **21** (3), 203–16.

Zellweger, T.M., Eddleston, K.A. and Kellermanns, F.W. (2010), 'Exploring the concept of familiness: introducing family firm identity', *Journal of Family Business Strategy*, **1** (1), 54–63.

Zellweger, T.M., Nason, R.S., Nordqvist, M. and Brush, C.G. (2011), 'Why do family firms strive for nonfinancial goals? An organizational identity perspective', *Entrepreneurship Theory and Practice*.

Zhao, H., Seibert, S. and Hills, G. (2005), 'The mediating role of self-efficacy in the development of entrepreneurial intentions', *Journal of Applied Psychology*, **90** (6), 1265–72.

11. Innovation in sustainable business practices: greening the family firm

Christina M. Scott-Young

INTRODUCTION

Eco-sustainability is focussed on wise stewardship of environmental resources and is defined as 'the ability of a company to continue indefinitely by making a zero impact on environmental resources' (Blowfield and Murray 2011, p. 59). Much of the eco-sustainability literature has focused on high visibility large enterprises (Bos-Brouwers 2009), largely overlooking small and medium enterprises (SMEs), which employ 250 or fewer workers (Levinsohn and Brundin 2011). However SMEs are the most common business form in the US (Heck and Trent 1999) and beyond, comprising up to 95 per cent of all businesses in both the developed and developing world (OECD 2011). These businesses create up to 70 per cent of the world's industrial waste and pollution (Hillary 2000), yet little is known about their behaviour in terms of eco-sustainable practices.

Scholars are only now beginning to recognize the importance of SMEs in managing environmental challenges (Battisti and Perry 2011; Levinsohn and Brundin 2011). Many of these SMEs are family owned and managed businesses. Despite their importance to environmental management, researchers have been slow to study eco-sustainability in the context of family businesses (Sharma and Sharma 2011). From the limited available research, the contribution that SMEs make to effective environmental management is contested. There is some evidence to suggest that SMEs are laggards in the uptake of sustainable practices (Collins et al. 2010), due to limited eco-awareness (Tilly 2000), or lack of resources (Hillary 2000), or to problems in creating a business case to justify their implementation (Revell and Blackburn 2007). More recent research though has suggested that SMEs may be becoming more proactive in adopting environmentally sustainable practices (Parker et al. 2009). A review of the literature reveals that our knowledge is sparse about what motivates family owned SMEs to demonstrate concern for the natural environment (Craig and Dibrell 2006).

In this chapter we will explore the factors that drive innovative adoption of sustainability practices in family owned SMEs by examining a case study of one environmentally innovative medium sized Australian family business, Ferguson Plarre Bakehouses. We draw together strands of the eco-entrepreneurship and family business literatures to provide a theoretical lens to interpret our case study. Ferguson Plarre Bakehouses is a leader in world best practice in sustainable food manufacturing and has received multiple awards, including the prestigious 2009 Gold Banksia environmental award for excellence in sustainability. The company is an exemplar of the successful integration of eco-sustainability with firm profitability and business growth. 'Ferguson Plarre Bakehouses' sustainability principles have been extended to all levels of the business from top level strategic planning through to staff recruitment, induction and position descriptions which identify sustainability as key performance indicators' (Victorian Employers' Chamber of Commerce 2012). Data for this case study was collected using a triangulated method of semi-structured interviews with the company's fourth generation director and CEO Steve Plarre, documents from the company website, together with media reports, and recorded interviews with a third generation owner-director Ralph Plarre.

According to Isaak (2005), there are two types of environmentally friendly businesses: 'green businesses' which are existing businesses that have adapted to environmental challenges by converting to eco-sustainable practices, and 'green-green businesses' that start up especially with the goal of eco-sustainability. Ferguson Plarre Bakehouses is the first type of business (a green business), which is an owned and operated partnership of the fourth and fifth generations of the two founding families. Ferguson Plarre Bakehouses was formed in 1980 through the amalgamation of two separate long running baking businesses that were originally established at the beginning of the 20th century by two immigrant families (the British Fergusons and the German Plarres) in Melbourne, Australia. In this partnership, the Ferguson family is responsible for the retail and marketing side of the business and the Plarre family is in charge of the operation of the manufacturing facility that supplies all its retail outlets. It is the Plarre family, headed by owner Ralph, which has spearheaded eco-sustainability in the business.

Ferguson Plarre Bakehouses has grown from a five bakery operation in 1980 to a medium sized firm of 55 family-owned and franchised bakehouses in 2012, employing 120 people. This strong growth necessitated the building of a new larger facility in 2007. Adopting a sustainable growth model, the firm built a new $10 million state of the art baking facility that is four times the size of its old premises. This new facility included more than $300 000 worth of eco-sustainability initiatives, the cost of which was recouped in one year through cutting the firm's total energy consumption by 40 per cent. Sustainability initiatives have included recovering heat from the refrigeration system to heat the water used in cake production, using recovered heat from freshly baked goods to heat or cool the production area, using solar heating in the offices, collecting rainwater in tanks to provide water for offices, truck washing and garden irrigation, cutting packaging waste through bulk silo storage of ingredients, disposing of baking waste to a local piggery and to their own onsite worm farm, using the state's first hybrid truck to distribute products, rerouting deliveries to cut emissions, and using a monitoring system that delivers real time energy consumption data to increase employee awareness. As well as creating considerable cost savings, the new initiatives have reaped considerable environmental benefits. 'By harnessing the waste heat from our refrigeration systems, redistributing heat recovered from freshly baked products, employing hybrid vehicle technologies and offsetting the remaining emissions via tree planting, we have reduced our carbon footprint by over 5,000 tonnes of CO_2 annually' (Ralph Plarre).

Ferguson Plarre's operational innovations constitute a model of corporate eco-entrepreneurial behaviour that may offer some lessons in explaining what drives sustainability innovation in family owned SMEs. 'Entrepreneurship centers on recognizing and exploiting opportunities by reconfiguring existing and new resources in ways that create an advantage . . . [and] that improve the company's responsiveness to the market' (Zahra 2005, p. 25). Currently, little is known about what motivates family businesses to become environmentally friendly, so we look to the eco-sustainability entrepreneurship and the family business literatures for theoretical guidance in interpreting our case. Levinsohn and Brundin's (2011) review of the sustainability entrepreneurship literature identifies a number of factors related to entrepreneurial innovation, including the importance of economic opportunity recognition and business case; owner-CEO environmental values; and the presence of an innovation culture. From the perspective of the family business literature, eco-sustainability has been associated with family socio-emotional capital and stewardship (Sharma and Sharma 2011). We now draw on these theoretical constructs to help unpack the factors that have driven the formulation and implementation of Ferguson Plarre Bakehouses' innovative eco-sustainability business strategy. We begin with the first stage of any entrepreneurial endeavour: opportunity recognition.

THE IMPORTANCE OF ECONOMIC OPPORTUNITY RECOGNITION

In traditional entrepreneurship theory, entrepreneurial behaviours are related to identifying new economic opportunities. Imperfections in the market, such as firm inefficiencies, present business opportunities (Cohen and Winn 2007) that are recognized and exploited by enterprising individuals. In the sustainability literature, eco-entrepreneurship has been linked to opportunity recognition of inefficiencies in the use of natural resources (Dean and McMullen 2007). At present many firms are only achieving a portion of the efficiencies possible (Cohen and Winn 2007). More efficient use of natural resources can reduce both resource waste and economic waste and produce environmental improvement and cost-savings for business (Hawken et al. 1999).

In order for opportunity recognition to occur, there needs to be some sort of organizational learning (Wiesner et al. 2011) and knowledge transfer. In their study of New Zealand firms, Collins et al. (2010) found that lack of knowledge was a major barrier to corporate sustainability innovation. This was true in Ferguson Plarre Bakehouses' case. It was a serendipitous government initiative that prompted opportunity recognition and organizational learning. While the firm was well aware that the baking industry is energy-intensive with high heating and cooling expenses, it was not until they were invited to participate in the Australian Government's Greenhouse Challenge program in 1989 that they learned how to conduct an environmental audit and discovered that there were initiatives they could introduce to reduce their energy consumption and create cost savings. Smaller companies often lack the knowledge to conduct energy audits and access other strategic tools that are the usual eco-sustainability entry points available to larger firms (Duh et al. 2010). The then CEO Ralph Plarre notes the critical importance of this external injection of sustainability knowledge:

> The Greenhouse Challenge was the start of our sustainable journey. In the Challenge we started to measure energy and carbon. Then we reduced our emissions through common sense, care and good housekeeping. [We realized that] environmental sustainability makes good business sense . . . Consequently when the time came to build a new central baking facility . . . I made sustainability a priority . . . Any business or organization can profit and grow by adopting sustainability as a positive change driver.

Ralph's son Steve Plarre, who took over as CEO in 2009, stresses the importance to his company of developing a strong business case for introducing sustainable practices, which was critical to convince others in the management team of the financial benefits. His perspective reflects the views of Loukes and Martens (2010, p. 186) who argue that 'given that theoretical grounding of any business is to increase the monetary value of the firm ... a clear case for how sustainable development strategies improve the economic situation of a company ... help[s] owners operationalize their values'. Since the old baking premises had always been inefficient in its use of energy, the Plarre family was convinced that a more energy efficient design would save money, an important consideration since the new facility was designed to be four times larger.

> We recovered over 100 per cent of the costs involved in setting up our energy-efficient bakery in the first year alone. Once you take into consideration the recent increases in the price of water and energy, our payback over the next 20 years will be far more than just penny-pinching – it will be a definite competitive advantage. (Steve Plarre)

Although the initial stimulus to opportunity recognition was external to the business, further business benefits became obvious internally after building the new premises. The energy savings encouraged further sustainability initiatives that produced more benefits through ongoing streamlining of the manufacturing process, continuous improvement in waste reduction, and in attracting and retaining staff.

> Since completion of the new bakery ... we have reduced our carbon emissions by over 5,000 tonnes and the initiative was a catalyst for a sustainable culture-change that continues in the business ... Best of all, our new facility has continued to make a positive impact on our culture, and our bottom line. The sustainable baking initiatives have been more effective than I could have imagined. (Ralph Plarre)

> Aside from the energy cost savings, sustainability and minimizing waste is perfectly aligned with 'lean' manufacturing. Not only have our staff embraced the concept of reducing energy, but lean techniques are being used across the entire business to improve efficiencies. Another key stakeholder for us is our staff. It's nice to work for a company that's doing the right thing. In a world where the youth are increasingly aware of the damage that prior generations have inflicted on the earth, it's valuable to be able to promote your company as one that is responsible and caring. We'd like to think we'll get a better share of the quality employees out there as a result of our environmental stance and passion. (Steve Plarre)

Business benefits have also emerged with regard to external stakeholders, like the bakehouses' customers. Aware that consumers are becoming increasingly sensitive to environmental issues, Ferguson Plarre Bakehouses' marketing and website now inform customers of the company's green awards and efforts towards environmental sustainability. 'We believe strongly that people will be increasingly happy that the cakes and savouries they purchase from us are not only family baked, award winning and full of quality ingredients, but less damaging to the environment than our competitors' products' (Steve Plarre). Ferguson Plarre Bakehouses' green credentials have also played a role in attracting new franchisees. 'The sort of person that looks at a franchise has more awareness of a business's vision, and if a business has got a vision of the future then that's a big tick' (Ralph Plarre).

THE IMPORTANCE OF THE FAMILY BUSINESS OWNER-CEO AS CHAMPION OF ECO-SUSTAINABLE PRACTICES

The entrepreneurship literature highlights the importance of the individual in driving innovation. The internal beliefs and values of the family business owner and CEO are key motivators of intentional sustainability actions (Linnanen 2005). In the family business literature also, the owner-manager's personal beliefs and values are considered to be a primary driver of the adoption of environmental sustainability (Battisti and Perry 2011). One study of thriving British SMEs found that 'strategy . . . is enacted in a highly personalized manner, and is strongly influenced by the actions, abilities, personality and success criteria of the key role players' (Beaver 2007, p. 16). Consistent with this, the initial thrust for eco-sustainability at Ferguson Plarre Bakehouses came from one key player, the owner and CEO Ralph Plarre. Although some in the business were not initially as passionate as Ralph, he worked hard to convince his management team that his quest for sustainable practices made good business sense.

> Passion is really important. Leadership is important in all of this. You've got to have someone in your business that's going to be passionate and who is really going to drive the environmental story . . . One of the decisions that we took after starting this journey was to say, right, we're going to do away with the argument of climate change and all that because there's still sceptics around. We took the decision that climate change is real and that we were contributing to it . . . it got everybody on board, right, we're all part of the team, we're all moving forward harmoniously . . . the whole team, all the team . . . It took a long time for it to get down through to [all] the 120 people, to engage with them all, but persistence is absolutely critical. (Ralph Plarre)

As well as being convinced of the economic opportunities of sustainable baking practices, Ralph Plarre is also deeply committed to the care of the environment and its natural resources for future generations. As with many eco-sustainability advocates, his drive stems from deep personal values (Castka et al. 2004). For such individuals, eco-sustainability activities have a strong moral component (Duh et al. 2010). Walley and Taylor (2005) describe such individuals as 'visionary champions', motivated to change the world. Ralph Plarre is passionate that 'business sustainability is about doing the right thing' in his own company, but he also has the sense of a wider mission that often characterizes environmental champions (Choi and Gray 2008). An important part of the company's environmental mission statement is 'to be an industry leader in environmental performance and an ambassador for positive environmental change'. Since passing on the management of Ferguson Plarre Bakehouses in 2009 to his two sons, Steve and Mike, Ralph has intensified his endeavours to educate other SMEs about the business benefits of eco-sustainability. His assistance has been practical, like providing mentorship to another baking business in the planning and development of a new, more environmentally sustainable bakehouse, and has also taken the form of education and information dissemination. Ralph regularly addresses local and national business groups through his association with the ICMI Speakers and Entertainers Group. He also is one of three business sustainability ambassadors for the Victorian Employers' Chamber of Commerce and Industry (VECCI), the state's peak body for employers, which services more than 15 000 members. Reflecting on his role at VECCI, Ralph Plarre observed:

> We're thrilled to be involved with VECCI and to assist others in their quest for sustainability. Every company – every person – needs a role model for this. We find that companies and people are often a reflection of who they spend time and network with, and this is where ambassadorships are vital. Sustainability is relatively new for people, especially those in hands-on manufacturing jobs where thinking beyond the day's production is limited. While we're thrilled that we've been able to reduce the impact of our own company on the environment, we recognize that it's our ability to influence others that can generate truly exponential results. My personal message is simple . . . Don't let yourself be overwhelmed by complexity, think outside the square and be prepared to challenge the status quo and most importantly . . . start now!

THE IMPORTANCE OF THE FAMILY SYSTEM AND STEWARDSHIP OF SOCIO-EMOTIONAL WEALTH

Until recently the literature has typically focussed upon the entrepreneur as an individual actor, ignoring that many entrepreneurs are members of a broader family system that supports their activities (Danes et al. 2009; Zachary 2011). Family business scholars now argue for the inclusion of the family system when considering the entrepreneurial activities of family firms (Heck et al. 2006; Sharma and Sharma 2011). In their study of nearly 200 US firms, Berrone et al. (2010) found that family ownership of public companies was related to superior environmental performance, regardless of whether the CEO was a family member or not. 'Over generations, [shared] "family values" become the basis of the family business culture ... The family's articulation and cohesive support of its expectations about how business should be conducted really can provide clarity for directors and executives concerning their decisions and actions' (Aronoff 2004, p. 56). When families have been involved for multiple generations in the firm, as is the case with Ferguson Plarre Bakehouses, the power and influence of the family's values become deeply embedded in the business strategy and policies (Sorenson et al. 2009).

According to the Sustainable Family Business Theory (SFBT), members of the owning family bring a wealth of social, emotional and human capital to the business (Danes et al. 2008), which creates the necessary resources to support and sustain entrepreneurial behaviour (Zachary 2011). Due to their close ties family members are more likely to trust and support the business decisions of the family owner. Ralph Plarre recognizes the advantage that family owned SMEs have in decision-making: 'Being a family business meant that we could make decisions that maybe some of the larger public companies with highly responsible boards would have trouble [doing]'. Additionally emotionally supportive family relationships provide encouragement for business innovation, along with extra family time, labour, and family financial support for new initiatives (Danes et al. 2008). Greater involvement of family members in the firm creates stronger socio-emotional attachment between members of the business (Gomez-Mejia et al. 2007), which can bring about positive performance outcomes (Sharma 2004; Eddleston and Kellermanns 2007). This has occurred in the case of Ferguson Plarre Bakehouses. Senior management is comprised of multiple members from both families. In the case of the Plarre family, Ralph, his wife, two sons, his daughter and daughter-in-law either work or have worked in the family firm and all share Ralph Plarre's environmental values and support his strategic vision for a sustainable, carbon neutral business.

Increasingly as the owning family invests emotional value in the family business (Berrone et al. 2010), the family's identity becomes more and more enmeshed with that of the firm, and this identity can be just as important to the family as the economic wealth derived from the business (Astrachan and Jaskiewicz 2008). Studies have shown that when families identify strongly with the firm name (as in the case of Ferguson Plarre Bakehouses), those firms are more likely to display responsible community citizenship behaviours (Craig and Dibrell 2006; Dyer and Whetton

2006) that build up even larger stores of socio-emotional wealth (Berrone et al. 2010). Stewardship theory outlines the family's concern with preserving the business for future generations (Le Breton-Miller and Miller 2006) through family unity, altruism, helping behaviours and positive reciprocal relationships (Eddleston and Kellermanns 2007). Since they care for future generations' welfare as much as they do for current profit, family businesses have longer term horizons than public companies (Zahra et al.; Mandl 2008), especially firms which have passed through the hands of multiple generations. Family businesses tend to prioritize 'the long-range implications and impact of decisions and actions that come to fruition after an extended time period' (Lumpkin et al. 2010, p. 245). Ralph Plarre acknowledges that this time frame difference between public and family companies allows family firms greater leeway in waiting for a return on their investment: 'We're doing this because we are a family business that's committed to taking a long-range approach to sustainability, which is something that public companies often cannot afford to do.'

The stewardship concerns of family businesses are highly compatible with the principles of sustainability. Both stances take a long term perspective, emphasizing the preservation of resources for future generations. According to the World Commission on Environment and Development, 'sustainable development means meeting the needs of the present without compromising the ability of future generations to meet their own needs' (Brundtland and Khalid 1987). Similarly family business leaders feel a strong sense of commitment and responsibility to the next generation of the family (Mandl 2008). The Plarre family's desire to nurture and grow their business sustainably for the upcoming younger generation is frequently expressed by Ralph Plarre.

> We're a family business that recognizes the need to plan for the future. We've been around for over 100 years and we want to be around for another 100! Our families have weathered and grown five generations of baking . . . and we want to play our part in helping future generations to continue to be able to grow by minimizing our environmental footprint.

THE IMPORTANCE OF A CULTURE OF INNOVATION

A strong mark of entrepreneurial firms is their commitment to innovation (Covin and Slevin 1991), which in turn stimulates firm growth (Trott 1998). Authors argue that innovation is one of the most important factors in entrepreneurial orientation (Lumpkin and Dess 1996). Innovativeness is 'a firm's tendency to engage in and support new ideas, novelty, experimentation, and creative processes that may result in new products, services, or technological processes' (Lumpkin and Dess 1996, p. 142). However in the eco-sustainability literature, Wagner (2009) draws attention to the omission of the dimension of innovation from current typologies of eco-entrepreneurship. Wagner's (2009) own research on sustainability suggests that for individuals, having a strong concern for the environment is not sufficient to drive eco-entrepreneurship; high green orientation must be paired with high propensity to innovate. Vollenbroek (2002) has also suggested that innovation is also a crucial mark of businesses that transition to sustainable development.

The family business literature has also tended to ignore the study of innovation, which may be why Sharma and Sharma's (2011) model of family firm eco-sustainable practices does not include innovation as a contributing factor. Family firms have traditionally been considered to be reluctant to innovate due to risk aversion (Allio 2004) and for fear of jeopardising the long term viability of the business (Habbershon and Williams 1999). However more recent research has found that family-owned businesses can in fact demonstrate the initiative and risk taking behaviours necessary for corporate entrepreneurship (Zahra et al. 2004; Gomez-Mejia et al. 2007) and that greater innovation is related to better family firm performance (Kellermanns et al. 2012). Ferguson Plarre Bakehouses is an example of a family business that has demonstrated an appetite for innovation and growth. In his 45 years in the family business, Ralph Plarre grew the company from five bakehouses in one city in 1980 to a 55-store bakery chain in three cities in 2012 through the adoption of innovative business models that created a partnership between two family businesses to combat growing competition from supermarkets, and through developing a franchising arm of the business.

Ferguson Plarre Bakehouses exhibits a strong culture of innovation in all aspects of its business, which Samson (2010, p. 4) calls 'systematic innovation capability' that 'assures them of a series of innovations that deliver business value'. This argument reflects the Enterprise Innovation System (EIS) theory (Shen et al. 2009) which posits that innovation is systemic and occurs interactively across all aspects of the business, including innovation in strategy, organization, culture, products, processes, and marketing. Ralph Plarre's attitude exemplifies Wagner's (2009) finding that sustainability and innovation are coupled: 'Business sustainability is about doing the right thing, but the process of investigating and discovering better ways to do things is also exciting.' According to Samson (2010, p. 4), 'innovation goes hand-in-hand with sustainable development initiatives, as both require progressive leadership and an appetite for change, combined with a tolerance of experimentation and some risk'.

The importance of the family system's influence on innovation has been largely overlooked in both the eco-entrepreneurship and family business literature, and scholars are only just beginning to recognize the family's importance. Studies are beginning to identify the benefits of multi-generational involvement in the family firm, which is associated with greater innovation (Zahra 2005) and also with the firm's identification and pursuit of entrepreneurial opportunities (Salvato 2004). Although both single and multiple generation ownership are positively related to innovation in the family firm, concentration of ownership in a single generation produces the highest level of innovation (Kellermans et al. 2012). In the case of Ferguson Plarre Bakehouses, the major thrust of the eco-sustainability innovation was executed during Ralph Plarre's term as CEO, with his sons assisting in a management capacity.

Together, the three Plarres have introduced a written environmental policy, an innovation that is a rarity in family businesses, which are usually less formal (Meers and Robertson 2007). Their environmental policy sets out Ferguson Plarre Bakehouses' mission 'to be an industry leader in environmental performance and an ambassador for positive environmental change . . . to achieve this we will be innovative in our approach to reducing our environmental impact'. The policy document identifies a number of initiatives, including implementing new innovations in world best practice baking technology, training employees in environmental best practice, working with suppliers to green the supply chain, as well as improving energy efficiency and transportation, preserving water and reducing waste and greenhouse gas emissions across their business. Another new initiative introduced by the next generation Plarre brothers has been a commitment to measurement and monitoring of the company's sustainability scorecard. An Environmental Management System (EMS) has been developed to 'set targets for our policy commitments, to measure our performance against these targets, and to transparently report on our achievements' (Ferguson Plarre Bakehouses 2012).

PRACTICAL IMPLICATIONS AND FUTURE RESEARCH

Despite increasing global attention to environmental issues and sustainability, CO_2 emissions are continuing to rise, with a global increase of 4.4 per cent between 2008 and 2010 (Busch et al. 2012). The need for efficient stewardship of natural resources is a pressing issue in the business world. Clearly researchers will need to increase their effort in identifying business solutions to efficient use of the world's depleting resources. Research to date has focussed mainly on eco-sustainability initiatives in large enterprises (Bos-Brouwen 2009), overlooking that the majority of companies around the world are SMEs (Levinsohn and Brundin 2011), which contribute up to 70 per cent of the world's pollution and environmental waste (Hillary 2000). Many of these SMEs are owned and operated by families (Chang et al. 2008). Family business researchers have argued that family owned firms are qualitatively different from public firms due to the overlapping interests of the family system and the firm (Danes et al. 2008) and their degree of access to resources (Hillary 2000). Given their large market share, there is a need for greater research into innovative behaviour in family firms (Kellermans et al. 2012), particularly in the area of eco-sustainable business practices (Bos-Brouwen 2009; Battisti and Perry 2011).

In this chapter we have used theories from the entrepreneurship, eco-entrepreneurial and family business literatures as lenses to study an exemplar of eco-sustainable innovation, the family-owned SME, Ferguson Plarre Bakehouses. In particular, we have explored whether there is evidence of the key drivers of eco-sustainable business practices identified from Levinsohn and Brundin's (2011) review of the eco-sustainability literature, namely, economic opportunity recognition and business case; owner-CEO environmental values; and the presence of an innovation culture. To capture the family ownership elements of the case, we drew on the family business theories of socio-emotional capital (Danes et al. 2008) and stewardship (Le Breton-Miller and Miller 2006). We found that these theories were able to explain to a large extent the drivers behind the change to eco-sustainability that occurred at Ferguson Plarre Bakehouses.

Of primary importance was opportunity recognition (Levinsohn and Brundin 2011), which convinced the company of the financial value of creating eco-efficiencies in their operations. Using the baking chain as an example, we were able to unpack the subtlety of the opportunity recognition process. An interesting finding emerged: opportunity recognition was a process, not an event. In our case study, opportunity recognition took the form of a progressive, incremental realization, rather than a sudden revelation. The owner-CEO Ralph Plarre had always been conscious that the old baking facility he inherited was inefficient in its energy use and that the lack of climate control impacted the quality of his baked goods. But it was only when a government environmental agency invited his company to participate in an energy auditing program that Ralph Plarre acquired the knowledge, skills and support to begin to implement eco-efficiencies in his operations. This initial external intervention ignited his motivation to create an eco-sustainable business. From there on the motivation grew internally from the firm's initial successes, but was also externally reinforced by continued support from government and growing media and industry interest in their innovations. The firm's eco-sustainable initiatives grew iteratively, building on early successes, and continued to be driven by successive financial, process and product quality gains. Each gain cemented the company's commitment to further spreading eco-sustainability to all areas of their operations, resulting in the development of what is now a systemic culture of sustainability.

Our case study also highlights the critical importance of creating a sound business case to overcome management team resistance to eco-sustainability initiatives. Our findings support Revell and Blackburn's (2007) contention that the need to create a business case to justify the implementation of sustainable initiatives can be a barrier for SMEs. A potential remedy to this lack of knowledge and resources is the provision of support and information through external intermediaries (Klewitz and Zeyen 2010). Our case study underscores the importance for SMEs of external sources of support in bringing about increased eco-sustainability in their business practices. In Ferguson Plarre Bakehouses' case, government support in catalysing opportunity recognition and providing the necessary knowledge and skills for change was critical to their success. This is an important finding since the literature has identified SMEs' lack of knowledge (Tilly 2000) and resources (Hillary 2000) as a primary barrier to eco-sustainable implementations. Clearly, government environmental agencies have a vital role in fostering opportunity recognition and in facilitating organizational learning in SMEs.

Our study also highlights the importance of access to other forms of external support for SMEs. Through their own experience, Ferguson Plarre Bakehouses has recognized that SMEs need greater knowledge about business eco-sustainability. The company now places high priority upon the external dissemination of sustainability knowledge via industry networks and associations, media coverage and informal mentoring of other businesses. This finding extends the eco-sustainability literature. The importance of the family business owner-CEO as a champion of eco-sustainable practices is not just critical for the individual business – the wider business community can also benefit from the passion of these eco-champions. Researchers are now beginning to recognize the importance of such external networks (Loucks et al. 2010) and intermediary organizations (Klewitz and Zeyen 2010) for initiating and fostering environmental change in SMEs. Our case study findings suggest that this promising area of intervention warrants further investigation.

Another area deserving of further research is how eco-sustainability champions acquire their environmental orientation. In our case study the strong desire to conserve natural resources for future generations was a powerful driver of business change. Future research is needed into what life experiences influence these eco-champions' thinking, foster their value system and motivate them to act on their values. Our study also highlights the importance of family buy-in and support of eco-sustainable practices. Strong family backing of the family environmental champion helped convince other team members to support the proposed changes. Despite the transition to new leadership (from father to sons), the solidarity of the family value system has meant that the eco-sustainable culture is being maintained. Further study of how families develop a cohesive united family value system around environmental issues would be of value. The final area deserving more research is the role of an established innovation culture in enabling eco-sustainability business initiatives. The study of innovation has been largely ignored in the family business literature. Our case study suggests that a firm's appetite for innovation is strongly related to openness to conservation and implementing environmentally friendly practices. We recommend further research to explore this relationship.

Whilst our in depth case study yielded rich insights into the key drivers of the greening of one family business, it suffers from the limitation of being a single company's experience. We recommend further qualitative and quantitative research using a large sample of family owned SMEs. Nevertheless, our case study has demonstrated that the principles of the entrepreneurship and family stewardship theories are useful in explaining how one family firm developed a successful sustainability culture that has produced proven economic, environmental and reputational benefits. This exemplar offers guidance for other SMEs to help them gain competitive advantage through voluntary implementation of eco-sustainability initiatives.

REFERENCES

Aldrich, H.E. and Cliff, J.E. (2003), 'The pervasive effects of family on entrepreneurship: toward a family embeddedness perspective', *Journal of Business Venturing*, **18** (5), 573–96.
Allio, M. (2004), 'Family businesses: their virtues, vices and strategic path', *Strategy and Leadership*, **32**, 24–5.
Aronoff, C. (2004), 'Self-perpetuation family organization built on values: necessary condition for long-term family business survival', *Family Business Review*, **17** (1), 55–9.
Astrachan, J. and Jaskiewicz, P. (2008), 'Emotional returns and emotional costs in privately-held family businesses: advancing traditional business valuation', *Family Business Review*, **21** (2), 139–50.
Battisti, M. and Perry, M. (2011), 'Walking the talk? Environmental responsibility from the perspective of small-business owners', *Corporate Social Responsibility and Environmental Management*, **18** (3), 172–85.

Beaver, G. (2007), 'The strategy payoff for smaller enterprises', *Journal of Business Strategy*, **28** (1), 11–17.

Berrone, P., Cruz, C., Gomez-Mejia, L.R. and Larraza-Kintana, M. (2010), 'Socioemotional wealth and corporate responses to institutional pressures: do family-controlled firms pollute less?', *Administrative Science Quarterly*, **55**, 82–113.

Blowfield, M. and Murray, A. (2011), *Corporate Responsibility: A Critical Introduction* (2nd edn), New York: Oxford University Press.

Bos-Brouwers, H.E.J. (2009), 'Corporate sustainability and innovation in SMEs: evidence of themes and activities in practice', *Business Strategy and the Environment*, **19**, 417–35.

Brundtland, G. and Khalid, M. (1987), *Our Common Future*, Oxford: Oxford University Press.

Busch, T., Bauer, R. and Orlitzky, M. (2012), 'Call for papers for special issue: sustainable development and financial markets', *Business and Society*, www.bas.sagepub.com (accessed 25 March 2012).

Castka, P., Balzarova, M.A., Bamber, C.J. and Sharp, J.M. (2004), 'How can SMEs effectively implement the CSR agenda? A UK case study perspective', *Corporate Social Responsibility and Environmental Management*, **11** (3), 140–49.

Chang, E.P.C., Chrisman, J.J., Chua, J.H. and Kellermanns, F.W. (2008), 'Regional economy as a determinant of the prevalence of family firms in the United States: a preliminary report', *Entrepreneurship Theory and Practice*, **23** (3), 559–73.

Choi, D.Y. and Gray, E.R. (2008), 'The venture development processes of "sustainable" entrepreneurs', *Management Research News*, **31** (8), 558–69.

Cohen, B. and Winn, M.I. (2007), 'Market imperfections, opportunity and sustainable entrepreneurship', *Journal of Business Venturing*, **22** (1), 29–49.

Collins, E., Roper, J. and Lawrence, S. (2010), 'Sustainability practices: trends in New Zealand businesses', *Business Strategy and the Environment*, **19** (8), 479–94.

Covin, J.G. and Slevin, D.P. (1991), 'A conceptual model of entrepreneurship as firm behavior', *Entrepreneurship Theory and Practice*, **16** (1), 7–25.

Craig, J. and Dibrell, C. (2006), 'The natural environment, innovation, and firm performance: a comparative study', *Family Business Review*, **19** (4), 275–88.

Danes, S.M., Lee, J., Stafford, K. and Heck, R.K.Z. (2008), 'The effects of ethnicity, families and culture on entrepreneurial experience: an extension of Sustainable Family Business Theory', *Journal of Developmental Entrepreneurship*, **13** (3), 229–68.

Danes, S.M., Stafford, K., Haynes, G. and Amarapurkar, S. (2009), 'Family capital of family firms: bridging human, social, and financial capital', *Family Business Review*, **22** (3), 199–215.

Dean, T. and McMullen, J. (2007), 'Toward a theory of sustainable entrepreneurship: reducing environmental degradation through entrepreneurial action', *Journal of Business Venturing*, **22** (1), 50–76.

Duh, M., Belak, J. and Mifelner, B. (2010), 'Core values, culture and ethical climate as constitutional elements of ethical behaviour: exploring differences between family and non-family enterprises', *Journal of Business Ethics*, **97**, 473–89.

Dyer, W.G. and Whetten, D.A. (2006), 'Family firms and social responsibility: preliminary evidence from the S&P 500', *Entrepreneurship Theory and Practice*, **30** (6), 785–802.

Eddleston, K. and Kellermanns, F.W. (2007), 'Destructive and productive family relationships: a stewardship theory perspective', *Journal of Business Venturing*, **22** (4), 545–65.

European Commission Enterprise and Industry (2010), *Small and Medium-Sized Enterprises (SMEs): SME Definition*, available at http://ec.europa.eu/enterprise/policies/sme/facts-figures-analysis/sme-definition/index_en.htm (accessed 17 May 2012).

Ferguson Plarre Bakehouses (2012), *Environmental Policy*, available at www.fergusonplarre.com.au (accessed 2 April 2010).

Gomez-Mejia, L.R., Hynes, K.T., Nunez-Nickel, M. and Moyano-Fuentes, H. (2007), 'Socio-emotional wealth and business risk in family-controlled firms: evidence from Spanish olive oil mills', *Administrative Science Quarterly*, **52**, 106–137.

Habbershon, T.G. and Williams, M. (1999), 'A resource-based framework for assessing the strategic advantage of family firms', *Family Business Review*, **12**, 1–25.

Hawken, P., Lovins, A. and Lovins, L.H. (1999), *Natural Capitalism: Creating the Next Industrial Revolution*, New York: Little, Brown and Company.

Hillary, R. (2000), *Small and Medium-Sized Enterprises and the Environment: Business Imperatives*, Sheffield: Greenleaf.

Hillary, R. (2004), 'Environmental management systems and the smaller enterprise', *Journal of Cleaner Production*, **12** (6), 561–9.

Heck, R.K.Z. and Trent, E.S. (1999), 'The prevalence of family business from a household sample', *Family Business Review*, **12** (3), 209–224.

Heck, R.K.Z., Danes, S.M., Fitzgerald, M.A., Haynes, G.W., Jasper, C.R., Schrank, H.L., Stafford, K. and Winter, M. (2006), 'The family's dynamic role within family business entrepreneurship', in P.Z. Poutziouris, K.X. Smyrnios, and S.B. Klein (eds), *Handbook of Research on Family Business*, Cheltenham, UK and Northampton, MA, USA: Edward Elgar, pp. 80–105.

Isaak, R.A. (2005), 'The making of the ecopreneur', in M. Schaper (ed.), *Making Ecopreneurs: Developing Sustainable Entrepreneurship*, Aldershot: Ashgate, pp. 13–26.

Kellermanns, F.W., Eddleston, K.A., Sarathy, R. and Murphy, F. (2012), 'Innovativeness in family firms: a family influence perspective', *Small Business Economics*, **38**, 85–101.

Klewitz, J. and Zeyen, A. (2010), 'The role of intermediary organizations in eco-efficiency improvements in SMEs. A multi-case study in the metal and mechanical engineering industries in Germany', Proceedings of 26th Canadian Council for Small Business and Entrepreneurship Conference, 28–30 October, Calgary, Canada.

Le Breton-Miller, I. and Miller, D. (2006), 'Why do some family businesses out-compete? Governance, long term orientation and sustainable capability', *Entrepreneurship Theory and Practice*, **30**, 731–46.

Levinsohn, D. and Brundin, E. (2011), 'Beyond "shades of green" – opportunities for a renewed conceptualisation of entrepreneurial sustainability in SMEs: a literature review', Conference Proceedings of the International Council for Small Business (ICSB), pp. 1–28.

Linnanen, L. (2005), 'An insider's experiences with environmental entrepreneurship', in M. Schaper (ed.), *Making Ecopreneurs: Developing Sustainable Entrepreneurship*, Aldershot, UK: Ashgate, pp. 72–88.

Loucks, E.S., Martens, M.L. and Cho, C.H. (2010), 'Engaging small and medium sized businesses in sustainability', *Sustainability Accounting, Management and Policy Journal*, **1** (2), 178–200.

Lumpkin, G.T. and Dess, G.G. (1996), 'Clarifying the entrepreneurial orientation construct and linking it to performance', *Academy of Management Review*, **21** (1), 135–72.

Lumpkin, G.T., Brigham, K. and Moss, T. (2010), 'Long-term orientation: implications for the entrepreneurial orientation and performance of family businesses', *Entrepreneurship and Regional Development*, **22** (3), 241–64.

Mandl, I. (2008), *Overview of Family Business Relevant Issues*, Final Report, Austrian Institute for SME Research, Vienna.

Meers, K.A. and Robertson, C. (2007), 'Strategic planning practices in profitable small firms in the United States', *The Business Review*, **7** (1), 302–309.

OECD (2011), *Centre for Entrepreneurship, SMEs and Local Development*, available at www.oecd.org (accessed 25 March 2012).

Parker, C.M., Redmond, J. and Simpson, M. (2009), 'A review of interventions to encourage SMEs to make environmental improvements', *Government and Policy*, **27** (2), 279–301.

Revell, A. and Blackburn, R.A. (2007), 'The business case for sustainability? An examination of small firms in the UK's construction and restaurant sectors', *Business Strategy and the Environment*, **16** (6), 404–420.

Salvato, C. (2004), 'Predictors of entrepreneurship in family firms', *Journal of Private Equity*, **7** (3), 68–76.

Samson, D. (2010), *Innovation for Business Success: Achieving a Systematic Innovation Capability*, report funded by the Australian Government's Department of Innovation, Industry, Science and Research Department.

Sharma, P. (2004), 'An overview of the field of family business studies: current status and directions for the future', *Family Business Review*, **17** (1), 1–36.

Sharma, P. and Sharma, S. (2011), 'Drivers of proactive environmental strategy in family firms', *Business Ethics Quarterly*, **21** (2), 309–334.

Shen, H., Wang, L., Qiang, X., Li, Y. and Xunfeng, L. (2009), 'Toward a framework of innovation management in logistics firms: a systems perspective', *Systems Research and Behavioural Science*, **26** (2), 297–309.

Sorenson, R.L., Goodpaster, K.E., Hedberg, P.R. and Yu, A. (2009), 'The family point of view, family social capital, and firm performance: an exploratory test', *Family Business Review*, **22** (3), 239–53.

Tilly, C. (2000), 'Mechanisms in political processes', *Annual Review of Political Science*, **4**, 21–41.

Trott, P. (2008), *Innovation Management and New Product Development*, Financial Times Press, Harlow.

Victorian Employers' Chamber of Commerce and Industry (2012), available at www.vecci.org.au (accessed on 15 March 2012).

Vollenbroek, F.A. (2002), 'Sustainable development and the challenge of innovation', *Journal of Cleaner Production*, **10** (3), 215–23.

Wagner, M. (2009), 'Advances in the study of entrepreneurship, innovation and economic growth', *Frontiers in Eco-entrepreneurship Research*, **20**, 127–52.

Walley, L. and Taylor, D.W. (2005), 'Opportunists, champions, mavericks . . .? A typology of green entrepreneurs', in M. Schaper (ed.), *Making Ecopreneurs: Developing Sustainable Entrepreneurship*, Aldershot, UK: Ashgate, pp. 27–42.

Wiesner, R., Chadee, D. and Best, P. (2011), 'Insights into sustainability change management from an organisational learning perspective: learning from SME sustainability champions', in 10th International Research Conference on Quality, Innovation and Knowledge Management, 15–18 February, Kuala Lumpur, Malaysia.

Zachary, R.K. (2011), 'The importance of the family system in family business', *Journal of Family Business Management*, **1** (1), 26–36.

Zahra, S.A. (2005), 'Entrepreneurial risk taking in family firms', *Family Business Review*, **18** (1), 23–40.

Zahra, S.A., Hayton, J.C. and Salvato, C. (2004), 'Entrepreneurship in family vs. non-family firms: a resource-based analysis of the effect of organizational culture', *Entrepreneurship Theory and Practice*, **28** (4), 363–81.

Zahra, S.A., Gedajlovic, E., Neubaum, D.O. and Shulman, J.M. (2009), 'A typology of social entrepreneurs: motives, search processes and ethical challenges', *Journal of Business Venturing*, **24** (5), 519–32.

12. Sustainability in the retail and services sector

Janet Sawyer and Nina Evans

INTRODUCTION

This chapter discusses a study of the attitudes and activities of small businesses located in the city of Whyalla towards strategies to enhance their sustainability through socially and environmentally responsible initiatives. Whyalla is an industrial city located on the upper Spencer Gulf in South Australia with a population of approximately 23 000 people. Over the years the city has experienced rapid expansion due to the introduction of a steel making plant in 1961 (population increased to approximately 38 000), followed by a decline with the closing of its shipbuilding operations in 1971. Whyalla is currently in an expansionary phase attributable to major growth in the surrounding mineral resources industry, which offers significant potential flow-on benefits for businesses in the city (WEDB, 2006).

The study of social responsibility is currently receiving much academic attention, and has also moved up the corporate agenda. The European Commission (2001) defines corporate social responsibility (CSR) as 'a concept whereby companies decide voluntarily to contribute to a better society and a cleaner environment' (European Commission, 2001, p. 5). CSR involves complex issues such as environmental protection, human resource management, health and safety, and relations with local communities, suppliers and consumers.

Two different perspectives on the concept of CSR have led to the 'stakeholder-shareholder' debate. The shareholder perspective is that the only responsibility of business managers is to serve the interests of shareholders by seeking profits. On the other hand more recent definitions of CSR describe it through the lens of the stakeholder theory, which suggests that in addition to shareholders, other groups and constituents are affected by a business's activities and that CSR is concerned with the way a company governs the relationship between the firms and all these stakeholders. Post et al. (2002) conducted research on firms in the United

States and Europe and describe stakeholders as the people and entities that contribute to an organization's wealth creating activities, and that are therefore its potential beneficiaries and/or risk bearers. CSR thus involves the performance of companies in monetary, social and environmental terms, and includes the impact of business activities on suppliers, customers, employees, local community and the environment. Accordingly companies should voluntarily integrate social and environmental concerns into their operations and interaction with stakeholders.

More specifically five key elements are usually attributed to CSR: business entities have responsibilities beyond the production of goods and services at a profit; their responsibilities involve helping to solve important social problems, especially those they have helped to create; they have a broader constituency than shareholders; they have impacts that go beyond simple marketplace transactions; and they serve a wider range of human values than can be captured by a sole focus on economic values (Branco and Rodrigues, 2007).

SMALL BUSINESS AND CSR

Hornsby et al. (1994) referred to 'business practices in light of human values' and called it business ethics. According to them ethics is 'the study of whatever is right and good for humans.' Studies on the ethical perceptions of small business owners (Hornsby, 1994; Spence and Rutherfoord, 2001) indicate that there are important differences in the nature of business ethics in small firms. Like all businesses, small businesses face many business decisions with ethical challenges, such as employee problems, product pricing, legal problems, product quality and government regulatory problems. Owner managed small firms where the owner makes personal choices about the allocation of resources, are able to be very adaptive. The studies indicate that there are underlying dimensions of the concepts of small business ethics which are broader than simple adherence to the law. The owner's value system is therefore a critical component of the ethical considerations that surround a business decision (Hornsby, 1994). In small to medium-sized enterprises (SMEs) in Ireland the acceptance of CSR was found to be largely a factor of personal attitudes of the owner/manager (Sweeney, 2007), and small firms are dominated by relationships of trust and openness (Spence and Rutherfoord, 2001).

Closely linked to ethical decision making is the view of and attitude towards the social and environmental responsibility of the business. SMEs are under increasing pressure to address environmental issues from a range of sources including legislation, supply chain, trade associations and customers. There are also an increasing number of commercial pressures, such as significant cost savings associated with effective management of waste and resources, protection against future cost increases (taxes, waste disposal and transport), market opportunities for environmental goods and services, demands made by insurers, financial institutions and shareholders and contract specifications (Friedman et al., 2000).

A study by Rutherfoord et al. (2000) investigated what is achievable in the engagement of small firms with environmental policy. They found that there was a difference in the practice of small firms, particularly in the levels of intervention and support, as well as the attitude of owner/managers to environmental issues. Smaller businesses are likely to be less 'eco-efficient' than larger firms, mostly because larger firms can benefit from economies of scale regarding resource efficiencies. For instance it is estimated that smaller firms contribute at least 60 percent to carbon emissions (Rutherfoord et al., 2000).

Addressing environmental awareness is a complex issue for SMEs, exacerbated by a lack of resources, including time and environmental expertise (Friedman et al., 2000). As SMEs are frequently constrained by time and financial resources, long term investment projects in CSR are often not of immediate concern. Spence and Rutherfoord (2001, p. 131) also acknowledge that owner/managers of small businesses have a limited capacity to deal with issues that are not directly affecting the survival of the firm, due to pressure of having to deal with multiple tasks, cash flow restrictions and other short-term problems. On the other hand, it has also been argued that being smaller and flatter may place SMEs in a better position than large firms to take advantage of the changing needs of society (Sweeney, 2007; Sawyer and Evans, 2010).

THE STUDY

The study was undertaken collaboratively by the University of South Australia's Centre for Regional Engagement and the Whyalla Economic Development Board (WEDB). It sought data on the following questions:

1. What is the attitude of small businesses in Whyalla towards social and environmental responsibility?
2. What are the drivers and barriers for and against implementation of socially and environmentally responsible initiatives?
3. What type of support, if any, is required to assist the small businesses to implement CSR initiatives? (Sawyer and Evans, 2009).

The participants in the study were the owner/managers of businesses operating in the retail and services sector. This sector was selected because it
had been identified by the WEDB as a sector in need of support to enable
it to take advantage of the benefits the mining boom may offer. Thirty
potential participants were identified from the WEDB database and a
written invitation to participate in the research project was sent to them.
Eighteen firms became involved in the study, giving a participation rate of
60 percent. Although there is no single, uniformly accepted definition of
a small business, the criterion of businesses with fewer than 20 employees
was used to select these (Burgess, 2003).

Structured face-to-face interviews were conducted with the owner/
managers because they potentially have the strongest influence on decision
making within the firm. The owner/managers were requested to define the
challenges and opportunities facing their business and outline any social
and environmental responsibility activities of their business. The study
was not presented to the participants as being about CSR, but about
business sustainability through social and environmental responsibility,
amidst the challenges and opportunities of implementing such responsible initiatives. This approach was taken in an effort to avoid 'socially
desired' responses. Interviews therefore allowed the contextualized discussion of how small businesses in Whyalla are operated and the emphasis
that is placed on social responsibility. The interviews also allowed the
opportunity to probe and expand the participant responses to structured
questions to give the participants a chance to explain their opinions. The
questions focused on the following issues: perceived challenges/risks and
opportunities in running the business and making it sustainable for the
future; attitudes and current initiatives (in relation to customers, suppliers,
employees, local community and environment); motives for the initiatives;
perceived barriers to being socially and environmentally responsible; and
any desired follow-up support.

The interview questions were piloted on owner/managers of two small
businesses in Whyalla that were not included in the main study. The aim
of this preliminary investigation was to check that the questions captured
the information required to complete the aims of the research and identify
any ambiguities or problem areas.

The interviewers encouraged the business owners to discuss the issues in
their own terms, related to their own business environment. All questions
explored the responses of business managers in as much detail as possible,
to uncover new factors and ideas. During the interview notes were taken
and the interviews were audio recorded. Recording the interviews allowed
the researchers to participate in the discussions as well as taking notes. The
interviews were transcribed and reviewed to ensure internal validity. The

data collected in the interviews were analysed and categorized according to the emerging themes using the NVivo8 software.

FINDINGS

The main themes emerging from the interviews in relation to the challenges and threats to the firm's sustainability were: attracting and retaining capable employees; competition from large businesses; attracting more customers; maintaining adequate cash flow; the characteristics of customers in Whyalla; keeping up to date with new products and business methods; long working hours; and the location of the business.

Attracting and Retaining Capable Employees

Attracting and retaining capable employees was the major challenge facing small business managers. The reasons varied from people leaving to join the mining industry, to the fact that there were not enough tradespeople in the city due to its ageing population. The manager of a service firm indicated that 'tradespeople were aging and difficult to acquire'; and there were 'no people currently studying through the local Technical and Further Education (TAFE) system in this field'. Further the methods of doing business were changing and the tradespeople had generally 'gone through the old school' and were not familiar with modern trends and techniques. There was an opinion that older people within the community who 'would be happy to pass on their experience with a view to getting some financial benefit and personal satisfaction' were a resource currently being under-utilized. The acquisition of suitable staff, particularly those with the 'soft skills' was also a challenge. Remuneration against other industries was a key issue as the small businesses did not have the ability to pay the high salaries provided by larger firms. Having staff who were 'locals with families' was the 'single biggest plus factor' in retaining employees.

Competition from Large Businesses

Competition from large businesses was a related challenge. Some of the comments received were:

> The challenge is keeping up with the multinationals that come in. It's a well-known fact that multinationals and franchises are going to all the regions; especially with the mining boom, they're just following.

Obviously other companies will see the opportunity to come to town and rape and pillage, so to speak, so the locals need to be prepared to provide that service to retain that business and not let it walk out of town.

The City Council's act of classifying buildings as a heritage site was expressed as a threat to the competitiveness and sustainability of existing firms as the small business 'can't expand and knock it down' whereas the larger businesses 'come in on new land and they'll have a clear run'. Already traders located in the older, eastern part of Whyalla were deemed to be suffering due to the competition from the large, modern, shopping mall established in the centre of the city.

Business owners operating in the clothing area found it a challenge 'to keep ahead of the game, because there are so many big retailers out there who are dominating the market'. They reported that local people preferred to shop at the larger stores (Target and Harris Scarfe) that were able to buy a large volume of different products at good prices. One owner commented: 'I'm always the third one on the list.' The additional freight charges incurred due to their regional location was also an issue in remaining competitive. Another risk was that the larger firms poached their staff ('they come in and they have no staff') and as a result the small businesses have to pay more to retain employees.

Finances

Cash flow was a challenge for some small business managers. The owner of a new business commented that: 'one has very limited funds until you've got a very well established business to draw out wages.' It appears that people in Whyalla are spending less on luxury items and more on housing and household goods. The manager of a business selling such non-essential items reported: 'everybody's building houses and most of the stores are finding that spending is down.'

Characteristics of the Customer

Some business owners referred to the unique characteristics of Whyalla customers due to the isolation of the city. One believed that 'if more people came into Whyalla and locals mingled with more people from outside, it might help open up a lot of closed-mindedness.' Customers in Whyalla were also seen to be price sensitive, 'they go for cheap not for quality', although this was considered to be turning around as 'younger people now in their 20s and 30s look more for quality.'

Attracting customers was a further challenge. Retailers complained that contractors came into Whyalla and took the money earned back to their families in other cities. These potential customers need to be educated to shop locally. Some business managers also believed that the location of their business in the eastern part of Whyalla presented a challenge to attract more customers, as the City Council was perceived to be directing more resources towards the large shopping mall located in the centre of the city. They indicated that customers also needed to be educated about the fact that there was more than one shopping precinct in Whyalla.

Business and Product Knowledge of Owner/Manager

Several managers referred to service and product knowledge as being challenges; keeping up with trends and constantly identifying what people want and trying to find it was difficult. For another owner, getting contacts and building up a list of suppliers was a problem. Others were challenged by the fact they had minimum purchase levels imposed upon them and needed to wait until they had sufficient orders before being able to buy from some suppliers.

Long Hours

Time management and having a strategic outlook were also challenges: 'You would really like to be able to make comprehensive lists of the direction you're going to take, the different things you want to do, but the day-to-day running of things just takes over.' One owner reported: 'I'm doing between 80 and 90 hours a week now and always have since the beginning. Some days you just feel like you're going to fall over.' This was partly due to being unable to afford more staff. The managers' health suffering due to working long hours was another risk. They referred to the impact on family: 'Family, kids, no time for your children.'

Many respondents referred to the growing number of people moving into Whyalla as an opportunity for their business: 'More people in Whyalla will make it better for everyone' . . . 'You get more demand for your products and the more profit you make the bigger and better business.' This increase in population was attributed to the developments in the mining area: 'I think it's more small industries, you know, to support the mining factor.' One manager commented that 'we're hoping by the year 2022 that we will have it [the population level] back to around 30 000 to 35 000 people.' They mentioned new premises being established, more accommodation being built, and the upgrade of the foreshore area. Interestingly the name 'Whyalla' was thought to create an opportunity, with one owner commenting: 'I will become more known once I'm online on the web; I might be easier to find just because people recognize the name Whyalla.'

The steps taken to protect their businesses, overcome risks, and take advantage of opportunities included: improving customer service; modernizing the business and keeping up to date with trends in the industry; employing capable staff and treating them well; diversifying product lines; and pricing competitively.

Improved Customer Service

Good customer and after sales service were considered the most important means of overcoming threats and challenges. Owners reported that 'customer service goes a long way to get people back into your shop' and 'some people don't mind paying a few dollars more if they're getting the service that they want.' Many were of the opinion that larger retail shops do not give the same quality service as a small business, and that the personal service they provided gave them an advantage:

> We go out of our way to help the customer and to treat a client in a personal way – if they've got any problems we're always out there to help them.

> In Whyalla many people work 12 hour shifts. We open the shop after hours for the customer, so the husband/partner has a chance to look at the product and select as well.

Keeping Up to Date with Products and the Business

Several business managers reported that they aimed to protect their business by keeping up to date with products and the nature of the retail sector in general. One manager commented: 'Old businesses tend to have old problems. We're trying to streamline everything; right now we're getting rid of dead stock that's been accumulating, and trying to get our staff right up with modern trends.'

Several managers benchmarked with shops located in Adelaide, travelling to the capital city to 'look at what's going on there and bring the information back to Whyalla.'

Capable Employees

Many businesses were already employing apprentices and qualified tradespeople and investing in new facilities in preparation for future expansion as a result of the anticipated 'boom'. The provision of competitive salaries and monetary incentives were used as a means to overcome the challenges of finding suitable employees. Maintaining a happy workplace was considered important for protecting the business against risks: 'The other thing that I think is very important, and we're doing, is creating a friendly working environment to provide a quality of life because it's not always just about money.'

Diversification

Diversifying and increasing the choice to customers was another step undertaken to protect their businesses. Providing different types of products and services that were not part of their core business enabled them to 'lure more customers into their store' and attract a larger variety of shoppers. Another strategy was to import product from overseas and wholesale it to other stores.

Good Prices

Competitive pricing was also a strategy for dealing with challenges, with one manager saying: 'Basically we just try to keep the costs down as low as we can but obviously we have to make money – that's what we're here for.' They try not to overprice, and mentioned the importance of good suppliers and backup.

DISCUSSION

General Attitudes and Values

'Superior customer service' and 'honesty' were the most important principles the owner/managers said they followed in conducting their business. Good staff, good manners, and friendly service were regarded as factors that would differentiate between competing stores. It was believed that 'with honesty comes trust'; honesty in 'the way we sell' and not misrepresenting products was regarded as vital, especially in a repeat business industry, where it 'pays to do the right thing'. It was considered important to maintain high standards; that there was no pressure put on the customer and that customers were able to 'feel as if they could ask for help.' Other important principles were: being approachable and welcoming, respect (towards the people who worked for the business and who came into the business to support it), reliability, confidentiality, adaptability and the ability to grow with the demands in the field.

Most owner/managers would like their businesses to be described as 'professional' and 'fun'. They wanted customers to think of their firm as a 'friendly, happy business'; that customers liked going into the store and found it an enjoyable, comfortable experience. The focus was also on the provision of prompt, quality, service; that they were perceived as being helpful, reliable, and trustworthy; and that customers were happy with their service, end product and back-up, so that they would want to return. Being 'unique' was also mentioned, along with 'having competitive pricing', being 'community minded', and 'a good one-stop shop'.

The majority of owner/managers believed their business had a responsibility other than being profitable. They acknowledged they were part of a community – part of the city and part of the business community – and that they should be good 'corporate' citizens. This included providing financial support to local clubs and societies. Generally they believed they had a responsibility to everybody they interacted with, including other traders, suppliers, contractors and customers. They also acknowledged that as employers they had responsibilities in relation to work conditions, safety, social issues and the well-being of their staff. This responsibility was seen to extend to the families of their staff. They believed they had a responsibility to provide good quality products that the customer can enjoy; to ensure that suitable products and services are available to meet needs; and to provide competition to benefit the community. It was considered important to have a social conscience, be environmentally responsible, to spend the dollars generated 'in the town' and buy Australian-made products rather than importing products made overseas.

Initiatives undertaken by the entities in relation to interaction with their customers focused on increasing customer satisfaction by building positive, personal relationships. They aimed to provide friendly and consistently high-quality service to each customer and made an effort to remember the customer and discuss their previous dealings. The businesses gave advice on their products and provided after sales follow-up. They would also help to source any goods they did not have available from other suppliers. The importance of giving some authority to and listening to feedback from their employees was acknowledged as a means of increasing customer satisfaction. While these businesses did not formally measure customer satisfaction, the majority did so informally by regularly talking to customers about the service they provided, their prices, the customer's experience with their product, and how their business compared with that of competitors. They monitored their marketing and asked how the customer had heard about their store. The managers watched and listened; often the customers volunteered feedback. The businesses tried to avoid complaints from customers. If there were problems, talking with the customer was again considered important and they tried to resolve issues without conflict. Some businesses offered a gift as a means of apology and to increase customer satisfaction.

Attitudes to CSR

Even though the attitude of businesses towards society and the environment was an important issue for most, the owner/managers were generally not able to take this into consideration when choosing their suppliers. Increasingly many of the products they acquired were made overseas and they were unable to be sufficiently informed in relation to the social and environmental practices of the businesses they had dealings with. Often no alternative suppliers were available for particular products. Some of the businesses sourced their products based only on price. However many of the firms would pay more to purchase their products from socially and environmentally responsible suppliers and believed their customers would be willing to absorb higher prices due to dealing with responsible firms. Others believed their customers would choose the cheaper goods available from competitors. This makes the decision to move to environmentally friendly suppliers even more difficult for already struggling small businesses. Also while some firms aimed to use local suppliers first, to support their community, small businesses rarely had the purchasing power to influence their local suppliers to provide environmentally and socially responsible products.

Responses regarding initiatives in relation to their employees revealed the main methods of attracting capable staff were 'word of mouth', using local knowledge and poaching from other organizations. Strategies to retain employees included maintaining a 'happy workplace', being proactive with personnel requirements, and providing competitive salaries and monetary incentives. Organizing regular social gatherings and making the business an enjoyable place to work were considered key factors in retaining employees. The owner/managers referred to the need to be cooperative and to have flexible work practices. They emphasized the importance of positive, 'open' staff relationships, based on trust and respect. Empowering employees by allowing them to share in decision making and by providing training and development opportunities were other strategies. Most businesses did not have formal mechanisms to ensure inclusivity in their staff composition and used the criterion of selecting the most suitable person for the position.

The businesses generally aimed to assist employees with their family responsibilities by providing flexible working hours, but few had formal job sharing arrangements in place. Most training and development of employees was provided internally on the job, although some firms offered traineeships and apprenticeships and would financially support staff who wished to complete study related to their work. The majority of businesses measured employee satisfaction informally by talking with staff and observing them at work, using their responses and actions to gauge their satisfaction.

Most owner/managers did not specifically encourage their employees to be socially responsible, but those who did understood the benefits that could be gained. These firms provided support to the clubs and service groups that their employees were part of, believing it would attract additional business, because 'if people want to buy our product, there's a fair chance they'll go to someone they know'. One manager supported the groups his staff were involved with through sponsorship, commenting: 'If I can expose my staff to a group of 300–400 members and the company is seen to be looking after their interests, it results in plus business.' Another manager, who is active in the community, has only employed people who are also involved in community activities, reporting: 'I meet my employees through my outside activities so therefore I've hand-picked them . . . I see what they're like in their outside world and think 'you would fit nicely into the team.'

Yet another manager was cautious, reporting that the business had carried out a lot of charity work in the past, but there became 'more and more demanding' expectations for very little return. Some managers believed that the employees' social responsibilities were part of their personal life and they should not 'interfere' with their private lives. However it was emphasized that the employees were made aware of the environmentally responsible processes to be undertaken within the business and that social and environmental responsibility initiatives were important.

The businesses generally had community engagement initiatives in place, ranging from donating goods and services to local organizations and charities to sponsoring events and school projects. While they were generally keen to assist organizations and activities within their local community, the high frequency of requests for support often became a burden and was expensive to them in terms of time and money. The owner/managers reported that 'small business gets hit a lot'; 'it's very hard to say no'; and that it was important for them to decide what charities or events they would support and to budget for it. One of the business owners described how he provided expertise to the community by giving talks about his business activities to schools, service groups and conferences, and using his boat and diving skills to assist in search and rescue. He added: 'We do a lot of work for the environmental companies and we don't often charge full commercial rates for let's say a study, or they might want some help or services or boat or whatever and we'll always supply that free of charge.'

Receiving lower payment for work appeared to be a feature of doing business in Whyalla. One owner commented: 'we don't charge in Whyalla the rate that would be charged in Adelaide.' All the businesses appeared to appreciate the importance of strong community links. While for some community engagement took up a lot of time, it provided opportunities to network and to promote the business: 'it's all advertising because you're supporting the community, sometimes it's more effective than a half page ad in the paper you know.'

A substantial number of businesses made efforts to minimize environmental damage. This was especially noticeable in their concern for the avoidance of unnecessary waste of energy and materials. Almost all the businesses were involved in waste recycling and approximately half had large recycle bins that they used for packaging material if it could not be reused. Drink containers, bottles and cans, glass, pieces of timber and plastic bubble wrap were regularly recycled but few reported that they recycled ink, toner and printer cartridges. The businesses generally ensured their lights and air-conditioning were switched on only when needed and that machinery was turned off until use. One firm conserved energy and reduced costs by only using every second row of lights; other firms had either converted to smarter lights that use less energy, or were trialling LED lighting to reduce the cost of electricity and the amount of heat and emissions. Many businesses turned off lights at night, or used only security lighting. Several owner/managers reduced fuel by planning sales and deliveries so that travel was reduced. One business had changed to using fuel efficient four-stroke motors and introduced a group-based transport system. Another commented: 'We've tried to streamline it now by using our trucks less and doing it smarter – where we used the one big truck we tend to use two small ones.'

Many businesses worked towards reducing their environmental impact in other ways such as putting kitchen waste into a compost bin; using bags, containers and cutlery that were compostable; using environmentally friendly cleaning products; and labels printed on recycled paper with vegetable dye inks. Items such as envelopes, small boxes, oil drums, coat hangers and paper were reused. Oil and coolants were disposed of in accordance with legal requirements. There appeared to be an appreciation that environmental awareness made good business sense and the importance placed on undertaking environmentally beneficial initiatives was indicated by the following comment: 'I think that most probably one is unwise if something is shown to be cost saving in that sense and better for the environment, not to do it, because I think in the longer term it will be more costly if you don't.'

There was also concern for aesthetics with many managers making an effort to keep their premises attractive and clean. One manager had taken steps to improve the neighbourhood around his premises by developing a network with the adjoining shops; they shared a recycling bin, advertising campaigns, and generally supported each other. Another owner indicated a lack of support for environmental awareness initiatives when he replied: 'It's enough keeping up with what's inside the shop let alone what's outside the shop.' In cases where there was a lack of environmental priority, it was not reflected in the owner/managers' general attitudes, as they recognized the importance of environmental issues. In some instances environmental care was associated with cost saving, not extra burdens. Often the owner/managers did not think of all the interventions that they were involved in during the first discussion. Princic (2003, p. 3) refers to this as 'doing good without knowing it.' Many of the Canadian SMEs that he investigated did not consider their practices as part of CSR, but just as 'good business' and referred to the business benefits resulting from these initiatives. However they did not make interventions only because they expected their business to benefit. The owner/managers generally implemented socially responsible behaviour because 'it is simply the right thing to do' and it gave them personal pride and enjoyment. The responses to a list of statements provided to them during the interview to determine their reasons for CSR initiatives are summarized in Table 12.1.

When asked to rank the three most important reasons for them implementing such initiatives, items (1) 'Is simply the right thing to do'; (2) 'Improves the image/profile of my business' and (12) 'Saves costs', were ranked equally (44 percent). Table 12.2 shows the main reasons for not implementing CSR initiatives were 'time constraints', 'lack of financial resources' and because 'only a minority of customers prefer to buy from ethical businesses.'

When asked to identify the three most important reasons for not implementing such initiatives, 'Time constraints' (56 percent), 'Lack of financial resources' (50 percent) and 'I'm not in a position to influence the nature of my supplier's products' (39 percent) were ranked highest (Evans and Sawyer, 2010).

Most owner/managers (67 percent) had never received support (moral, financial, technical or educational) for implementing CSR. The respondents when asked to identify strategies that would help them to design and implement socially responsible initiatives in their business suggested a strong demand for assistance (Table 12.3).

Programs relating to the principles of being socially and environmentally responsible ranked highest (67 percent) followed by programs to educate consumers on the impacts of their purchasing decisions (61 percent), and

Table 12.1   *Motivation of small business owner/managers to implement socially responsible behaviour*

	Item	%
1	Is simply the right thing to do	78
2	Improves the image/profile of my business	67
3	Helps me make more money	50
4	Is what my clients/customers expect from me	50
5	Is what a law forces me to do	33
6	Helps me create a market niche	39
7	Gives us a competitive advantage	39
8	Is necessary due to the increased public demand for ethical products and services	22
9	Gives me personal pride and enjoyment	78
10	Boosts staff morale	44
11	Increases staff empowerment	22
12	Saves costs	67
13	Is part of a continuing process of building long-term value	67
14	Minimizes the risk of damage to our own reputation due to dealing with socially responsible suppliers	39
15	Cut utility bills	61
16	Cut waste disposal costs	39
	Other	0

Table 12.2   *Barriers to small business owner/managers implementing socially responsible behaviour*

	Item	%
1	Lack of financial resources	61
2	Time constraints	72
3	My customers do not demand it from me	22
4	I don't think it will really make a difference to society	6
5	My business will not benefit from it financially	11
6	I'm not in the right industry to make a difference	6
7	I am burdened by industry regulations	6
8	I am burdened by technological overheads	6
9	I'm not in a position to influence the nature of my supplier's products	44
10	Customers are bottom-line oriented and base purchasing decisions on price above other factors	33
11	Only a minority of customers prefer to buy from ethical businesses	56
	Other	0

Table 12.3   Strategies that would assist small business owner/managers to implement socially responsible initiatives

	Item	%
1	Awareness programs on the principles of being socially and environmentally responsible	67
2	Awareness programs to educate consumers on the impacts of their purchasing decisions	61
3	Information sessions on the business benefits of environmentally and socially responsible practices	56
4	Information sessions on policies regarding quality, the environment and stakeholders	39
5	Information sessions on general business principles	50
6	Workshops to learn from your peers about their experiences	56
7	Hands-on support programs in aspects of running your specific business	50
8	Assistance with the strategy/strategic plan for your specific business	56
9	Tools to measure the impact of the initiatives on your business	44
	Other	0

'information sessions on the business benefits of environmentally and socially responsible practices', 'workshops to learn from your peers about their experiences' and 'assistance with the strategy/strategic plan for your specific business' (56 percent). 50 percent of participants indicated they would benefit from information sessions on general business principles and hands on support in aspects of running their business (Sawyer and Evans, 2009).

CONCLUSIONS

The focus of previous CSR research has been predominantly on larger firms with little attention given to the socially responsible activities of SMEs; small businesses are often not researched because it is too expensive to reach them (Rutherfoord et al., 2000). This was confirmed by research done by Aragón-Correa et al. (2008) in the automotive sector in the south of Spain. However in today's marketplace it is becoming more important for all firms to demonstrate that they are operating in a manner that is supportive of society and its objectives. This study provides a useful basis for assisting the development of sustainable, socially responsible small businesses. It identified key challenges: difficulties in recruiting and retaining good staff; competition from larger firms; the need to attract more customers; higher freight charges; and an inability to purchase in high volume to take advantage of bulk discounts, and to innovate and differentiate products/services. These challenges and business realities prevent the firms from embarking on and benefiting from CSR activities.

The business owner/managers believed they were accountable to their broader community. They participated in recycling, worked to reduce their energy use, and supported their local organizations where practical. Generally they did so because it was the 'right thing to do' and gave them a sense of pride, but also because it could save costs, improve the image of the business and build long term value. These findings align with the comments of Fassin (2008) who conducted research among Belgian SMEs and found that it is often wrongly assumed that CSR is non-existent in SMEs because they do not formally report on CSR. According to him, most SMEs regard their informal responsible behaviour as normal, simply because they 'feel right' and it is the 'decent thing to do'. The main reasons for not undertaking CSR initiatives were lack of time and money. However the inability to influence the nature of suppliers' products and the belief that only a small proportion of customers would be concerned with the ethical nature of a business when considering a purchase, were also notable factors (Sawyer and Evans, 2009).

Most of the businesses had never received any support for implementing CSR. They indicated their desire to participate in programs and workshops to learn about CSR practices and the experiences of their peers. The WEDB can now assist these firms with strategic planning and creating a forum for sharing experiences and for giving and receiving ideas; to inform about the business benefits of being responsible; and to distribute information about the latest initiatives for businesses to become socially and environmentally responsible. Awareness programs are required regarding the principles, policies and tools to integrate CSR strategy and activities into business strategy so that both CSR and business benefits can be achieved simultaneously.

The owner/managers could also encourage their employees to participate in voluntary community activities that benefit the community as well as promoting the business profile. This in turn may enable the employees to become more skilful and receptive to new initiatives and innovative activities that will assist the small businesses to develop and introduce new products and services vital to future business growth. The businesses may then become more confident and able to form alliances to compete against larger firms and create a market niche.

REFERENCES

Aragón-Correa, J.A., Hurtado-Torres, N., Sharma, S. and García-Morales, V.J. (2008), 'Environmental strategy and performance in small firms: a resource-based perspective', *Journal of Environmental Management*, **86** (1), 88–103.

Branco, M.C. and L.L. Rodrigues (2007), 'Positioning stakeholder theory within the debate on corporate social responsibility', *Electronic Journal of Business Ethics and Organisation Studies*, **12** (1), 5–15.

Burgess, S. (2003), 'A definition for small business?', available at www.businessandlaw.vu.edu.au/sbirit (accessed 4 October 2007).

European Commission (2001), 'Promoting a European framework for corporate social responsibility', Green Paper, European Commission, Directorate-General for Employment and Social Affairs.

Evans, N. and Sawyer, J. (2010), 'CSR and stakeholders of small businesses in regional South Australia', *Social Responsibility Journal*, **6** (3), 433–51.

Fassin, Y. (2008), 'SMEs and the fallacy of formalising CSR', *Business Ethics: A European Review*, **17** (4), 364–78.

Friedman, A.L., Miles, S. and Adams, C. (2000), 'Small and medium-sized enterprises and the environment: evaluation of a specific initiative aimed at all small and medium-sized enterprises', *Journal of Small Business and Enterprise Development*, **7** (4), 325–42.

Hornsby, J.S., Kuratko, D.F., Naffziger, D.W., LaFollette, W.R. and Hodgetts, R.M. (1994), 'The ethical perceptions of small business owners: a factor analytic study', *Journal of Small Business Management*, **32** (4).

Post, J.E., Preston, L.E. and Sachs, S. (2002), 'Managing the extended enterprise: the new stakeholder view', *California Management Review*, **45** (1), 6–28.

Princic, L. (2003), 'Engaging small business in Corporate Social Responsibility: a Canadian small business perspective on CSR', *Canadian Business for Social Responsibility*, available at www.cbsr.ca/files/ReportsandPapers/ (accessed 4 October 2007).

Rutherfoord, R., Blackburn, R.A. and Spence, L.J. (2000), 'Environmental management and the small firm', *International Journal of Entrepreneurial Behaviour*, **6** (6), 310–25.

Sawyer, J. and Evans, N. (2009), 'Supporting regional small business: a collaboration between higher education and the economic development board', *The Australasian Journal of University-Community Engagement*, **3** (2), 103–114.

Sawyer, J. and Evans, N. (2010), 'An investigation into the social and environmentally responsible behaviours of regional small businesses in relation to their local community and immediate environment', *Australasian Journal of Regional Studies*, **16** (2), 253–65.

Spence, L.J. and Rutherfoord, R. (2001), 'Social responsibility, profit maximisation and the small firm owner/manager', *Journal of Small Business and Enterprise Development*, **8** (2), 126–39.

Sweeney, L. (2007), 'Corporate Social Responsibility in Ireland: barriers and opportunities experienced by SMEs when undertaking CSR', *Corporate Governance*, **7** (4), 516–23.

Whyalla Economic Development Board Incorporated (WEBD) (2006), 'Facilitating business growth in Whyalla', *Whyalla Economic Development Board: Annual Report 2006*, Whyalla Economic Development Board, Whyalla, S.A.

13. Appraising corporate sustainability of construction contractors: concepts and approaches

Jian Zuo, Lou Wilson, George Zillante, Stephen Pullen and Nicholas Chileshe

INTRODUCTION

The last few decades have seen a growing public concern for sustainability issues associated with the construction industry across various stages of the project life cycle. For example construction activities are responsible for a large amount of on-site environmental impacts such as noise, dust, traffic congestion and water pollution (Glass and Simmonds 2007). Once completed, the buildings and facilities can have a large effect on sustainability issues. According to statistics from the World Business Council for Sustainable Development, buildings contributed to more than 40 per cent of energy consumption in most countries (WBCSD 2007). Indeed the building sector is one of the biggest energy consumers and carbon emitters (Zuo et al. 2012a). The demolition of buildings is also energy intensive and has large environmental impacts such as waste, environmental pollution and disturbance of surrounding communities. As a result there is an increasing level of attention by the industry to pursue sustainable business. For instance a study conducted by the Australian Centre for Corporate Social Responsibility (ACCSR) indicated that the property development/construction industry recorded a slightly above average budget for Corporate Social Responsibility (CSR) when compared to other industries (ACCSR 2011). Year 2011 saw the release of the Sector Supplement for the Construction & Real Estate industries by the Global Reporting Initiative, re-confirming the importance of sustainability issues in construction related businesses (GRI 2011a).

This chapter starts with a review of the concepts of corporate sustainability and is followed by a review of the approaches used to evaluate corporate sustainability. We propose an innovative conceptual framework to appraise corporate sustainability in the construction industry with a consideration of unique characteristics of construction businesses. The focus of this chapter is directed towards construction companies (contractors) with a potential to be extended to other construction related companies such as architectural and engineering consulting firms, quantity surveying firms and facility management consultancies. Future research opportunities are discussed.

CORPORATE SUSTAINABILITY

Some fundamental concepts need to be understood prior to the design of an approach to measure corporate sustainability:

1.   What is corporate sustainability?
2.   Why is corporate sustainability required?

The concept of corporate sustainability stems from a global debate of 'what is a good corporate citizen?' This is basically a challenge to the traditional business model of corporations: that is, profit driven.

Corporate sustainability is defined by the Dow Jones Sustainability Indexes (2012) as:

> . . . a business approach that creates long-term shareholder value by embracing opportunities and managing risks deriving from economic, environmental and social developments. Corporate sustainability leaders achieve long-term shareholder value by gearing their strategies and management to harness the market's potential for sustainability products and services while at the same time successfully reducing and avoiding sustainability costs and risks.

Azapagic (2003) developed this concept by identifying a number of risks associated with unsustainable business practices such as penalties for pollution, damage to company reputation, being unattractive to talented employees, and financial inefficiency.

A study by Dyllick and Hockerts (2002) translated the Brundtland definition of sustainable development to the business level, defining corporate sustainability as: 'meeting the needs of a firm's direct and indirect stakeholders (such as shareholders, employees, clients, pressure groups, communities, etc.), without compromising its ability to meet the needs of future stakeholders as well' (p. 131). They further pointed out that companies needed to focus on growing social and natural capitals as well as developing economic capital. This approach was confirmed by Steurer et al. (2005) who argued that '. . . Sustainable development is commonly perceived as a societal guiding model, which addresses a broad range of

Table 13.1   *Benefits associated with corporate sustainability by research study*

Benefits	Aras and Crowther (2009)	IFC (2004)	MIT SMR (2009)	EXCEL Partnership (2005)	Lee and Saen (2012)
Better image of the corporate and/or product	✓	✓	✓		
Increased sales and revenues	✓	✓			✓
Cost savings	✓	✓	✓		✓
Increased productivity	✓	✓	✓		✓
Lower staff turnover	✓	✓	✓		✓
Improved relationship with stakeholders		✓	✓	✓	✓
Easier access to finance	✓	✓	✓	✓	✓
Health and safety benefits		✓		✓	
Effective risk management			✓	✓	✓
Innovation of products and business models			✓		✓

quality of life issues in the long term, Corporate Sustainability is a corporate guiding model, addressing the short and long term economic, social and environmental performance of corporations' (p. 274). In other words the responsibilities of companies are not only generating profits but also contributing towards environmental sustainability, community development and interaction with stakeholders (Lo and Sheu 2007).

There are a number of benefits associated with corporate sustainability (Table 13.1). Based on a study of large non-financial companies in the United States, Lo and Sheu (2007) found that sustainability investment is positively correlated to the market value of the company and sales growth. On the other hand there are costs derived from pursuing corporate sustainability. The extra cost needs to be justified so that a business case can be put forward for pursuing corporate sustainability. According to Figge and Hahn (2004), the sustainability value to a firm equals the benefits from the sustainability investment minus the cost.

It is worth noting that there is a debate on the relationship between sustainability initiatives and final performance of corporates. Many studies found that there is positive correlation between CSR and corporate financial performance (CFP) even though they admitted that CFP is affected by other factors as well, such as the age of corporate asset and the level of risk (for example Cochran and Wood 1984; McGuire et al., 1988). In contrast Pava and Krausz (1996) emphasized there is a complex relationship between CSR and financial performance. Indeed McWilliams and Siegel (2000) argued that there is neutral relationship between CSR and financial performance if rectification is made on the existing models. Other studies found a negative relationship exists between CSR and financial performance (for example Wright and Ferris 1997). Therefore the financial return should not be the only indicator to measure the outcome of corporate sustainability commitments.

SUSTAINABILITY PRACTICES IN THE CONSTRUCTION INDUSTRY

In the construction context sustainability issues have also gained an increasing level of attention from industry practitioners, authorities and academics. The majority of current studies are heavily environmentally oriented: for example, innovations on construction technologies and building materials to help achieve sustainable construction. A number of studies have been undertaken to explore how construction and demolition waste can be recycled and reused. For instance Snelson et al. (2009) found that fly ash and waste tyres can be used for road construction, which helps to reduce the waste to the landfill. A study by Shen et al. (2009) found that there are a number of benefits of using precast slabs for temporary construction works, such as reduction of obsolescence and cost savings (that is, contributing to sustainable construction performance). Prefabrication is found as a useful tool to reduce the amount of construction and demolition waste (Jaillon et al. 2009). Numerous studies have also been undertaken to improve the energy efficiency and carbon emission reduction in buildings as well as during the construction process (for example Ortiz et al. 2010; Manoliadis et al. 2006; Zuo et al. 2012a). To better achieve the environmental sustainability goal, it has been suggested that companies adopt an Environmental Management System (EMS) such as ISO14001 (Zeng et al. 2003; Turk 2009). Senior management's commitments are crucial for achieving better sustainability performance at both company and project levels (Beheiry et al. 2006). Other scholars have suggested the use of management tools such as green specifications and green project management with the aim of promoting sustainable practice in the construction industry (for example Lam et al. 2009; Wu and Low 2010). A change of culture and attitude is equally important.

Recent research in the construction context has started to focus more on another dimension of sustainability, social sustainability. This is arguably due to the fact that construction is a social process (Abowitz and Toole 2010). There is a recent demand from various stakeholders such as the government, clients and the public community, for products and services to be 'socially responsible'. The common criteria of social sustainability in the construction context include: ecological impacts, quality of life, health and safety, security, equity, provision of infrastructure, future professional development opportunities, etc. (Hill and Bowen 1997; Labuschagne and Brent 2006; Shen et al. 2007). According to a study conducted by the Chartered Institute of Building (CIOB), an increasing number of clients demand that contractors demonstrate CSR commitment as a critical factor for awarding contracts in some cases (CIOB 2006). Petrovic-Lazarevic (2008) interviewed the senior management of 17 large, global companies in Australia. Her study found that a corporate governance structure needs to be in place for construction companies to consider health, safety and environment issues from all stakeholders' perspectives so that the corporate social responsibility can be fully developed.

Sustainability reporting in construction companies has also gained considerable attention in the last five years. For instance large enterprises such as Colliers International, Stockland and Bovis Lend Lease have taken action to address social and environmental issues. As the first property group in Australia to be listed on the Corporate Responsibility Index (CRI), Colliers International recognizes that CSR provides a framework for the company to accelerate its future efforts and share knowledge with other leading companies. On this matter, research at the University of South Australia on the sustainability reporting practices adopted by the top 50 international contractors listed by Engineering News Record (ENR) 2009 found an increasing level of disclosure of corporations' commitments and achievements on sustainability by contractors. Disclosure tended to relate mainly to environmental aspects such as the energy efficiency, greenhouse gas emission reduction and application of renewable energy on sites (Zuo et al. 2012b).

APPROACHES TO APPRAISE CORPORATE SUSTAINABILITY

Most of these sustainability initiatives described above are voluntary. A number of guidelines have been developed to measure corporate

Table 13.2   Corporate sustainability measurement framework by Dow
           Jones Sustainability Indexes

	Criteria – general (40%)	Criteria – industry specific (60%)
Economic	• Corporate governance • Risk and crisis management • Codes of conduct	• Media and stakeholder analysis • Brand management • Innovation management
Environment	• Environmental reporting	• Media and stakeholder analysis • Environmental management system • Sustainability strategy • Biodiversity • Eco-efficiency
Social	• Human resources management (for example professional development, employee retention) • Social reporting • Corporate citizenship	• Media and stakeholder analysis • Social integration • Occupational health and safety • Supplier management

Source: Adapted from Dow Jones Sustainability Indexes (2011).

sustainability, as in the Dow Jones Sustainability Index and the Global Reporting Initiative. As shown in Table 13.2 and Table 13.3, both guidelines broadly cover three dimensions: environmental, social and economic. Under this are some sub-categories where the indicators are developed. Both guidelines have considered the industry specific criteria or indicators. In particular the Dow Jones Sustainability Indexes specified that these industry specific criteria account for 60 per cent of the total score. GRI 3.1 does not specify the weight of industry specific indicators but does highlight the issues specific to the construction sector such as building energy intensity and building and material certification in the Sector Supplement for the Construction and Real Estate sector. In this sector supplement GRI also acknowledges the lifecycle aspects of the construction industry; that is, considering the GHG emission reduction in both the construction stage and the operation stage.

There is also a substantial amount of academic research on the evaluation of corporate sustainability performance (e.g. Keeble et al. 2003; Orlitzky et al. 2003). These studies generally follow the tri-dimensional architecture of the corporate sustainability assessment framework developed by the

Table 13.3   Sustainability reporting framework by GRI

Category	Sub-category	GRI indicators for the construction and real estate sectors
Environmental	Material, water, energy, biodiversity, emissions, waste, transport, etc.	Building energy intensity, building water intensity; GHG emission intensity from building operation and construction activities; reuse and recycling of building materials, etc.
Human rights	Investment and procurement practices; non-discrimination, freedom of association and collective bargaining; child labour, security practices, etc.	
Labour practices and decent work	Employment; relations between labour and management; occupational health and safety; professional development; diversity and equity, etc.	Health and safety management system recognized internationally
Society	Local community; corruption and bribery; public policy; anti-competitive behaviour	Number of people displaced and/or resettled as a consequence of the development
Product responsibility	Customer health and safety; product and service labelling; marketing communication; customer privacy, etc.	Sustainability certification, rating and labelling schemes
Economic	Economic performance; market presence; indirect economic impacts, etc.	

Source: Adapted from GRI (2011a, GRI 2011b).

Dow Jones Sustainability Indexes and the Global Reporting Initiatives. Efforts have been made to develop a comprehensive set of indicators to cover this structure.

In practice, some large construction companies have adopted this structure and indicators to plan and report their sustainability performance. For instance HOCHTIEF AG, the top ranking international contractor by the Engineering News Record (ENR), reported key performance indicators of corporate sustainability in the stand-alone sustainability report 2011 (HOCHTIEF 2011), such as:

1. Volume of works completed and commenced
2. Number of employees
3. Number of LEED certified projects
4. GHG emission per region
5. Water consumption
6. Obtain ISO14001 certification
7. Recycling rate of construction waste
8. Number of fatal incidents
9. Proportion of females in workforce
10. Obtain OHSAS 18001 certification
11. Resources made available to R&D on sustainability technologies
12. Professional development opportunities to employees such as training, PhD, etc.

The Lend Lease Group, the highest ranking Australian contractor in the Engineering News Record's top international contractor list, reported key corporate sustainability performance indicators in the annual report 2011 (Lend Lease 2011), such as:

1. Energy consumption and reduction rate per region
2. Number of completed projects that are accredited by environmental sustainability rating schemes
3. Proportion of workforce that have received sustainability related training
4. Recognized by independent organizations such as Dow Jones Sustainability World Index
5. Proportion of females holding senior positions
6. Proportion of female employees
7. Commitments from employees to help communities
8. Number of fatalities
9. Reduction of lost time injuries

Both HOCHTIEF AG and the Lend Lease Group have recognized the critical role of corporate governance and communication to achieve corporate sustainability, as described in their standalone sustainability report and annual report respectively. For instance HOCHTIEF AG established a dedicated committee to deal with corporate wide sustainability issues. This committee is responsible for development of corporate strategy on sustainability and communicates with the Executive Board, internal departments and other external stakeholders. Lend Lease adopted a centralized approach where the Group Head of Sustainability coordinates four Regional Heads of Sustainability (Australia, Asia, America, and Europe and Middle East) and reports to the Board.

CONCEPTUAL FRAMEWORK TO APPRAISE CORPORATE SUSTAINABILITY FOR CONSTRUCTION CONTRACTORS

There are a number of stakeholders within the context of construction. These stakeholders often have conflicting interests and needs (Moodley et al. 2008). Developed by Freeman (1984), stakeholder theory aims to integrate a variety of stakeholders into the decision making process where these stakeholders may have different needs, sometimes even conflicting (Garriga and Melé 2004). Walker et al. (2008) asserted that stakeholder management forms a critical component of project management process in various sectors such as construction. The stakeholder analysis provides a useful input for prioritizing different stakeholders' short-term and long-term interests and subsequently making decisions (Carroll 1991). Figure 13.1 describes the stakeholder structure in a typical construction project/company.

Given that the construction industry is project-based (Black et al. 2000; Whyte et al. 2002), the evaluation of corporate sustainability in the construction context should be conducted at both the project and company levels. This is evidenced by the significant amount of research on sustainability issues at both the company and project levels in the construction context. At the project level design process modelling and visualization tools provide useful mechanisms to minimize design process waste and to achieve high performance green building design goals (Korkmaz et al. 2010). This is further reinforced by the fact that a number of building/project sustainability assessment tools have been developed in recent decades such as the Green Star (Australia), LEED (United States), BREEAM (UK). Recently the Australian Green Infrastructure Council released a rating tool to assess the sustainability performance of infrastructure projects. Indeed a proper use of indicators helps in addressing corporate sustainability in both company-wide issues and project related issues (Keeble et al. 2003).

Another issue of the evaluation of corporate sustainability is timing. In other words, are we measuring the corporate sustainability performance right now from the efforts of the construction contractor or in the

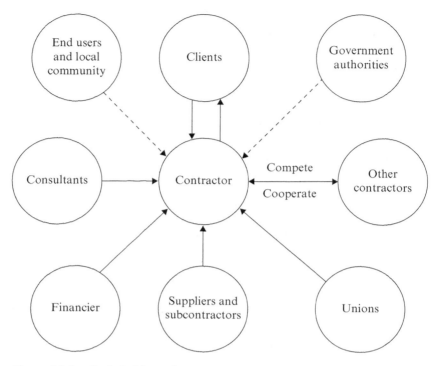

Figure 13.1   Stakeholders of construction companies

subsequent performance of the asset constructed? The previous studies have shown that it takes time for the efforts to be reflected in the performance. Therefore the time horizon forms another dimension of the appraisal of corporate sustainability by construction contractors. Aras and Crowther (2009, p. 285–6) argued:

> Many of these benefits are not just intangible but will take some time to realise. Hence, there is a need to select an appropriate time horizon for the evaluation of the risk and associated effects. This time horizon will very likely be a longer one than under a traditional financially based evaluation.

This is supported by Lee and Saen (2012) suggesting that the tangible benefits derived from corporate sustainability need to be looked at from a long term perspective.

Another issue worth noting is that the current approaches to measuring corporate sustainability vary, with some focusing on the process, others focusing on the product (or result). In other words are we going

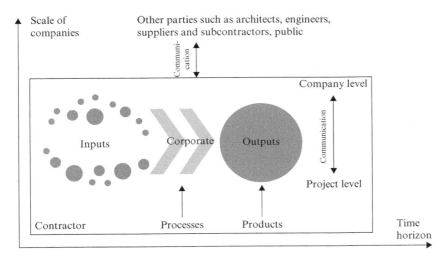

*Figure 13.2   Conceptual framework of appraisal of corporate
sustainability of construction contractors*

to measure the efforts that have been made by the corporate on sustainability (for example, plans, targets, clarity of sustainability related goals) or simply their sustainability performance and outcomes? We propose to measure both the process and product for the evaluation of corporate sustainability by construction contractors.

According to Lingard et al. (2009) the dominance of the private sector and small and medium size enterprises (SMEs) in construction presents a challenge for the development of corporate social responsibility initiatives within the industry. They further comment that the Australian construction industry appears to be socially irresponsible. Therefore the scale of an individual company needs to be taken into consideration when assessing its corporate sustainability performance.

We propose the following conceptual framework to measure the corporate sustainability in construction contractors with consideration of the aforementioned factors.

As shown in Figure 13.2, different focuses may exist with sustainability issues at the company level compared with the project level:

1.   At the company level the focus is on strategic issues such as sustainability planning, establishment of governing bodies, etc.
2.   At the project level the major focus is to execute the plans and achieve these targets on each site.

Therefore, efforts are required to ensure that strategic sustainability oriented plans are executed properly at project (site) level. There is no point for a company level sustainability policy to be in place if it is ignored or not implemented properly on the company's construction sites. This is compounded by the fact that there are a number of organizations involved in a typical construction project, such as the client, architect, engineers, building surveyors, contractors, subcontractors and quantity surveyors. As a consequence, effective communication plays a critical role in ensuring that the message is conveyed to all team members. As such it is recommended that a project culture (defined as the collective attitude and behaviour of all project team members) that leads to awareness and commitments towards sustainability be developed. Indeed the knowledge of contractors and suppliers about environmental impacts of construction activities, building materials and plant plays a critical role in improving the sustainability performance of construction projects (Shen et al. 2010). The early involvement of other stakeholders from an early stage of the project assists the decision making process on sustainability issues (Ortiz et al. 2010).

CONCLUSION

The sustainability performance of corporations has gained an increasing level of public awareness and concern. The construction companies are no exception. This chapter reviewed the concepts of corporate sustainability and the current practices used to measure it and proposed a new conceptual framework to appraise corporate sustainability for construction contractors. As a project based industry, the construction industry needs more insights into the corporate sustainability issues at both the company level and the project level. Other key factors such as time horizon and the scale of companies need to be taken into consideration as well. Future research opportunities exist to develop comprehensive indicators for the proposed conceptual framework. Empirical data should be sought to validate the conceptual framework proposed in this study. Case studies can be undertaken in order to illustrate how construction related businesses pursue corporate sustainability and the effectiveness of their sustainability strategies.

REFERENCES

Abowitz, D.A. and Toole, T.M. (2010), 'Mixed method research: fundamental issues of design, validity, and reliability in construction research', *Journal of Construction Engineering & Management*, **136**, 108–116.

ACCSR (2011), *The State of CSR in Australia: Annual Review 2010/2011*, Australian Centre for Corporate Social Responsibility, Victoria, Australia.

Aras, G. and Crowther, D. (2009), 'Corporate sustainability reporting: a study in disingenuity?', *Journal of Business Ethics*, **87** (S1), 279–88.

Azapagic, A. (2003), 'Systems approach to corporate sustainability: a general management framework', *Process Safety and Environmental Protection*, **81** (5), 303–316.

Beheiry, S.M.A., Chong, W.K and Haas, C.T. (2006), 'Examining the business impact of owner commitment to sustainability', *Journal of Construction Engineering and Management*, **132** (4), 384–92.

Black, C., Akintoye, A. and Fitzgerald E. (2000), 'An analysis of success factors and benefits of partnering in construction', *International Journal of Project Management*, **18** (6), 423–34.

Carroll, A.B. (1991), 'The pyramid of corporate social responsibility: toward the moral management of organizational stakeholders', *Business Horizons*, **34** (4), 39–48.

CIOB (2006), *Corporate Social Responsibility and Construction*, Sydney: Chartered Institute of Building Australasia.

Cochran, P.L. and Wood, R.A. (1984), 'Corporate social responsibility and financial performance', *The Academy of Management Journal*, **27** (1), 42–56.

Dow Jones Sustainability Indexes (2011), *Dow Jones Sustainability World Indexes Guide Book*, Version 11.6, September.

Dow Jones Sustainability Indexes (2012), *Corporate Sustainability*, available at http://www.sustainability-index.com/07_htmle/sustainability/corpsustainability.html, accessed 12 January 2012.

Dyllick, T. and Hockerts, K. (2002), 'Beyond the business case for corporate sustainability', *Business Strategy and the Environment*, **11**, 130–41.

EXCEL Partnership (2005), *A Sustainability Lens for Capital Decisions. A Corporate Sustainability Approach to Reduce Business Risk*, November, Vancouver, Canada.

Figge F. and Hahn, T. (2004), 'Sustainable value added – measuring corporate contributions to sustainability beyond eco-efficiency', *Ecological Economics*, **48** (2), 173–87.

Freeman, R.E. (1984), *Strategic Management: A Stakeholder Approach*, Boston: Pitman.

Garriga, E. and Melé, D. (2004), 'Corporate social responsibility theories: mapping the territory', *Journal of Business Ethics*, **53** (1–2), 51–71.

Glass, J. and Simmonds, M. (2007), 'Considerate construction: case studies of current practice', *Engineering, Construction and Architectural Management*, **14** (2), 131–49.

GRI (2011a), *Sustainability Reporting Guidelines & Construction and Real Estate Sector Supplement*, Global Reporting Initiative, September.

GRI (2011b), *G3.1 Sustainability Reporting Guidelines*, Global Reporting Initiative, March.

Hill, R.C. and Bowen, P.A. (1997), 'Sustainable construction: principles and a framework for attainment', *Construction Management and Economics*, **15** (3), 223–39.

HOCHTIEF (2011), *Sustainability Report 2011*, Aktiengesellschaft, Essen, Germany: HOCHTIEF.

IFC (2004), *The Business Case for Sustainability*, Washington DC: International Finance Corporation.

Jaillon, L., Poon, C.S. and Chiang, Y.H. (2009), 'Quantifying the waste reduction potential of using prefabrication in building construction in Hong Kong', *Waste Management*, **29** (1), 309–320.

Keeble, J., Topiol, S. and Berkeley, S. (2003), 'Using indicators to measure sustainability performance at a corporate and project level', *Journal of Business Ethics*, **44** (2/3), 149–58.

Korkmaz, S., Messner, J.I., Riley, D.R. and Magent, C. (2010), 'High-performance green building design process modeling and integrated use of visualization tools', *Architectural Engineering*, **16** (1), 37–45.

Labuschagne, C. and Brent, A. (2006), 'Social indicators for sustainable project and technology life cycle management in the process industry', *International Journal of Lifecycle Cost Analysis*, **11** (1), 3–15.

Lam, P.T.I., Chan, E.H.W., Chau, C.K., Poon, C.S. and Chun, K.P. (2009), 'Integrating green specifications in construction and overcoming barriers in their use', *Journal of Professional Issues in Engineering Education and Practice*, **135** (4), 142–52.

Lee, K.H. and Saen, R.F. (2012), 'Measuring corporate sustainability management: a data envelopment analysis approach', *International Journal of Production Economics*, dx.doi.org/10.1016/j.ijpe.2011.08.024

Lend Lease (2011), *Annual Report 2011*, Sydney: Lend Lease Group.

Lingard, H., Blismas, N. and Stewart, P. (2009), 'Corporate social responsibility in the Australian construction industry', in Michael Murray and Andrew Dainty (eds), *Corporate Social Responsibility in the Construction Industry*, Abingdon, UK: Taylor and Francis, pp. 351–80.

Lo, S.F. and Sheu, H.J. (2007), 'Is corporate sustainability a value-increasing strategy for business?', *Corporate Governance: An International Review*, **15** (2), 345–58.

Manoliadis, O., Tsolas, I. and Nakou, A. (2006), 'Sustainable construction and drivers of change in Greece: a Delphi study', *Construction Management and Economics*, **24** (2), 113–20.

McGuire, J.B., Sundgren, A. and Schneeweis, T. (1988), 'Corporate social responsibility and firm financial performance', *The Academy of Management Journal*, **31** (4), 854–72.

McWilliams, A. and Siegel, D. (2000), 'Corporate social responsibility and financial performance: correlation or misspecification?' *Strategic Management Journal*, **21** (5), 603–609.

MIT SMR (2009), *The Business of Sustainability: Findings and Insights from the First Annual Business of Sustainability Survey and the Global Thought Leaders Research Project*, Cambridge, MA: Massachusetts Institute of Technology.

Moodley, K., Smith, N. and Preece, C. (2008), 'Stakeholder matrix for ethical relationships in the construction industry', *Construction Management and Economics*, **26** (6), 625–32.

Orlitzky, M., Schmidt, F.L. and Rynes, S.L. (2003), 'Corporate social and financial performance: a meta-analysis', *Organization Studies*, **24** (3), 403–441.

Ortiz, O., Pasqualino, J.C., Díez, G. and Castells, F. (2010), 'The environmental impact of the construction phase: an application to composite walls from a life cycle perspective', *Resources, Conservation and Recycling*, **54** (11), 832–40.

Pava, M.L. and Krausz, J. (1996), 'The association between corporate social-responsibility and financial performance: the paradox of social cost', *Journal of Business Ethics*, **15**, 321–57.

Petrovic-Lazarevic, S. (2008), 'The development of corporate social responsibility in the Australian construction industry', **26** (2), 93–101.

Shen, L.Y., Hao, J.L., Tam, V.W.Y. and Yao, H. (2007), 'A checklist for assessing sustainability performance of construction projects', *Journal of Civil Engineering and Management*, **13** (4), 273–81.

Shen, L.Y., Tam, V.W.Y. and Li, C.Y. (2009), 'Benefit analysis on replacing in situ concreting with precast slabs for temporary construction works in pursuing sustainable construction practice', *Resources, Conservation and Recycling*, **53** (3), 145–8.

Shen, L.Y., Tam, V.W.Y., Tam, L. and Ji Y.B. (2010), 'Project feasibility study: the key to successful implementation of sustainable and socially responsible construction management practice', *Journal of Cleaner Production*, **18** (3), 254–9.

Snelson, D.G., Kinuthia, J.M., Davies, P.A. and Chang, S.R. (2009), 'Sustainable construction: composite use of tyres and ash in concrete', *Waste Management*, **29** (1), 360–67.

Steurer, R., Langer, M.E., Konrad, A. and Martinuzzi, A. (2005), 'Corporations, stakeholders and sustainable development I: a theoretical exploration of business–society relations', *Journal of Business Ethics*, **61**, 263–81.

Turk, A.M. (2009), 'The benefits associated with ISO 14001 certification for construction firms: Turkish case', *Journal of Cleaner Production*, **17** (5), 559–69.

Walker, D.H.T., Bourne, L.M. and Shelley, A. (2008), 'Influence, stakeholder mapping and visualization', *Construction Management and Economics*, **26** (6), 645–58.

WBCSD (2007), *Energy Efficiency in Buildings, Business Realities and Opportunities*, World Business Council for Sustainable Development, October.

Whyte, J., Bouchlaghem, D. and Thorpe, T. (2002), 'IT implementation in the construction organization', *Engineering Construction & Architectural Management*, **9** (5/6), 371–7.

Wright, P. and Ferris, S. (1997), 'Agency conflict and corporate strategy: the effect of divestment on corporate value', *Strategic Management Journal*, **18** (1), 77–83.

Wu, P. and Low, S.P. (2010), 'Project management and green buildings: lessons from the rating systems', *Journal of Professional Issues in Engineering Education and Practice*, **136** (2), 61–70.

Zeng, S.X., Tam, C.M., Deng, Z.M. and Tam, V.W.Y. (2003), 'ISO 14000 and the construction industry: survey in China', *Journal of Management in Engineering*, **19**, 107–115.

Zuo, J., Read, B., Pullen, S. and Shi, Q. (2012a), 'Achieving carbon neutrality in commercial building developments – perceptions of the construction industry', *Habitat International*, **36** (2), 278–86.

Zuo, J., Zillante, G., Wilson, L., Davidson, K. and Pullen, S. (2012b), 'Sustainability policy of construction contractors: a review', *Renewable and Sustainable Energy Reviews*, doi: 10.1016/j.rser.2012.03.011.

PART IV

International Environment of Sustainable
Business

14. International trade law, climate change and carbon footprinting

Vicki Waye

INTRODUCTION

Sustainable development is now thoroughly integrated into international and national governance and policy making, and widely accepted within the business community (Matthew and Hammill, 2009; Keijzers, 2005). Through organizations such as the World Business Council for Sustainable Development and the International Chamber of Commerce, global business leaders have committed to sustainable business practice and, by means of initiatives such as the Sustainability Reporting Guidelines (Global Reporting Initiative, 2011; Carbon Disclosure Project, 2011) have also committed to ensuring that sustainability standards are transparently monitored. Business everywhere is keen to spruik its sustainable development credentials.

Climate change poses a significant threat to sustainable development and has been classified as 'the greatest and widest-ranging market failure ever seen' (Stern, 2006). Projected increases in global temperatures not only endanger human welfare by reducing the supply of potable water and by putting global food production at risk, they also have a devastating impact upon the environment and biodiversity. As the costs of mitigation and adaptation increase, climate change places immense pressure on the adaptive capacity of developing nations (Intergovernmental Panel on Climate Change, 2007a; UNFCCC, 2011). Climate change also puts the economic prosperity of fully developed countries at risk.

Globally, business accounts for around 35 percent of greenhouse gas (GHG) emissions (UN Principles for Responsible Investment and UNEP Finance Initiative, 2011). However, companies that mitigate their GHG emissions and manage their climate change risk are perceived as more competitive than those that fail to respond to the climate change challenge (Lash and Wellington, 2007; Hoffman and Woody, 2008). Consequently, business has been exhorted to quantify and reduce its GHG footprint, to develop lower GHG emitting products, to evaluate supply chain GHG risk, and to investigate the carbon market. Approximately 85 percent of the world's largest businesses now embed climate change and carbon management into their executive decision making (Carbon Disclosure Project and PricewaterhouseCoopers LLP, 2010). Moreover, as the political and scientific consensus regarding the causes and impact of climate change has grown, many larger businesses have become active lobbyists in favour of mandatory GHG reduction targets and other efforts to facilitate the transition to a low carbon global economy (Pinkse and Kolk, 2009).

As global business shifts to the new carbon-constrained paradigm, so too has the legal system, albeit more slowly and less uniformly. Unfortunately, this lack of uniformity poses problems of complexity and regulatory arbitrage, which, in turn, adversely affect competitive advantage. The purpose of this chapter is to outline some of the general features of the international legal system and, in particular, laws governing international trade that may help promote or impede sustainability and to consider how this may impact upon businesses' pursuit of sustainable practice. Following a general outline of the law relating to international trade, the chapter will focus upon the specific example of carbon footprinting to illustrate the difficulties that may arise for business as a result of the 'prisoner's dilemma' of legal development in the climate change milieu (Golub and Marechal, 2011).

THE LEGAL FRAMEWORK

The legal system has responded to the two pronged need of mitigating and adapting to climate change at various levels and in various ways. Globally, the Kyoto Protocol, negotiated under the UN Framework Convention on Climate Change (UNFCCC), aims to mitigate climate change by setting binding GHG reduction targets that average around 5 percent on former 1990 GHG levels on industrialized countries up to 2012. These obligations are primarily implemented on a national basis, but may be supplemented by international market measures including emissions trading, trading in certified emission reduction credits, and cross-border emission reduction projects. Importantly, however, under Kyoto no binding targets are imposed on developing countries including the world's largest GHG emitter, China.

The European Union (EU) has led the field in implementing legally binding GHG reduction targets. Under the so-called 20-20-20 policy, the EU will reduce GHG emissions by 20 percent and increase the share of renewable energies in EU energy consumption to 20 percent by 2020 (European Commission, 2008). Consequently, at this stage the EU is well ahead in delivering its Kyoto Protocol commitments. Outside of the EU there are few national examples of legally binding frameworks to cut GHG emissions. Brazil's Law 12.187, which establishes GHG reduction targets of between 36.1 percent and 38.9 percent of projected emissions by 2020, is the exception rather than the rule, although a number of other countries including Thailand and Indonesia may soon follow suit. Nonetheless, worldwide at national and provincial levels there is a plethora of climate change regimes designed to reduce or stabilize GHG concentrations, encompassing: the imposition of GHG taxes; cap-and-trade systems; emissions reporting; emissions caps; land use restriction; mandatory deployment of renewable energy; product and production standards; as well as pollution control. There are many examples, including the United States' Clean Fuel Emissions Standards, limiting the amount of GHG from vehicle exhaust systems, and Thailand's Royal Decree No. 514, which exempts corporate income tax on profits earned from the sale of carbon credits. In some jurisdictions, private forms of legal action may also be available to individuals and entities adversely affected by climate change (Ghaleigh, 2010).

With a view to enhancing adaptation through international co-operation, parties to the UNFCCC have also established the Cancun Adaptation Framework (CAF). The CAF requires individual nations: to prepare national adaptation planning documentation that assesses environmental and institutional vulnerabilities to climate change; to implement reliable monitoring and reporting; and to address the regulatory coherence of mitigation and adaptation instruments. National programs must address matters such as water resources, health, food security, socio-economic activities and coastal zoning. Commitment to addressing these matters secures access to substantial amounts of multilateral funding from the Green Climate Fund as well as technology development and transfer. The CAF has also set up a process for consideration of how loss and damage resulting from climate change might be quantified and compensated. Under this approach, for example, the Ecuadorian government has offered to refrain from exploiting 1 billion barrels of its Yasuni crude oil reserves, thereby saving emissions of 410 million tons of CO_2, in exchange for international economic compensation of $US7 billion (United Nations, ECLAC, 2010).

Although the CAF obligations are political in nature, it is expected that once the Green Climate Fund becomes fully operational in 2012 there will be a stronger basis for moving toward adoption of legally binding obligations (The Climate Institute, 2010).

In the meantime, in preparation for a post-2012 Kyoto Protocol instrument, the secretariat of the UNFCCC has been attempting to renew and enhance existing binding reduction targets. Despite initial reluctance, at the Durban Climate Change Conference (COP17/CMP7), governments agreed to extend the commitment period of the Kyoto Protocol to 1 January 2013 and, more importantly, finally agreed to begin working on a new universal legal agreement incorporating quantified GHG reduction targets. It is anticipated that the new agreement will be adopted no later than 2015.

Meanwhile, as the existing Kyoto targets only apply to industrialized nations, these countries have tended to become net importers of GHG emissions from developing nations. Consequently, although some, like the United Kingdom, appear to be meeting their Kyoto targets, because their carbon trade balance has substantially worsened very little progress has been made overall (Minx, 2009). The international legal response to climate change to date thus remains largely ineffective and fragmented (Boyd, 2010). Accordingly, global temperatures will continue to increase, leading to adverse changes in the world's hydrological cycle, extreme weather events, rising sea levels, and desertification (IPCC, 2007b). Indeed, the International Energy Agency has predicted that on current trends GHG levels will increase 100 percent by 2050, which will seriously undermine the viability of many life forms on our planet (Storm, 2009).

While they are inextricably linked, international trade, sustainable development and climate change are addressed by independent legal regimes which only cross-reference to each other in minimal fashion. Thus Article 3.5 UNFCCC and Article 2.3 Kyoto Protocol provide that measures taken to combat climate change should not constitute a means of arbitrary or unjustifiable discrimination or a disguised restriction on international trade. Conversely, subject to the requirement that measures should not constitute disguised impediments to international trade, Article XX of the General Agreement on Tariffs and Trade (GATT) permits member countries to impose restrictions on international trade relating to the conservation of exhaustible natural resources or where necessary to protect human, animal or plant life or health. Similar concessions appear in the text of other World Trade Organization (WTO) Agreements including Article 2.2 of the Agreement on Technical Barriers to Trade (TBT Agreement) and Article 2.1 of the Agreement on the Application of Sanitary and Phytosanitary Measures (SPS Agreement).

Notwithstanding minimal annotation between the texts of the multilateral treaties, at an institutional level there is a greater degree of cross-fertilization. The UNFCCC participates in the WTO Committee on Trade and Environment (CTE) meetings and acts as an observer to the Committee managing trade and environment negotiations (CTESS). Similarly, the WTO Secretariat participates in UNFCCC Conference of

Parties meetings. The WTO also claims that its trade rules ensure a liberalized market for trade in environmentally beneficial goods and services (World Trade Organization, 2011) such as wind and solar power technology and equipment. According to the WTO, trade is a fundamental tool for sustainable development (Singh, 2011).

While there is no jurisprudence that operates as precedent within the WTO system, decision-making under the auspices of the WTO Dispute Settlement Understanding (DSU) provides further elaboration upon the intersection between international and national environmental obligations, and the WTO international trade rules. The DSU is a set of procedures that operate where one or more nation member(s) of the WTO believes another nation member has violated the terms of a WTO Agreement. Under the DSU, following consultations and negotiation between disputing members, the WTO establishes panels of experts to arbitrate the dispute. Panel findings can be appealed to an Appellate Body, comprised of three members of a permanent seven-member Appellate Body established by the Dispute Settlement Body (DSB) made up of WTO members. After the Panel Report has been handed down and any appeal determined, the DSB must accept the report as modified unless there is a consensus to reject it.

The DSB has addressed a number of disputes where environmental considerations have appeared to conflict with trade liberalization. The two case studies discussed below are indicative of the approaches that may be taken.

1. Mexico–US Tuna Dispute (World Trade Organization, 15 September 2011)

Mexico complained that United States' regulations restricting the use of 'dolphin safe' labelling where tuna was harvested using purse seine nets in the eastern tropical Pacific Ocean contravened Articles 1:1 and III:4 of the General Agreement on Trade and Tariffs (GATT) 1994, and Articles 2.1, 2.2 and 2.4 of the Technical Barriers to Trade (TBT) Agreement. According to Mexico, even though it had maintained sustainable means of harvesting tuna and participated in all multilateral initiatives to protect dolphins, including the Agreement on the International Dolphin Conservation Program endorsed by the United Nations, the US regulations prohibited it from using the dolphin safe label, whereas other foreign tuna producers operating outside of the eastern tropical Pacific Ocean were not subject to the same restrictions. The restrictions included requiring independent observer verification that no dolphin deaths or injuries occurred during tuna harvest. Mexico submitted evidence that large US grocery chains refused to stock Mexican tuna products that did not bear a US approved dolphin safe label. Responding to Mexico's complaints, the US defended its measures explaining that tuna fishing resulted in many thousands of dolphin deaths. According to the US, any deaths greater than zero were unacceptable.

Without determining whether the GATT provisions were violated, the Panel found that the US regulations were not discriminatory and therefore did not offend Articles 2.1 or 2.4 TBT because they applied to capture method rather than the national origin of the fish. In particular, the Panel noted that Ecuador which also fished in the eastern tropical Pacific Ocean was able to access dolphin safe labelling in the US because it had disavowed the harvesting techniques employed by Mexico.

However, the Panel did find that the US regulations infringed Article 2.2 of the TBT Agreement determining that they were more trade restrictive than was necessary, taking account of the legitimate objectives of properly informing consumers as to whether tuna was harvested in a manner adverse to dolphins, and of protecting dolphin stock. This finding rested on the fact that dolphins caught outside of the eastern tropical Pacific Ocean zone were not subject to the same stringent restrictions that applied to Mexican tuna. Furthermore, according to the Panel, US independent verification requirements were too costly given the low likelihood of dolphin deaths and injuries arising from Mexican methods of tuna harvest.

2.   US–Gasoline (United States – Standards for Reformulated and Conventional Gasoline, 1996)

Venezuela brought a complaint to the WTO based upon regulations enacted by the United States' Environmental Protection Agency (EPA) pursuant to the Clean Air Act 1990. So as to reduce toxic air pollutants the regulations required that gasoline sold in certain areas of the US (whether imported or domestic) had to be reformulated pursuant to specifications founded upon 1990 baselines. Domestic refiners were required to set an individual refinery baseline that represented the quality of gasoline produced in 1990, whereas foreign refiners were subject to a statutory baseline fixed by the EPA on the basis of US average 1990 gasoline quality. The EPA justified the differential treatment because of difficulties related to verification and enforcement. Venezuela complained that the regulations breached Article III.4 GATT (the 'national treatment' principle) because foreign refineries were subject to more exacting standards than domestic refineries. Venezuela also argued that the regulations could not be justified as health or environmental measures under Article XX.

At first instance the Panel found that imported and domestic gasoline were like products and had to be subject to the same standards, but that under the EPA's regulations, imported gasoline was treated less favourably. The Panel also found that although clean air was a natural exhaustible resource with Article XX (g), the regulations did not relate to its conservation. The US appealed. Unlike the Panel, the Appellate Body found that the baseline establishment rules fell within Article XX (g). However, according to the Appellate Body, the regulations failed to meet the requirements of the chapeau to Article XX. Notwithstanding administrative difficulties faced by the EPA, the Appellate Body regarded the more stringent baseline requirements for foreign refiners as unjustifiable or arbitrary measures that impeded international trade. The regulations thus breached the WTO rules.

North American Free Trade Agreement (NAFTA)

An analogous situation applies to significant preferential trade agreements such as the NAFTA between Canada, the United States and Mexico. Article 104 NAFTA, for example, provides that pre-existing international environmental obligations such as the Montreal Protocol on Substances that Deplete the Ozone Layer are to prevail over NAFTA's trade liberalization obligations provided the parties choose the least inconsistent means of compliance. In addition, Article 1106 (6) NAFTA adopts similar language to Article XX GATT by stating that environmental protections are permitted provided they are not unduly trade restrictive.

Unlike WTO disputes that are limited to State-to-State matters, NAFTA also provides investors affected by trade restrictive measures in host countries recourse to arbitral mechanisms such as the World Bank's International Centre for the Settlement of Investment Disputes (ICSID). In relation to foreign investment, Article 1114 provides that NAFTA tolerates national measures requiring that investment activity be undertaken in an environmentally sensitive manner.

Articles 1106 and 1114 were interpreted in *Methanex v United States* (*Methanex Corporation v United States*, 2005), an international investment arbitration initiated by a Canadian corporation claiming that Californian legislation phasing out methyl tertiary butyl ethers in Californian gasoline constituted discrimination against a foreign producer (because it gave preferential treatment to US ethanol producers) and an invalid expropriation of its business. Methanex sought $US970 million in compensation. The Tribunal found against Methanex, determining that Methanex's position as a methanol producer could not be compared to that of an ethanol producer, and that general environmental measures enacted in good faith did not constitute compensable expropriations.

NAFTA members have specifically pledged to 'promote sustainable development based on cooperation and mutually supportive environmental and economic policies' in the North American Agreement on Environmental Cooperation 1993 and have established a Commission for Environmental Cooperation (CEC). Among other things the CEC has been involved in improving enforcement activity to prevent illegal trade in environmentally hazardous material and protected flora and fauna. The CEC has also undertaken an ongoing environmental assessment of NAFTA, commissioning independent experts to provide reports on the impact of NAFTA on various environmental indicators such as fisheries and freshwater. Unfortunately, the consensus appears to be that while the composition of NAFTA industries has become less pollution intensive, this has not been outweighed by the effect of scale. Increased investment in GHG producing industry has overwhelmed the capacity of domestic regulators to respond effectively to the climate change agenda (Wold, 2010).

Mercado Común Del Sur (MERCOSUR)

The MERCOSUR comprised of Argentina, Brazil, Paraguay, Uruguay, Venezuela and associate members Bolivia, Chile and Ecuador, has taken similar steps. In 1992 MERCOSUR members signed a Cooperation Agreement on Environmental Issues that established a Commission to harmonize regional environmental regulations and to promote programs leading to improvements in environmental quality. In addition, MERCOSUR's executive body, the Common Market Council, has adopted a number of resolutions requiring Member States to pursue environmental objectives, such as the enactment of gas emission controls, the formulation of sustainable energy policies, and the implementation of an action plan for cooperation on bio-fuels (Morosini, 2010). An Environmental Framework Agreement 2001 and supplementary Environmental Framework Agreement Regarding Cooperation and Assistance in Environmental Emergencies 2004 have also been approved. However, as with NAFTA and the WTO Agreements, MERCOSUR's more explicit and expansive commitment to sustainability does not necessarily permit environmental considerations to trump trade and commerce. Article 3 of the Environmental Framework Agreement likewise requires members to avoid environmental measures that unjustifiably or arbitrarily restrict trade between MERCOSUR members, and has been used to defeat national environmentally motivated regulations such as bans on the importation of re-treaded tyres. Using its bargaining power as a trade bloc, MERCOSUR has also, at times, prioritized its members' trading interests above those of the environment. Thus, MERCOSUR vehemently opposes EU regulations that prohibit cyanide in mining to protect water resources and biodiversity. MERCOSUR regards the EU initiative as an attack on its members' mining industries, which are responsible for significant economic and social development in the region (Yakovleva and Vazquez-Brust, 2011). This position has led one writer to conclude that trade liberalization in Latin America has had a net negative environmental effect, and that any gains in environmental standards have been the result of demands from external markets (Ballesteros, 2009).

IMPLICATIONS FOR BUSINESS

Although a number of large international businesses have embraced sustainability, because the law does not mandate corporate social responsibility it remains the case that many other businesses will continue to act in ways that might be characterized as indifferent or even harmful to the environment. Industry responses to climate change diverge significantly between sectors, between firms within sectors, and across countries. However, it appears that pressure from regulatory agencies acting pursuant to a robust legal mandate is a good predictor of the likely strength of business engagement with sustainability (Jeswani et al., 2008). Where the Kyoto Protocol is supplemented by strong national policies and legal regimes, heavier investment in green technologies has followed and business has reduced its GHG more rapidly and more uniformly (Dessler and Parson, 2010). A good example is the position taken by the United States' EPA as a result of the Supreme Court decision in *Massachusetts v EPA* (*Massachusetts v Environmental Protection Agency, 2007*). Following this decision, the EPA determined that GHG endanger public welfare and so began rulemaking under the Clean Air Act, specifying standards for fuel economy and maximum GHG vehicle emissions. The EPA has also published draft rules to impose clean air technology standards upon coal powered energy utilities in the near future. Without such drivers it is unlikely that vehicle manufacturers and coal powered utilities would universally adopt sustainable practices at their own initiative. Major concerns are that costly actions taken to mitigate GHG emissions where regulation is absent make businesses less competitive, causing the 'leakage' of production to areas or countries where climate change regulation and business commitment to sustainability are weak. Unless strong parallel actions are undertaken, the incentive for business to make major cuts to GHG emissions can be stymied.

Regulation is not just a more effective driver of GHG mitigation than business goodwill alone. It also overcomes the coordination and collective action problems that arise from the formulation and implementation of mitigation and adaptation strategies. Collective action problems surrounding climate change are well known: climate change is a multiscalar problem spanning borders, governance units, and business enterprises; the efforts of a few to slow climate change are unlikely to make any significant difference; and committed warming caused by the actions of others in the past continues to lead to higher temperatures despite efforts to mitigate and adapt today. Global business response to climate change is also hindered by the variegated and non-linear effects of climate change, where differential environmental tipping points throughout the world affect the speed with which climate change accelerates (Ruhl and Salzman, 2010).

Coordination problems are particularly acute for carbon trading. Without a uniform and ubiquitous means of measuring, verifying and monitoring GHG emissions and agreement on matters such as the permissibility of carbon offsets, carbon trading is unlikely to significantly ameliorate climate change. Information asymmetries and enforcement problems also underpin the need for government action (Storm, 2009).

Consequently, the failure of the international community to set globally binding GHG reduction targets, the lack of clear signalling in favour of sustainability in international trade law, uncertainties concerning the pace and level of climate change, as well as the cost and efficacy of mitigation strategies, make it difficult for business to plan for and respond to climate change. Although there is a consensus that investment in energy efficient infrastructure and green technologies will be a major driver of growth (European Commission, 2010), continued poor economic outlook flowing on from the global recession of 2008 has exacerbated that difficulty (Garnaut, 2010).

As the failure to co-ordinate conflicting national climate change regulation continues, the likelihood of international trade conflict increases (Atik, 2011). Disputes are predicted in relation to border adjustments that reflect the embedded energy within imported products, for example, climate-related tariffs; rebates on exports of carbon intensive products; unilateral countervailing duties and sanctions imposed against carbon free riding; GHG performance standards; and subsidies for renewable energy initiatives (Hufbauer et al., 2009). Recent analysis suggests that exports from countries such as China and India might be subject to an average applied tariff of 8–10 percent, if a carbon tax of $50 is imposed on imports by the US or the EU (Mani, 2010). If such measures are put in place it is highly likely that they will be heavily scrutinized by the WTO for their environmental efficacy and for their cost compared with less trade restrictive alternatives (*Brazil – Measures Affecting Imports of Retreaded Tyres*, 2007; McLure, 2010). From the perspective of businesses in developing nations, attempts to marry international trade and climate policies are sometimes viewed as means to conceal trade protectionism, whereas developing countries are not well placed to monitor and respond to climate-related trade measures (Ghosh, 2009).

CARBON FOOTPRINTING

The problems posed by the failure to secure global climate change regulation are exemplified by the case of carbon footprinting. Carbon footprinting refers to the measurement and reporting of GHG emissions associated with production and consumption activity and which can be measured on a national, regional, enterprise, company, household or per product basis (Peters, 2010). At the enterprise/company level carbon footprinting helps business to better understand the sources of its GHG emissions, and to identify cost effective opportunities to reduce energy consumption and carbon intensity.

Internationally, there are two main groups of standards:

- Greenhouse Gas Protocol Initiative (the GHG Protocol) published by the World Resources Institute/World Business Council for Sustainable Development (WRI/WBCSD)
- International Standards Organization 14064 – 69 Greenhouse Gases Collection.

In addition to the above there are a number of officially recognized standards operating at national level, including: Britain's Publicly Available Specification 2050; New Zealand's Greenhouse Gas Footprinting Strategy; Thailand's Greenhouse Gas Management Organization's Carbon Footprint Assessment Guidelines; China's Panda Standard for measuring off-set project activities; and carbon footprinting rules devised by AFNOR, the French Standards Agency. Pursuant to its Sustainable Consumption and Production Action Plan, the European Commission DG Environment is also developing carbon footprinting technologies and standards (European Commission, 2011). Although the carbon footprint standards employ similar methodologies, each varies in scope, unit of measurement, reliability of data, verification, and communication mode (Micallef-Borg, 2010; Pandey et al., 2011). Thus, the size of carbon footprints will vary according to how they are calculated, making comparisons of performance difficult across sectors. Additionally, the standards themselves are still evolving. As yet there is no scientific consensus on the best way to accurately measure GHG emissions (Wright et al., 2011). Thus the holy grail of a universal carbon footprinting standard seems to be falling well behind existing technology and collaborative effort.

Most of the existing standards distinguish between three tiers of measurement:

- Scope 1 – all direct emissions
- Scope 2 – indirect GHG emissions from electricity, heat or steam
- Scope 3 – other indirect emissions related to the supply chain, such as the extraction and production of purchased materials and energy, transport-related activities in vehicles not owned or controlled by the reporting entity, outsourced activities, waste disposal, etc.

Regardless of the lack of international standardization, a number of national and supra-national jurisdictions already legally mandate carbon footprinting on an enterprise or company level. These include Europe, Australia, the United States, Japan, Canada and the United Kingdom. Under Europe's (EU) Directive 2003/87, which established the EU's GHG trading scheme, stationary sources emitting greater than 25,000 CO_2 equivalent (CO_2e) tonnes per annum must report their GHG emissions. Similarly, Australia's National Greenhouse and Energy Reporting Act 2007 requires corporations with GHG emissions, energy consumption or production above 25 000 CO_2e tonnes to report their emissions data to the Australian government. An analogous law has been introduced in the United States by the Consolidated Appropriations Act 2008 and has subsequently led the EPA to issue a Mandatory Reporting of Greenhouse Gases Rule (74 FR 56260) obliging reporting of GHG data and other relevant information from large sources and suppliers. As a result of cost and 'double counting' both the United States and the EU legally mandated reporting requirements only apply to Scope 1 emissions, whereas the Australian and British requirements extend to Scope 2 GHG emissions. Some jurisdictions like France and Japan are also considering mandatory per product carbon footprinting.

In addition to regulatory initiatives, a few large businesses like Britain's Tesco and the United States' Wal-Mart impose their own environmental credentialing along their supply chains. Industry organizations are also attempting to assist their constituents by developing industry specific carbon footprint technologies and standards. Examples include the International Dairy Federation, which has established a methodology to determine the carbon footprint of dairy products regardless of the geographic origin; and the International Wine Industry Greenhouse Gas Protocol and Accounting Tool.

This raises a number of dilemmas for policy makers attempting to target particular business sectors or particular business practices. Uncertain and conflicting carbon footprinting results undermine the efficacy of policy formulation (Minx, 2009). It also poses problems for business itself regarding the standard(s) that ought to be applied so as to best support sustainability strategies. Businesses with an export orientation are likely to be subject to several different standards, imposing extra costs affecting production, packaging and labelling. When forced to comply with multiple carbon footprinting procedures emanating from both private and public domains so that different carbon labels are required to be applied on the same products, many small to medium businesses, especially those from developing nations, will face substantial access to market barriers. Allied to this is the problem of insufficient and expensive datasets that are required for carbon footprint analysis (Baddeley et al., 2011). In many developing countries there is simply not enough data available to determine enterprise or product footprints. Thus, if a large retailer or distributor in a fully developed nation requires carbon footprinting or demonstrable low carbon production standards, or both, producers from less carbon oriented countries will effectively be shut out of the market.

The Mexico–US tuna dispute outlined previously and *EC – Trademarks and Geographical Indications (European Communities – Protection of Trademarks and Geographical Indications for Agricultural Products and Foodstuffs – Complaint by Australia,* 2005) demonstrate that even where labelling is not obligatory, if regulatory or quasi-regulatory standards for labelling are developed which are unduly trade restrictive or which impose discriminatory measures against imported products, this can raise WTO concerns. Standards such as those for carbon footprinting may fall within the Code of Good Practice for the Preparation, Adoption and Application of Standards set out in Annex 3 to the TBT Agreement. Under the Code, WTO members are required to encourage their standards bodies (both public and private) to prepare and apply their standards in accordance with the Code. The Code imposes obligations similar to those that apply more generally under the WTO Agreements, including the prohibition against discriminatory treatment of imports and a requirement that standards are not designed or applied with a view to creating unnecessary obstacles to international trade. Consistency with relevant international standards is also promoted under the Code. As long as the relevant standard is consistent with a pertinent international standard, it is presumed not to amount to an unnecessary obstacle to trade (TBT Agreement, Article 2.5).

Nonetheless it remains to be determined whether carbon footprinting standards will be characterized as product or production process related standards. If they are not product or production process related they will fall outside of the TBT Agreement altogether. Presumably, however, since the carbon intensity of any product or production process will attract different levels of demand from consumers, wholesalers and retailers, and different taxation, subsidy and regulatory treatment from government, this will be sufficient to classify it as a product/production characteristic. Consequently, it is likely that they will attract WTO protection where the relevant measure fails to conform to international standards and/or imposes unreasonable restrictions on trade.

The pathway forward is the obvious one of harmonization. The International Standards Organization is making considerable progress towards it. The WTO's Committee on Trade and Environment has also been meeting regularly to consider the impact of carbon footprinting on trade and has initiated a number of studies to evaluate how carbon footprinting schemes may affect market access; to address transparency in the implementation of carbon footprinting regulation; and to respond to the proliferation of non-uniform carbon footprinting standards (World Trade Organization, Committee on Trade and Environment, 2011). Clearly the development of an accurate, efficient and commonly used tool to measure carbon intensity will be essential for both policy makers and business in their effort to mitigate climate change. Technological assistance is also required for developing countries whose capacity for collecting and interpreting GHG data is limited.

CONCLUSION

The trend toward constructive business engagement with the climate change agenda has been hindered by the failure to match this with binding international commitments for GHG emission reduction and climate change adaptation. Although legally some significant progress has been made at national and international levels, GHG levels continue to rise as global population and the volume of international trade increase. The international trade law framework itself sends mixed messages that underscore the lack of priority that has historically been given to the threat of climate change. This is reflected in the glacial pace toward harmonization of carbon footprinting methodologies. Without accurate and comparable performance indicators of carbon intensity, businesses' efforts to transform to a low carbon model will be limited. The sooner harmonization is addressed the better.

REFERENCES

Atik, J. (2011), 'Inventing trade remedies in response to climate change', available at http://papers.ssrn.com/sol3/papers.cfm?abstract_id=1934431 (accessed 19 October 2011).

Baddeley, S., Cheng, P. and Wolfe, R. (2011), *Trade Policy Implications of Carbon Labels on Food*, s.l., Canadian Agricultural Trade Policy and Competitiveness Research Network.

Ballesteros, D. (2009), 'Examination of the environmental consequences of trade regimes in Latin America, *Opera*, **24**, 173–95.

Boyd, W. (2010), 'Climate change, fragmentation, and the challenges of global environmental law: elements of a post-Copenhagen assemblage', *University of Pennsylvania Journal of International Law*, **32** (2), 457–550.

Brazil – Measures Affecting Imports of Retreaded Tyres (2007), Appellate Body Report, WT/DS332/AB/R, adopted 17 December 2007, DSR 2007:IV, 1527.

Carbon Disclosure Project and PricewaterhouseCoopers LLP (2010), *Carbon Disclosure Project 2010: Global 500 Report*, London and New York: Carbon Disclosure Project.

Carbon Disclosure Project (2011), *Carbon Disclosure Project*, available at https://www.cdproject.net/en-US/Pages/HomePage.aspx (accessed 13 September 2011).

Dessler, A.E. and Parson, E. (2010), *The Science and Politics of Global Climate Change: A Guide to the Debate I*, 2nd edn, Cambridge: Cambridge University Press.

European Commission (2008), *Communication from the Commission to the European Parliament, the Council, the European Economic and Social Committee and the Committee of the Regions – 20 20 by 2020 – Europe's Climate Change Opportunity*, available at http://eur-lex.europa.eu/LexUriServ/LexUriServ.do?uri=CELEX:52008DC0030:EN:NOT (accessed 14 November 2011).

European Commission (2010), *Communication from the Commission to the European Parliament, the Council, the European Economic and Social Committee and the Committee of the Regions – Analysis of options to move beyond 20% greenhouse gas emission reductions and assessing the risk*, available at http://www.ipex.eu/IPEXL-WEB/dossier/dossier.do?code=COM&   year=2010&number=0265 (accessed 14 November 2011).

European Commission (2011), *European Sustainable Development Consumption and Production Policies*, available at http://ec.europa.eu/environment/eussd/escp_en.htm, (accessed 25 October 2011).

European Communities – Protection of Trademarks and Geographical Indications for Agricultural Products and Foodstuffs (2005), Panel Report, WT/DS290/R, adopted 20 April 2005, DSR 2005:X, 4603.

Garnaut, R. (2010), 'Policy framework for transition to a low-carbon world economy', *Asian Economic Policy Review*, **5** (1), 19–33.

Ghaleigh, N.S. (2010), '"Six honest serving-men": climate change litigation as legal mobilization and the utility of typologies', *Climate Law*, **1**, 31–61.

Ghosh, A.M, (2009), 'Enforcing climate rules with trade measures', in R.B. Stewart, B. Kingsbury, B. and Rudyk, B. (eds), *Climate Finance: Regulatory and Funding Strategies for Climate Change and Global Development*, New York and London: New York University Press, pp. 272–80.

Global Reporting Initiative (2011), *Global Reporting Initiative: Reporting*

Framework Overview, available at http://www.globalreporting.org/ ReportingFramework/ReportingFrameworkOverview/ (accessed 13 September 2011).

Golub, P.S. and Marechal, J.-P. (2011), 'Overcoming the planetary prisoners' dilemma: cosmopolitan ethos and pluralist cooperation', in P.G. Harris (ed.), *Ethics and Global Environmental Policy*, Cheltenham, UK and Northampton, MA: Edward Elgar, pp. 150–74.

Hoffman, A.J. and Woody, J.G. (2008), *Climate Change: What's Your Business Strategy*, Boston: Harvard Business School Publishing Corporation.

Hufbauer, G.C., Charnovitz, S. and Kim, J. (2009), *Global Warming and the World Trading System*, Washington DC: Peter G Peterson Institute for International Economics.

Intergovernmental Panel on Climate Change (2007a), *Climate Change 2007: Impacts, Adaptation and Vulnerability*, Cambridge, UK: Cambridge University Press.

Intergovernmental Panel on Climate Change (2007b), *IPCC Fourth Assessment Report: Climate Change 2007, Synthesis Report*, Geneva: Intergovernmental Panel on Climate Change.

Jeswani, H.K., Wehrmeyer, W. and Mulugetta, Y. (2008), 'How warm is the corporate response to climate change? Evidence from Pakistan and the UK', *Business Strategy and the Environment*, **18**, 46–60.

Keijzers, G. (2005), *Business, Government and Sustainable Development*, Oxford and New York: Routledge.

Lash, J. and Wellington, F. (2007), 'Competitive advantage on a warming planet', *Harvard Business Review*, **85** (3), 94–102.

Mani, M. (2010), *Creating Incentives for Clean Technology Trade, Transfer and Diffusion: The Role of Non-Distorting Policies*, Geneva: The Graduate Institute: Centre for Trade and Economic Integration.

Massachusetts v Environmental Protection Agency (2007), 549 US 497.

Matthew, R.A. and Hammill, A. (2009), 'Sustainable development and climate change', *International Affairs*, **85** (6), 1117–28.

McLure, C.E. (2010), 'The carbon-added tax: an idea whose time should never come', *Carbon and Climate Law Review*, **4** (3), 250–59.

Methanex Corporation v United States of America (2005), 44 ILM 1345.

Micallef-Borg, C. (2010), 'Product carbon footprinting: calculation and communication standards in the making', *Carbon and Climate Law Review*, **4** (2), 178–89.

Minx, J. (2009), 'Input-output analysis and carbon footprinting: an overview of applications', *Economic Systems Research*, **21** (3), 187–216.

Morosini, F. (2010), 'The MERCOSUR trade and environment linkage debate: the dispute over trade in retreaded tires', *Journal of World Trade*, **44** (5), 1127–44.

Pandey, D., Agrawal, M. and Pandey, J.S. (2011), 'Carbon footprint: current methods of estimation', *Environmental Monitoring and Assessment*, **178** (1–4), 135–60.

Peters, G.P. (2010), 'Carbon footprints and embodied carbon at multiple scales', *Current Opinion in Environmental Sustainability*, **2** (4), 245–50.

Pinkse, J. and Kolk, A. (2009), *International Business and Global Climate Change*, Oxford and New York: Routledge.

Ruhl, J. and Salzman, J. (2010), 'Climate change, dead zones, and massive problems in the administrative state: a guide for whittling away', *California Law Review*, **98** (1), 59–120.

Singh, D. (2011), *Assessing the Evolution of the International Trading System and Enhancing Its Contribution to Development and Economic Recovery,* Geneva: World Trade Organization.

Stern, N. (2006), *Stern Review on the Economics of Climate Change: Executive Summary,* United Kingdom: HM Treasury.

Storm, S. (2009), 'Capitalism and climate change: can the invisible hand adjust the natural thermostat?', *Development and Change,* **40** (6), 1011–38.

The Climate Institute (2010), *The Cancun Agreement: A Preliminary Assessment,* available at http://www.climateinstitute.org.au/our-publications/reports/772-the-cancun-agreement-a-preliminary-assessment (accessed 4 September 2011).

UN Principles for Responsible Investment and UNEP Finance Initiative (2011), *Universal Ownership: Why Environmental Externalities Matter To Institutional Investors,* London, Boston and New York: Trucost.

UNFCCC (2011), *Assessing Climate Change Impacts and Vulnerability: Making Informed Adaptation Decisions,* Bonn, Germany: Climate Change Secretariat (UNFCCC).

United Nations, ECLAC (2010), *Sustainable Development in Latin America and the Caribbean: Trends, Progress, and Challenges in Sustainable Consumption and Production, Mining, Transport, Chemicals and Waste Management,* Santiago: United Nations.

United States Standards for Reformulated and Conventional Gasoline, WT/DS2/R, adopted 20 May 1996, modified by Appellate Body Report, WT/DS2/AB/R, DSR 1996:I, 29.

USCAP (2009), *United States Climate Action Partnership,* available at http://www.us-cap.org/ (accessed 13 September 2011).

US Global Change Research Program (2009), *Global Climate Change Impacts in the United States,* New York: Cambridge University Press.

Wold, C. (2010), 'Taking stock: trade's environmental scorecard after twenty years of "trade and environment"', *Wake Forest Law Review,* **45**, 319–54.

World Trade Organization, Committee on Trade and Environment (2011), *Committee on Trade and Environment Work,* available at http://www.wto.org/english/tratop_e/envir_e/wrk_committee_e.htm (accessed 30 October 2011).

World Trade Organization (2011), *Climate Change and the Potential Relevance of WTO Rules,* available at http://www.wto.org/english/tratop_e/envir_e/climate_measures_e.htm (accessed 19 September 2011).

Wright, L.A., Kemp, S. and Williams, I. (2011), '"Carbon footprinting": towards a universally accepted definition', *Carbon Management,* **2** (1), 61–72.

Yakovleva, N. and Vazquez-Brust, D. (2011), 'Stakeholder perspectives on CSR of mining MNCs in Argentina', *Journal of Business Ethics,* forthcoming, available online at http://www.springerlink.com/content/4l36658726883255/ (accessed 14 November 2011).

15. The economics of climate change: the Stern and Garnaut reports and their implications for business

Martin P. Shanahan

INTRODUCTION

Over a century ago the Nobel Prize winning chemist Svente Arrhenius (1896), calculated that doubling the concentration of carbon dioxide (CO_2) in the atmosphere would increase global temperatures by 5 degrees Celsius. His work however did not attempt to identify the economic impact such a change might have on the economy. Nor did he examine the possible cost of attempting to prevent this increase.

While scientific research into the link between global temperatures and increased carbon dioxide wavered over the next 90 years, emissions did not decrease and by 1988 scientists and politicians were sufficiently concerned about global warming trends and the possible link to human activity that they established an Intergovernmental Panel on Climate Change (IPCC).[1] The United Nations Framework on Climate Change Convention (UNFCCC) followed in 1992, initiating a series of international conferences, the most notable being the 1997 Kyoto meeting that established specific targets to reduce greenhouse gases. Unfortunately adherence to this agreement by the original parties (mostly developed countries) was not unanimous, and later meetings that aimed to improve and extend the protocol (including recently Copenhagen 2009, Cancun 2010, Durban 2011, and Bonn 2012) have not been overwhelmingly successful. Nonetheless at the international level the number of countries agreeing to reduce greenhouse gas emissions continues to increase, and negotiations on how to coordinate reductions in greenhouse gases persist.[2]

Coordinating an international response is difficult, in part because each country faces different problems. Individual countries differ in their stage of development, production of carbon dioxide, the living standards of their population, the structure of their economy, their political processes and their ability to make change. Within the context of an international agreement, countries must also have sufficient flexibility to design their own methods to tackle the problem. One important part of the solution that both facilitates flexibility of response and accommodates differences in national objectives and stages of development, lies within the domain of economics.

The key to understanding current efforts to price carbon is that until recently, markets have not accounted for the true environmental cost of producing energy. Without the cost to the natural environment being properly factored into their market price, goods such as coal, oil or other energy producing resources were underpriced, leading to their overproduction and profligate use, and creating little incentive to move toward more efficient and less costly sources of energy.

The Stern Review written in 2006 for the United Kingdom Government, was one of the first truly comprehensive attempts to examine the issue of climate change using an economic perspective. The impact of the report, which extended well beyond the UK, was in large measure due to its 'translation' of global environmental and scientific issues into matters of economic and market consequence.

THE STERN REVIEW

The *Stern Review* (Stern 2006a, 2006b) first examined the existing scientific evidence on global warming and the contribution of humans to this and concluded that there was sufficient evidence to be concerned given current and projected trends. It then examined the economic aspects of climate change, and the costs and benefits of stabilizing greenhouse gas emissions. Third, it examined policy implications of shifting to an economy that was less reliant on carbon-based fuels.

An initial and important conclusion from the review was that the benefits of strong, early action on climate change outweighed the costs. This controversial finding was based on a series of logical steps that were detailed in the almost 700 page report. Briefly, Stern found that the available scientific evidence pointed to the increasing risks of serious, irreversible impacts from climate change associated with business-as-usual (BAU) paths for emissions. Such climate change threatened the basic elements of life for people around the world, including access to water, food production, health and their use of land, as well as the environment generally. The damage that would be done by climate change would accelerate as the world warmed, but the effects would not be evenly distributed. The poorest countries and people would suffer earliest and most.

Critically, for Stern's conclusions, if and when the damage appeared, it would be too late to reverse the process except at extreme cost and after considerable (and in some cases, irreversible) damage had occurred. Complicating the issue further he found that climate change may initially have small positive effects for a few developed countries, but was likely to be very damaging when the much higher temperature increases occurred; something that was expected by mid to late century under BAU scenarios. The review also re-estimated the total impact of climate change and found that at 5 to 20 percent of global GDP, its impact was likely to be considerably higher than previously estimated.

Stern found that for the past two hundred years, CO_2 emissions had been driven by economic growth, and would continue in the future. Nevertheless he concluded that economic growth could also be achieved while stabilizing greenhouse gas concentrations in the atmosphere, if there was a shift to a 'low-carbon' economy. He estimated that the cost of undertaking this shift at around 1 percent of global GDP by 2050. The cost of not making such a change he estimated at a minimum of 5 percent of global GDP, and perhaps over 20 percent if action was not taken quickly.

Importantly Stern's estimates, while open to challenge, were transparent and made serious efforts to be realistic. For example he assumed that China and India would continue to use coal for 80 percent of their electricity production for at least the next thirty or forty years. Hydrocarbon-based fuels would continue to contribute to over half of the world's energy generation in 2050. An assumption that countries could shift to less carbon-intensive methods of power generation more quickly was neither politically nor financially realistic. He thus attempted to balance the urgency of the need for change, with the reality of existing markets and resource costs. A fundamental change in the price of carbon, in almost all its forms, was a key element to advancing this change.

The transition to a lower carbon-based global economy posed challenges and opportunities, and required several elements, including putting a price on carbon, changing technology policies and removing barriers that prevented behavioural change. Policies to adapt to the consequences of climate change (such as rising sea levels) would also be required by many countries.

Increasing the market price of carbon (and consequently the price of all carbon-based products) could be achieved in several ways, specifically via taxation, trading or regulation. Placing a tax on carbon was a method available to individual governments to raise prices quickly. Such an approach also allowed countries to set their 'own' agenda and accommodate the price changes in different ways and at different rates. In theory the price could be raised to offset fully the cost of damage done to the environment. Unless there was coordination between tax regimes, however, there was also a danger that countries could either overtax and damage their economy excessively, or undertax, and so not contribute enough to the changes necessary to drive down the use of carbon-based products.

Trading schemes offered the potential to establish a more global price for carbon. In this case the difficulties lay with establishing the international trading 'architecture' (definitions, regulations, enforcement mechanisms, institutions) to establish a global market. The benefit of such an approach is that it allows the price of carbon to be signalled to all other markets (such as transportation, power generation, food production, etc), simultaneously and rapidly – and so establishes a fundamental shift in relative prices that could provide the incentive to change technologies. The third option, regulation, had the benefit of being relatively quick to implement. The downside, however, was that many unintended consequences could emerge, in many different countries, as relative prices overshot or undershot the prices needed to induce changes in carbon use.

Stern argued that international collective action was critical if the target range of 450 to 550 parts per million of CO_2 equivalent (the upper limit to a stable global air temperature) were to be achieved. Rich and poor countries would have to play their part. While the better off might adjust relatively quickly, poorer countries would require new finance mechanisms, such as 'carbon finance' to afford the necessary changes to their economies and adapt to global warming. Wealthier European Union member countries had the opportunity to develop their existing emission trading schemes further to assist with this. For example existing schemes could be used to assist the funding of technological developments and help create a global carbon market, and so facilitate the different rates of change that would be required in different countries according to their resources and challenges.

At the international level, Stern suggested addressing a range of issues from the establishment of international product standards (to improve efficiency in thousands of markets and transactions) to large global projects, such as halting deforestation or developing more drought and heat resistant food crops.

While Stern included several examples of how individual countries and the world community might shift to a lower carbon economy, perhaps his clearest message was also the simplest: business as usual was not an option if global warming was to be stabilized, while delaying the response would greatly increase the costs incurred later.

Almost immediately after the launch of his review, Stern's work was criticized on a number of fronts.[3] Some criticized technical aspects of his work such as the particular models used to predict future rates of emissions, or the discount rates used to calculate the net present value of current expenditures. Other criticized the science underlying the link between carbon emissions and global warming, or questioned the empirical evidence, while still others suggested that the uncertainty involved with Stern's predictions invalidated his strong recommendations. Others suggested that he had overstated the dangers and consequences of global warming so as to drive responses through fear, and understated the costs of taking remedial action. Less extreme voices, however, suggested that even though there was uncertainty with the models and the predictions the outcomes were so catastrophic that prudent governments would be better advised to take strong action and be proved wrong later, than to do nothing and later attempt to cope with the consequences.[4]

In Australia, the government asked Professor Ross Garnaut to examine the issues from Australia's perspective.

THE GARNAUT REPORTS

In 2007 the Australian Commonwealth, state and territory governments commissioned economist Ross Garnaut to conduct an independent study of the impacts of climate change on the Australian economy. The *Garnaut Climate Change Review: Final Report* was presented in September 2008 (Garnaut 2008). In November 2010 he was asked to update that report, and this was presented in the *Garnaut Climate Change Review Update 2011: Australia in the Global Response to Climate Change* (Garnaut 2011).

Garnaut reported his estimate of the costs and benefits to the Australian economy of taking action to reduce the damage caused by human initiated climate change in 2008. Accepting that on the balance of probabilities the science was correct, the report concluded that it was in Australia's national interest to do its part in a global effort to mitigate climate change. He was also relatively pessimistic that enough would be done in time to avert the worst impacts of global warming.

His 2011 follow-up report responded to criticism of his earlier work as well as incorporating more recent evidence on global warming and economic responses. Garnaut found the evidence for climate change was now even stronger – 'beyond reasonable doubt' – and that Australia had not yet shifted from a 'business as usual' approach, unlike some other developed countries. Garnaut too argued for a market-based approach to climate change mitigation strategies, although, unlike Stern, he especially focused on the practical responses available to a small, relatively rich industrialized country like Australia.

Specifically Garnaut recommended that Australia target emissions reductions proportionately to the global effort. If the international agreement was to stabilize greenhouse gases at 450 parts per million CO_2 equivalent (Stern's preferred target) this would mean that by 2020 Australia should reduce its carbon pollution by 25 percent below that produced in the year 2000. He also suggested that this should be revisited and recalibrated as the world's targets shifted over time.

Garnaut recommended that an emissions trading scheme be established by mid-2012, beginning with a fixed price for carbon and transitioning to a floating market-based price (and hence influenced by international prices) by 2015. He also suggested methods such as sale by auction of undated permits for use after 2015 to encourage market participation and development. At a carbon price of $26 per tonne of carbon dioxide equivalent, permits would generate about $11.5 billion in revenues. This level of revenue would enable the government to finance a large range of compensating and restructuring policies, including actually increasing the incomes of the less well off. Overall he noted that the impact of increasing the price of carbon would be roughly equivalent to a 5–7 cent per litre increase in petrol prices, the fluctuations that occurred due to the US/Australian dollar exchange rate in 2010 and, for households (before compensation) the equivalent of increasing interest rates on the average mortgage by 0.25 percent (Garnaut 2011, p. 10).

The report was careful to specify some of the governance structures that would be necessary, including a carbon bank to administer the scheme and a regulatory authority such as the Productivity Commission, to take submissions from emissions-intensive trade-exposed industries.

Given Australia's particular economic structure, which had a number of such exposed industries, Garnaut also recommended specific assistance be targeted at these sectors, and the regions in which they operated, to assist in their transition. A modified version of the former Carbon Pollution Reduction Scheme was recommended for implementation and to run for at least three years, before a more comprehensive review of their situation was made.

The electricity generation industry was to receive specific assistance in the form of low cost loans, to minimize the impact of changes on consumers and guarantee stability, both in prices and in the supply of electricity as producers altered their methods of electricity generation. Farmers who relied on agricultural exports were to be specifically targeted for assistance via the introduction of a carbon farming initiative to provide incentives to reduce emissions through carbon offsets. Different options were suggested as to how these offsets could work with the emission trading scheme, but in all cases these aimed to assist the transition to a lower carbon production process. The ultimate objective, predicted to occur after 2020, was to include the agricultural sector of the economy in a comprehensive carbon price scheme.

Garnaut also recommended that income taxes and social security be used to provide direct financial assistance to households. This process would enable the government to compensate low income households in particular. Properly implemented, this recommendation would mean that while goods and services that were intensive in their use of carbon-based energy would become relatively more expensive, households would have the extra income necessary to transition to less carbon-based goods and services. Specific support was recommended to assist low-income households in the purchase of energy-efficient technologies as well as supporting businesses to develop technological advances that resulted in lower carbon emissions, via a low-emissions innovation council.

Mindful of the power of vested interests to avoid change, the report argued that restructuring the economy using a more accurate carbon price had the potential to enhance greatly Australia's future productivity. Garnaut suggested that this restructuring, if begun without delay, would enable Australia to maintain and enhance its standard of living in the future. Failure to restructure would mean lower living standards as Australia's energy exports became less desirable and its ability to produce became compromised under the burden of old technologies.

Like Stern's, Garnaut's work was also criticized after its release.[5] Unlike the Stern Review, however, many of these criticisms came from people who considered his recommendations did not go far enough, or that as a relatively rich country, Australia should take the lead in reducing carbon emissions. Still others argued that his suggestions were too bold, and that as a relatively small country Australia should wait and follow others.

ECONOMIC CONSIDERATIONS

At their cores both the Stern and Garnaut reports take an economic approach to the consequences of climate change and the policies necessary to reduce carbon emissions. Both signal a critical market imperative: an increase in the relative price of carbon-based goods and services. Why this is so critical for the economy is of course because of the ubiquitous nature of cheap carbon; it has been central to driving technological development and raising material living standards for the past 200 years. Raising the relative price of carbon and thus signalling the true cost of burning carbon, acts to encourage individuals to change behaviour and seek alternatives. A persistent and consistent increase in the relative price of carbon will presage an important reallocation of resources to technologies that use carbon-based products either more efficiently or in much smaller quantities than currently.

Increasing the relative price of carbon sends a signal to all market participants – producers, consumers and governments – that the relative price of carbon has been too low, and its price should better reflect its 'true cost'; in this case its true social cost to the environment.

As with any change in relative prices there are short-term winners and losers. Increasing the price of carbon will mean that those who are currently dependent on low-cost carbon, either because they produce it or because they use it extensively, will lose in the short run. It is not surprising, therefore, that some of the most vocal in their questioning the science behind climate change or the market response to decrease the use of carbon, are those who have significant investments in technologies and processes that rely on cheap carbon-based energy. Those who are locked into a reliance on carbon-intensive energy, be this due to location, supply chain or production process, lack of finance or low income, will also lose, if prices change 'overnight'.

Those who will win in this situation are less easy to identify in the short term. A virtue of the market is that it allows individuals to react in the way they view as best for their own interests. Among suppliers, it will be those who can use carbon-based energy more efficiently or produce technologies that lower the demand for such energy. The market is a competitive and dynamic place, and a relative increase in the price for carbon will also result in innovations. Some will just offset these price increases, while others will reorganize and reframe production processes and increase efficiency.

While in such a dynamic situation being too far out in front is risky, it is also a position that can produce large financial gains to individual firms. Less risky but still often rewarding, has been the strategy of 'wait and see' followed by moving quickly, so that once new technologies and methods are developed, they are exploited quickly. Such change can happen rapidly. Consider for example the global adoption of communication technologies such as the internet, mobile phones and personal computers. Barely in existence 30 years ago, today such devices are distributed across the planet, demonstrating that the right technology, correctly priced, can quickly establish itself as an important element of the economy.

These types of responses to change have however been well described before. Over 70 years ago Joseph Schumpeter introduced the idea of 'creative destruction' to describe capitalism's ability to destroy outmoded production processes and refashion new systems and relationships (Schumpeter 1942). In Schumpeter's analysis, not only relative prices and price competition, but technological change and innovation create fundamental shifts that sweep away old firms and structures and replace them with new. Both Stern and Garnaut argue that such a fundamental shift is needed to respond to global warming, and both describe some of the signals that will cause these changes to occur.

What is true at the aggregated national and international level is also true for businesses and individuals. Rich nations, which have the resources, and frequently the policy frameworks, that are better able to change, will do better than poor nations or those countries whose political and social structures empower lobby groups and slow change. Garnaut in particular highlights that for countries such as Australia, responding rapidly to a shift in carbon prices provides an opportunity to obtain a comparative advantage over slower- moving competitors so that the shift to a lower carbon economy provides opportunities as well as challenges.

Here too history can serve as a guide. Countries that have transformed their competitiveness in the past half century, such as Japan, and the Asian Tigers after World War II, or more recently the emergence of China, provide multiple examples of the gains to be made from responding to international markets and grasping opportunities to innovate and transform 'old' economies to 'new'.[6]

IMPLICATIONS FOR BUSINESS

Regardless of the uncertainties about relative prices, future regulations, technological change, the changes in expectations that result from global warming or the policies used to offset it, several things are certain.[7]

First, change will occur. Second, at least in the short run, the cost of doing business will increase. Third, the expectation that businesses will move away from carbon-intensive production processes will increase. All of these are certain regardless of whether the worst case scenarios of climate change occur or CO_2 emissions are stabilized and the extreme effects of global warming avoided.

If the worst predictions of global warming and climate change do occur, it seems likely that costs will rise in many areas, and rapidly. For example extreme weather events may well increase the disruption of business supply chains and the frequency with which crops are destroyed, raising food prices. Such events may also increase the incidence of disease and injury. Businesses are likely to be exposed to more extreme weather events, disrupting communications, increasing insurance premiums, transportation costs and the general cost of doing business. In the longer term, populations may be forced to shift – some have even predicted the creation of climate change refugees (Sachs 2007).

If on the other hand national and international markets for carbon are established and policy and behavioural change occurs so that the worst effects of climate change are abated, these responses by themselves will also increase the cost of business. Uncertainty about regulations will increase. The regulations necessary to offset global warming will demand changes in firm behaviour and processes. Not only will carbon-intensive goods and services become relatively more expensive, but national and international regulations will be implemented that raise the cost of doing business. Even if a country does nothing, a global shift in regulations and expectations is likely to occur. This by itself will likely increase the need to demonstrate adherence to international best practice in order to access trading blocs and engage in overseas trade.

The costs of investment and obtaining business capital will increase in the short term. Either the negative impact of climate change will increase the cost of capital, as demand increases to replace or rebuild infrastructure, or the incentives to invest in newer, less carbon-intensive goods and services will divert resources from current 'standard' areas of investment ('old technology' industries) toward new opportunities. The cost of business as usual therefore will rise in the short run, even where some businesses choose to do nothing. Delay in investing in new, less carbon-reliant technologies will also mean a slow decline in the relative productivity of companies using old technology.

Offsetting these increased costs in the longer term, however, are the gains that are made from innovation and enhanced competitiveness. Changes to environmental regulations, new standards in production, and new investment can also result in lower production costs. Using resources more efficiently and wasting less can also result in better profit margins (Porter and van der Linde 1995). As these changes and technologies move across the economy, so the efficiencies they generate can actually decrease real costs. Firms that are flexible, astute and able to take advantage of these more efficient processes will gain more than firms that are slow to respond; over time the latter will find themselves less and less price- and quality-competitive.[8]

Investment opportunities in transportation, logistics, infrastructure, food production and storage, health, construction, education, energy and services, will potentially be large. Innovative firms and industries that consciously seek out opportunities, take risks and respond to new circumstances will find that new markets emerge. Existing companies that are aware of, and take steps to take up, the challenges posed by changed regulations and expectations will do better. Even in the process of offsetting costs, opportunities will exist for firms to make profits.

Such dynamic change is not new – it has occurred before.[9] What is new, however, is the global nature of the environmental changes that underpin these signals. A key lesson from Stern and Garnaut is that not only is the environment inseparable from the market place, but that all markets are connected. Changes in one market will cause changes in others either directly (via shifts in relative prices and quantities) or indirectly (via spill-over effects).

For the individual firm operating in a competitive market, the need to respond to changes in the market place and in the economic and regulatory environment is continuous. The simple acts of surviving as a business, selling products or services, buying inputs and operating within legal and social regulations and expectations will not change. The pressure to shift to a less carbon-intense economy must, therefore, be accommodated within this framework. It is not an impossible task, but it may well mean far more attention is paid to this task than ever before.

As with other external risks the individual firm must assess its own situation. It needs to know, for example, how exposed it is to increasing costs. This can be a complicated question to answer, as in all likelihood there will be areas about which it has little knowledge, such as the impact of rising costs on its suppliers. Without a close scrutiny of regulatory developments it may well be 'blind-sided' by changes to governance or technological standards. It is critical, therefore, especially in the case of medium and large businesses, that they devote time to understanding the potential impact of rising carbon prices to their business.

Perhaps most importantly, the key question for every competitive firm to ask is what are its competitors doing? Crucial to the individual firm's survival is this question: is the firm doing at least as well as its competitors in adjusting to the new low carbon economy?

CONCLUDING REMARKS

It is a very human response that individuals, when faced by looming danger, often 'wait and see', to be sure of the nature and direction of the danger, before acting. This can make a great deal of sense when sensing a predator up ahead. It may even seem to make sense for an individual firm to wait and see what will happen to environmental regulation or to supply costs before starting to take action. But both Stern and Garnaut argue that responding now, through raising the price of carbon, providing incentives, and reframing regulations, will be less costly than waiting to see the impact of global warming.

Governments set and enforce the legal and economic framework in which markets and individuals operate. Governments can, and will, make mistakes in this process, just as individuals and firms will make mistakes when responding to change. Despite the probability that mistakes will be made, however, the Stern and Garnaut reports are ultimately optimistic documents. Communities and economies have the ability and the ingenuity to burn less carbon and change their patterns of operation. The market mechanism can be harnessed to help change people's behaviour and provide incentives to invent technologies. Changing the price of carbon is just the first step in this process.

ACKNOWLEDGMENT

I would like to thank David Round for several helpful suggestions in constructing this chapter, but not implicate him in any errors, which remain my responsibility.

NOTES

1. The IPCC published a series of reports in 1995, 2001 and 2007.
2. There has been an International Conference of the Parties each year since 1995. Given the range of issues involved, each year several working parties have met in different international locations.
3. While there were many critics, only some addressed the issues. Two of the more thoughtful of these are Weitsman (2007) and Nordhaus (2007, 2008).
4. Statistically this issue is a classic 'Type I' or 'Type II' error. In this case the null hypothesis is that global warming will not occur. Critics of Stern would accuse him of making a Type I error (a false positive). Supporters of Stern's argument, however, would accuse 'climate sceptics' of a Type II error (a false negative). In deciding which error to avoid, statisticians suggest that the consequence of the error be considered: in this case the costs of making a Type I error, and diverting resources to avoid something that doesn't happen, against a Type II error, doing nothing, with the costs of BAU.
5. For one of the better commentaries on carbon taxes and emission trading schemes see Porter (1990).
6. For numerous cases, studies and detailed discussion see Porter (1990).
7. There are now hundreds of publications in this field. See for example Gunningham (2009); Hitchcock and Willard (2006); Hoffman and Woody (2008); Pappis (2011), and Quaddus and Siddique (2011).
8. For a broader discussion on the economics of the environment see Wills (2006), and on the implementation of economic policies targeting global warming see Helm (2005, 2008).
9. Mokyer (1990).

REFERENCES

Arrhenius, Svente (1896), 'On the influence of carbonic acid in the air upon the temperature of the earth', *Philosophical Magazine*, **41**, 237–76.

Garnaut, Ross (2008), *Garnaut Climate Change Review*, Canberra: Australian Commonwealth Government, available at http://www.garnautreview.org.au/ (accessed 28 December 2011).

Garnaut, Ross (2011), *Garnaut Climate Change Review Update 2011: Australia in the Global Response to Climate Change*, Canberra: Australian Commonwealth Government, available at http://www.garnautreview.org.au/ (accessed 11 March 2012).

Gunningham, N. (ed.) (2009), *Corporate Environmental Responsibility*, Aldershot, UK: Ashgate.

Helm, D. (ed.) (2005), *Climate Change Policy*, Oxford: Oxford University Press.

Helm, D. (2008), 'Climate-change policy: why has so little been achieved?', *Oxford Review of Economic Policy*, **24**, 211–38.

Hitchcock, D. and Willard, M. (2006), *The Business Guide to Sustainability: Practical Strategies and Tools for Organizations*, London: Earthscan.

Hoffman, A.J. and Woody, J.G. (2008), *Climate Change: What's Your Business Strategy?*, Boston, MA: Harvard Business Press.

Mokyer, J. (1990), *The Lever of Riches: Technological Creativity and Economic Progress*, New York: Oxford University Press.

Nordhaus, W. (2007), 'A review of the *Stern Review* on the economics of global warming', *Journal of Economic Literature*, **45** (3), 686–702.

Nordhaus, W. (2008), *A Question of Balance: Weighing the Options on Global Warming Policies*, New Haven, CT: Yale University Press.

Pappis, C.P. (2011), *Climate Change, Supply Chain Management and Enterprise Adaptation: Implications of Global Warming on the Economy*, New York: Information Science Reference.

Porter, M. (1990), *The Competitive Advantage of Nations*, London: Macmillan.

Porter, M. and van der Linde, C. (1995), 'Toward a new conception of the environment-competitiveness relationship', *Journal of Economic Perspectives*, **9** (4), 97–118.

Quaddus, M.A. and Siddique, M.A.B. (eds) (2011), *Handbook of Corporate Sustainability: Frameworks, Strategies and Tools*, Cheltenham, UK and Northampton, MA, USA: Edward Elgar.

Sachs, J.D. (2007), 'Climate change refugees', *Scientific American*, **296** (6), 43.

Schumpeter, J. (1942), *Capitalism, Socialism and Democracy*, New York: Harper.

Stern, N. (2006a), *Stern Review on the Economics of Climate Change*, London: H.M Treasury, Cabinet Office, available at http://webarchive.nationalarchives.gov.uk/+/http://www.hm-treasury.gov.uk/Independent_Reviews/stern_review_economics_climate_change/sternreview_index.cfm (accessed 28 December 2011).

Stern, N. (2006b), *Stern Review*, 'Executive summary', available at http://www.hm-treasury.gov.uk/d/Executive_Summary.pdf (accessed 30 December 2011).

Weitsman, M.L. (2007), 'A review of the Stern Review on the economics of climate change', *Journal of Economic Literature*, **45** (3), 703–724.

Wills, I. (2006), *Economics and the Environment. A Signalling and Incentives Approach*, 2nd edn, Crows Nest, NSW: Allen & Unwin.

Index